Teach Yourself®

#LANGUAGE HACKING

FRENCH

A CONVERSATION COURSE *FOR BEGINNERS*

Learn how to speak French – with actual people – right from the start!

BENNY LEWIS

THE IRISH POLYGLOT

First published in Great Britain in 2016 by John Murray Learning. An Hachette UK company.
First published in US 2016 by Quercus.

British Library Cataloguing in Publication Data: a catalogue record for this title is available from the British Library.

Library of Congress Catalog Card Number: on file.

9781473633094
4

Cover image © Allison Hooban
Illustrations © Will McPhail
Typeset by Integra Software Services Pvt. Ltd., Pondicherry, India
Printed and bound by Clays Ltd, St Ives plc

John Murray Learning policy is to use papers that are natural, renewable and recyclable products and made from wood grown in sustainable forests. The logging and manufacturing processes are expected to conform to the environmental regulations of the country of origin.
John Murray Learning Ltd

Carmelite House
50 Victoria Embankment
London EC4Y 0DZ
www.hodder.co.uk

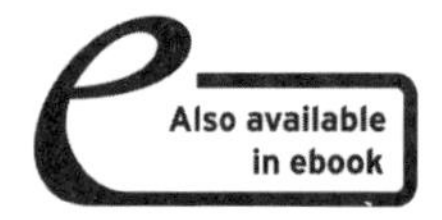

YOUR MISSIONS

INTRODUCTION

UNIT 1: TALKING ABOUT ME

UNIT 2: ASKING ABOUT YOU

UNIT 3: SOLVING COMMUNICATION PROBLEMS

A NOTE FROM BENNY

It's true that some people spend years studying French before they finally get around to speaking the language.

But I have a better idea. Let's skip the years of studying and jump right to the speaking part.

Sound crazy? No, it's language hacking.

#LanguageHacking is a completely different approach to learning a new language.

It's not magic. It's not something only 'other people' can do. It's simply about being smart with *how* you learn: learning what's indispensable, skipping what's not and using what you've learned to have real conversations in French right away.

As a language hacker, I find shortcuts to learning new languages – tricks and techniques to crack the language code and make learning simple so I can get fluent faster. When it comes to learning new languages, I focus on getting the biggest bang for my buck.

There's no need to learn every word and grammar rule before you start using the language. You just need to know *the most common* and *the most versatile* phrases you'll need in most situations, and how to 'speak around' the problem when there's something you don't understand or know how to say yet.

#LanguageHacking isn't just a course. It's a new way of thinking about language learning. It shows you how to learn a language as well as giving you all the language you need – and none of what you don't. You can use it on your own or with any other book to start speaking languages faster.

I'd like to show you how it's done. See you on the inside.

Benny

Benny Lewis, Language Hacker

HOW TO USE THIS COURSE

The most common complaint I hear from language learners is:

'I studied French for years in school. I can understand a few words when I see them, and even sometimes when I hear them, but I still can't speak the language.'

#LanguageHacking isn't like traditional courses. It's a *conversation* course, which means you will focus on building the language skills you need to have meaningful, real-life conversations with other people in French – right away. By the end of this course, you'll be able to introduce yourself and ask and answer hundreds of typical questions in French. You'll know how to find and connect with other French speakers no matter where you live. And you will gain the skills and strategies to have countless conversations entirely in French – as well as the confidence to keep them going.

#LanguageHacking can be used either on its own or alongside any other language course – whether written, online, or in the classroom. Just grab your notebook and get started!

WHAT YOU'LL FIND INSIDE

This course will challenge you to speak from day one by completing ten missions, which will grow your conversational abilities in French. To keep that promise, I invite you to become a part of the language hacking community, built with this course in mind, that gives you a safe and fun place to communicate with other like-minded and determined learners. You can complete the missions on your own, but you'll progress much faster if you use the language with real people, so I encourage you to submit your missions to the #LanguageHacking online community www.teachyourself.com/languagehacking for feedback (and secret mini-missions!).

SPEAKING FROM DAY 1

You can't learn to play the piano until you sit down and put your fingers on the keys. You can't play tennis until you pick up the racquet. And you can't learn a language if you don't speak it. By speaking from day one, you will:

- pick up expressions and language from others
- notice the expression gaps in your language you need to fill
- become aware of how other people say things
- get feedback from others
- improve your pronunciation and fluency
- conquer the fear of speaking a new language
- feel motivated by hearing your own progress.

BUILD YOUR LANGUAGE SKILLS

Build language through typical conversations

Each unit takes you through three **conversations** in French that show you how the language is used in common, everyday contexts. The conversations build on each other to grow your vocabulary and prepare you for your mission. Treat each conversation like a lesson, and make sure you understand everything before you move on to the next conversation.

Figure it out exercises

You'll read each conversation and listen to the audio, then I'll help you **Figure it Out**. These exercises train you to start understanding French on your own – through context, recognizing patterns and applying other language learning strategies – without relying on translations. By figuring out language for yourself, you'll internalize it better and recall it faster when you need it.

Notice exercises

Every conversation is followed by a **phrase list** with the key phrases, expressions and vocab to know from that conversation, with English translations and pronunciation to help you. **Notice** exercises get you thinking about the new language and noticing how the language works, so you're gaining an intuitive understanding of French.

Practice exercises

Practice exercises reinforce what you learn. You'll piece together different parts of what you know to figure out how to create new French phrases on your own.

Put it together

Finally, you'll take everything you've learned and **Put it Together** to create your own repertoire in French. I'll help you prepare 'me-specific' language you can use in real-life conversations that's actually relevant to you.

SUPPORT, TECHNIQUES AND STRATEGIES

In language hacking, your ability to have conversations in French is not limited by the number of words you know.

#LanguageHacks

You'll **learn unconventional shortcuts** to boost your language abilities exponentially. I reveal the different patterns, rules and tools to help you crack the code and get fluent faster. Each of the ten hacks equips you with techniques you can use in this course and throughout the rest of your learning journey.

As you go along, you may develop your own shortcuts for making learning simple. If you do, share them with others and me, and use the hashtag #languagehacking.

Conversation strategies

You'll learn essential conversation strategies, like **conversation connectors, filler words, and survival phrases** to strike up conversations and keep them flowing.

Grammar & pronunciation

We'll cover the foundation of the **grammar you need to know**, but I won't overload you with what's not essential to communication. I'll help you understand the important parts of French **pronunciation** and share techniques to help you get them right.

You don't need to learn all the grammar. A lot of the time you can **learn language in 'chunks'** – the same way you learned your native language. You learned to say 'there it is' before you ever understood what each individual word meant on its own… and you still got your point across.

Side notes

I'll share more insights as we go along – like culture tips about French speakers and French-speaking countries, vocab tips on how to get creative with new phrases and mini-hacks for better learning.

Progress you can see

You will see your progress build steadily throughout this course. Before you finish each unit, you'll **check your understanding** with audio practice that acts as a 'virtual conversation partner'. This practice gives you time to collect your thoughts and speak at your own pace. Before you move on to your mission, you'll do a **self assessment checklist** to make sure you're prepared and to keep a visual record of the progress you're making.

MISSIONS

Each unit ends with **three tasks** that you'll complete as your final mission.

STEP 1: build your script

To get ready for spoken practice with other people, you'll build 'me-specific' scripts with the language you need to talk about your life. These scripts make sure you're learning useful French phrases that are truly relevant to you.

STEP 2: speak French with other people... *online.*

Speaking from day one is the best way I've found to quickly reach fluency. I'll help you implement this strategy, no matter where you live, with the missions you'll complete as part of the language hacking community. You'll record yourself speaking your scripts aloud in French and upload them to the community where you'll get feedback from other learners and keep the conversation going. This is the best practice you can get – aside from one-to-one conversations with a native speaker. By speaking in front of others you'll become more confident using French in the real world.

STEP 3: learn from other learners

When you share your missions with other learners, you'll get more comfortable speaking French – and more importantly, you'll get comfortable speaking the imperfect beginner's French that everyone must use on the road to fluency. You'll gain insight into how conversations flow in French, and you'll learn where the 'expression gaps' are in your scripts that you need to fill to expand your conversation skills.

In other words, you'll have everything you need to genuinely start having conversations with other people in French. After all, isn't that the point?

Let's get started.

WHAT YOU'LL FIND ONLINE

Go to www.teachyourself.com/languagehacking to:

- Submit your missions
- Download or stream the course audio
- Find an up-to-date list of the best free online resources to support your learning
- Review transcripts for the audio
- Discover additional materials to help you on your learning journey
- Find out more about Language Hacking and Benny Lewis

Check back frequently as we add new language hacks.

THE LANGUAGE HACKER CONTRACT

In this course you will:

- **get shortcuts (#languagehacks)** to learn a new *langue* fast
- **learn the words and** *les phrases* you need to have real conversations immediately
- **gain the confidence** to start speaking *le français* from day one
- **have access** to a *communauté* of like-minded language learners

That's my side of the bargain. It's what I'm giving you.

Now here's your side of the contract. I recommend you read it every day so it embeds in your memory and becomes part of who you are.

I will speak French today and every day – if only a little. It will feel awkward and uncomfortable at times. And that's okay.

I will accept that the only way to speak perfectly is to first make mistakes. The only way to overcome my fear is to face it. The only thing preventing me from speaking French is... speaking French.

I will embrace my inner Tarzan. I will say things in French like 'I Benny. Me writer. I Ireland.' I'll do this because I'm still learning, and because I don't take myself too seriously. I will communicate effectively instead of perfectly. Over time, I will make massive leaps.

I will build 'me-specific' scripts – mini monologues about myself. I will memorize these scripts and rely on them whenever I'm asked questions. I will discover time and time again that I can manage the most common situations I come across in a new language. I will quickly feel my confidence build as I equip myself with the language I need.

I will speak at every opportunity and be an active participant in the language hacking community. I will learn from giving and getting feedback.

I will build my skills, day by day, piece by piece.

I will learn smarter. I will be self-sufficient. I will make learning French part of my daily routine. I will become fluent faster than I ever imagined possible.

I am a language hacker.

Sign here: ____________________ Date: ________________

PRONUNCIATION GUIDE

French words will *usually* follow the rules outlined here, but there are exceptions (which will be pointed out throughout the book as needed). While we will try to draw some parallels with English for all sounds, I highly recommend you listen to the audio samples as a priority, and try to mimic them as best as you can.

VOWELS

🔊 00.01

Seen in	Explanation	Represented by	Examples
eu, e	Similar to the sound you'd make when hesitating	uh	deux, bleu, je veux, un peu, demain
ou	Like in 'food'	oo	où, jour, nous
eau, o	Like the 'o' in 'no' or 'go', but cut short	oh	beaucoup, mot, bientôt
o	Like the 'o' in 'pot' or 'hop'	o	je donne, dehors
é	Like the 'ay' in 'tray', but cut short	ay	café, bébé
e, ê, è	Like in 'head'	eh	merci, tête, très
i, y	Like in 'free', but cut short	ee	il, ici
oi	Like 'wa' in 'wag'	wa	fois, moi
eille		ay-uh	oreille, mireille
u	Form your lips to say 'oo' but say 'ee' instead. A close approximation is the 'ew' sound in 'dew'	ew	menu, culture, tu
ui	Take the 'ew' from above, and add the 'ee' sound (also above) to the end	ew-wee	puis, nuit, huit

CONSONANTS

🔊 00.02

Seen in	Explanation	Represented by	Examples
r	The French 'r' sounds more like an English 'h', and could even be compared to the English 'k' sound. Until you get it right, a strongly aspirated 'h' works well – but never an English r!	R	après, rien
j	This sound is similar to the 's' sound in 'measure', 'usual' and 'version', or the 'g' sound in 'mirage' or 'beige' – never pronounced like the 'j' in jam	zh	je veux, jeune, garage
h	Not pronounced	–	hôtel, huit
ch	Always pronounced like the soft 'sh' in 'shop' – never like 'chat'	sh	champagne, acheter
ç	Always pronounced as an 's'	s	français, ça

NASALS

🔊 00.03

Seen in	Explanation	Represented by	Examples
in, ain, ein, un	These sounds don't have any true parallels in English. Listen to the audio and try to mimic them as best as you can	ahN	fin, pain, plein, simple, un, lundi, brun
an, am, en, em	This is the 'o' sound in 'not' nasalized, or like the end of 'long', cut short	awN	camp, grand, enfant
on, om	Somewhat like the [awN] sound, but brought forward in your mouth	ohN	bon, nom, long

TALKING ABOUT ME

Mission

Imagine this – you've arrived in France. You step up to get your passport checked, and the agent asks you about yourself.

Your mission is to convince the agent to let you through. Be brave and say *Bonjour.* Then have a basic exchange – entirely in French – for 30 seconds. Be prepared to **say your name**, **where you're from**, **where you live**, why you're coming to France, and especially **why you're learning French.**

This mission will prepare you for the inevitable questions you'll be asked in any first conversation you have in French.

Mission prep

- Learn basic phrases for talking about yourself: *je...*
- Create simple sentences to talk about your likes and wants using *je veux, j'aime*
- Develop a conversation strategy: turn the tables by asking, *et toi ?*
- Learn the words for countries, nationalities, professions and interests
- Use the connector words *parce que, et, mais.*

BUILDING SCRIPTS

Most first conversations in a new language are predictable. As a beginner, this is great news for you. We're going to start by building your first 'script' to help you prepare for what you'll need to say most, right away. We'll start slow and build as we move on.

If you've studied French before, some of the words in this unit may be familiar to you. But we'll be doing much more than just learning words in each unit: we're going to start building scripts. Once you learn a script, you can customize it to your needs. This will help you build your language so you can use it from the start.

#LANGUAGEHACK
get a head-start with words you already know

CONVERSATION 1

The first words you'll use in every conversation

PRONUNCIATION: *ça va ?*
With *ça va* we meet a brand new letter – ç. This *cédille* is like a 'c' with a tail on it. When you see the tail, pronounce it as an 's'.

Let's follow the story of Lauren, an author and French learner who just arrived in Paris to spend the summer immersing herself in French while doing research for her book. She decides to attend a French lesson at a local *brasserie*. Today she's meeting her teacher, Pierre, for the first time.

01.01 This is a typical introductory conversation. Listen to the conversation and pay attention to the way Lauren asks *et toi ?*

As a beginner, your first step is **building a basic introductory conversation**. After an initial greeting, a typical first conversation usually turns towards topics about where you live and what you do.

Lauren :	Bonjour. Je m'appelle Lauren, et toi ?
Pierre :	Bonjour! Je m'appelle Pierre. Ça va ?
Lauren :	Ça va. Et toi ?
Pierre :	Ça va, merci. Alors, parle-moi de toi !
Lauren :	Ben, je suis américaine. Mais j'habite ici à Paris. Et je suis auteur. Et toi ?
Pierre :	Moi, je suis de France, bien sûr ! Et j'habite ici, à Paris.

When you see or hear new French words for the first time, they are going to seem like random noise. But if you train yourself to look and listen a little closer, you'll realize that there's a lot you can figure out based on the context of the conversation and how the words relate to English. The key is to try to notice the language for yourself.

CONVERSATION STRATEGY: ***et toi ?***
If you're uncomfortable doing a lot of talking at first, a trick I like to use is to simply bounce the question back to the other person, so I can listen for a while. In French, it's easy to do, with a simple ***et toi ?***

Time to think about the conversation you just heard! Notice how French sentence structure differs from English. The more you actively think about the different ways French uses word order and expressions, the faster you'll learn.

FIGURE IT OUT

1 Based on the context of the conversation, what does *je suis* mean?

____

2 What are the two different ways 'I' is written in the conversation? Highlight them and write them here. ________ ________

3 What phrase does Lauren use to bounce the question back to Pierre?

____

4 Find the French word that answers each question, and write it out.

Example: Where is Pierre from? France

a What's Lauren's job? _______________

b What nationality is she? _______________

c Where does Lauren live? _______________

While you may not be able to figure out what a word means in isolation, the words around it give you clues you can combine with what you already know to deduce the meaning. You can figure out the answers to all these questions even if you don't know a word of French, thanks to **context**. Pretty cool, huh?

5 Find the two uses of *ça va* in the conversation. What is this phrase used for in each instance? _______________ _______________

POWER PHRASE = a phrase you can use in a variety of different ways and situations.

01.02 *Ça va* is a power phrase and has lots of meanings. Listen to the audio to hear how *ça va* is used in different ways. Pay attention to how the intonation of the words creates new meaning.

Ça va ?	Ça va.	Ça va... ? (How is...?)	Ça va ! (It/he/she is, they are...)
How are you doing?	I'm fine.	... la famille ? (your family?)	Ça va, ça va. (fine)
How are you?	OK.	... Paris ? (your time in Paris?)	Ça va super ! (great!)
How are things?	Not bad.	... Sandra ? (Sandra?)	Sandra, ça va ! (she's good!)
How have you been?	Good!	... ton régime ? (your diet?)	Ça va pas... (not well)

PRONUNCIATION: questions and answers

Learn questions and answers together. In French, you'll rely on intonation to tell you whether a phrase is a question or a statement.

All you need to do is change your intonation upwards for a question and downwards for an answer, while using the same words: *Ça va ?* ↗ *Ça va.* ↘

1 🔊 **01.03** Listen to the audio and repeat to mimic the speaker. Use intonation to determine whether you are hearing a question or a statement, then highlight the answer.

a *Ça va ?* *Ça va.* b *Et toi ?* *Et toi.*

Bonjour is the most famous go-to greeting you can use in French, especially early in the day. An alternative in more casual situations would be ***Salut !*** (Hi!)

NOTICE

🔊 **01.04** Listen to the audio and study the table.

Essential phrases for Conversation 1

French	Meaning	Pronunciation
bonjour	hello	bohN-zhooR
je m'appelle…	my name is (I myself call)	zhuh mah-pehl
ça va ?	how's it going?	sah vah
ça va.	I'm fine.	sah vah
et toi ?	and you?	ay twa
alors…	so…	ah-loR
parle-moi de toi	tell me about yourself (speak-me of you)	pahRl mwa duh twa
ben…	well…	bawN
je suis américaine	I'm American	zhuh sew-wee zah-may-Ree-kehn
j'habite ici à Paris	I live here in Paris	zhah-beet ee-see ah pah-Ree
je suis auteur	I'm an author (I am author)	zhuh sew-wee zoh-tuhR
moi	me	mwa
je suis de France	I'm from France	zhuh sew-wee duh fRawNs

GRAMMAR TIP:
spelling
Some words change in French depending on whether they refer to a man or woman. For instance, If this were a male speaking, he would say ***je suis américain*** - without an 'e' at the end.

LEARNING STRATEGY:
word-for-word translations
Use the translations you see in brackets to help you understand how the French phrases translate word-for-word to English. This will help you gain an intuitive understanding of how French works, without actively studying the grammar for now.

1 The French phrase for 'I'm an author' doesn't translate word-for-word from English. Which English word does the French phrase omit?

____

2 Translate these phrases into French:

a I am ________________

b I live in (city) ________________

c I'm from Paris. ________________

d I'm from France. ________________

You'll notice the different ways *je* is spelled. French uses an apostrophe to blend word sounds together if the next word starts with a vowel (*a, e, i, o, u*) or usually with an *h*. But don't worry – if you say 'je habite' instead of *j'habite*, French people will understand you. Perfectionism is never your goal – communication is!

PRONUNCIATION: *j*
The French *j* doesn't sound like 'j' in 'jam'. It has a softer sound, like the middle sound in 'measure'. Keep that in mind whenever you see it.

3 Decide whether to use *je* or *j'*.

a ____ *aime* (I like)

b ____ *danse* (I dance)

c ____ *habite* (I live)

d ____ *parle* (I speak)

e ____ *étudie* (I study)

f ____ *pense* (I think)

PRACTICE

Though some of this language may be familiar, you should still pronounce these words out loud now to start building muscle memory. This will help you develop your French accent right away. Make sure you understand the conversation before moving on.

SPEAKING: *take a risk!*
Something I hear all the time from French learners is, 'Benny, I've studied French for years, but I still can't speak it!' This happens when you spend all your time reading, listening or studying French, but not actually speaking it. Whatever you do, don't study French in silence. You have to use the language, even if it feels weird or silly, and even if your accent is terrible at first. It will only get better with use!

When you meet a new vocab list (like this one), don't try to memorize all the words – just the ones you can imagine yourself needing in your own conversations. In fact, as you go through this list, give yourself the pleasure of **striking out any words** you can't imagine yourself using in the next month or so.

01.05 Here's some new vocab to help you keep building your language script. Listen to the audio and study the table.

Countries	Nationalities	Professions	Interests
les États-Unis	américain	dentiste	la danse
le Canada	canadien	médecin	la photographie
l'Italie	italien	pilote	la musique, le piano
la Chine	chinois	artiste	la cuisine
l'Australie	australien	journaliste	la télévision
la Russie	russe	programmeur	le cinéma, le théâtre
la France	français	photographe	le shopping
le Mexique	mexicain	ingénieur	le jogging
le Japon	japonais	vétérinaire	faire du codage
l'Irlande	irlandais	blogueur	les langues

If you don't already have one, find a good French dictionary. This will help you build vocabulary that's what I call 'me-specific'. As we go along, you'll need to look up your own words that apply to your life to make your script more useful. Let's start now.

GRAMMAR TIP:
le and *la*
Le and *la* roughly translate to 'the' in English, but *le* is for masculine nouns and *la* is for feminine nouns. Some nouns may take either one, such as the professions you see here without an article. More on this later in Unit 3!

1 What are the professions and interests of the people in your life? What countries are they from?

a Look for any professions, interests and nationalities of people you know in the table and highlight them.

b Add three new words to each category (use words that are specific to you or people close to you).

2 Use a dictionary to help you create four phrases starting with *je suis* to describe yourself.

Example: Je suis Benny. Je suis végétarien. Je suis blogueur.

3 Now, answer these questions in French. How do you…

Example: ... say your name? Je m'appelle...

a ...say where you're from? ______________________

b ...say your profession? ______________________

c ...tell someone what city you live in? ______________________

Cover up the translations in the phrase list and see if you can remember what the French expressions mean.

PUT IT TOGETHER

Parle-moi de toi ! Now let's keep building your script. Use the conversation as a model, as well as the vocab and 'me-specific' words you just looked up, to create four of your own sentences about yourself. Write out in French:

I've listed some good free online dictionaries and apps in our **Resources** section. You can also use a good learner-friendly ink-and-paper dictionary.

- your name
- where you're from
- where you live
- what you do for a living

Moi, je m'appelle...

Throughout this course, I'll help you keep building this script. You'll draw on this again and again as you start having your first conversations in French with actual people.

CONVERSATION 2

Describing your interests

There's so much French you already know thanks to **cognates** – words that are the same, or nearly the same, in both English and French. Almost half of French words in the dictionary look and mean nearly the same in English!

As part of their first conversation, Pierre asks Lauren about her interests.

HACK IT: *word chunks*
It helps to learn words in chunks rather than understanding each part of every word. ***Qu'est-ce que*** is a great example. Learn this as a whole chunk. It simply means 'what?'

01.06 Listen for familiar-sounding words to see if you can understand the gist of what the speakers are saying.

Pierre : Alors, qu'est-ce que tu aimes ?

Lauren : J'aime mes amis, j'aime le cinéma, j'adore voyager. J'aime la pizza ! Mais, je déteste les spaghettis. Et toi ?

Pierre : Moi, j'adore mon travail comme professeur. J'aime visiter les musées, et j'adore le tennis. Le tennis, mais pas le tennis de table !

FIGURE IT OUT

When you talk to someone for the first time, you'll often get a question like, 'So, what do you like to do?'

1 What phrase does Pierre use to ask Lauren what she likes?

____

2 What does the word *mais* mean? ______________________

3 What does Lauren *not* like? Highlight the phrase she uses to say what she doesn't like.

4 What things *do* the speakers like? Highlight the two words they use to describe things they like.

NOTICE

01.07 Listen to the audio and study the table.

Essential phrases for Conversation 2

French	Meaning	Pronunciation
qu'est-ce que tu aimes ?	what do you like?	kehs kuh tew ehm
j'aime…	I like…	zhehm
mes amis	my friends	may-zah-mee
la pizza / le cinéma	pizza / cinema	lah pee-zah / luh see-nay-mah
mais	but	meh
je déteste...	I hate...	zhuh day-tehst
les spaghettis	spaghetti	lay spah-gay-tee
mon travail	my job	mohN tRahvah-ee
j'adore…	I love…	zhah-doR
voyager	to travel	vwa-yah-zhay
visiter les musées	to visit museums	vee-zee-tay lay mew-zay
le tennis	tennis	luh tay-nees

CULTURE TIP: *tu* or *vous*
French has two ways of saying 'you': one is informal, ***tu* / *toi***, and the other is formal, ***vous***. For this book, we're sticking with the informal form, because honestly, that's the form you'll use most when you're casually chatting with people your age.

1 Notice the question phrase from the list above, and complete the sentence:

What do you like? → ______________ *tu aimes?*

#LANGUAGEHACK: get a head-start with words you already know

I've already introduced you to a lot of cognates in this unit. Here are some simple tips to help you use them to quickly build up your vocabulary.

Can you guess the English meaning of these French cognates (or near cognates)?

pizza	télévision	voyage
culture	personne	langue
acteur	moderne	France

English has borrowed many words from French and, more recently, French has borrowed many words from English. Sometimes the spelling of these words is the same in both languages, and sometimes there are slight changes.

Luckily, you can follow straightforward patterns to guess when a word is likely to be a (near) cognate in French, so you can use something like the English word you know already. It's a safe bet to guess with cognates when you're talking about...

Professions, concepts, technical vocabulary or scientific words	pilote, beauté, trigonométrie, cohésion
Words ending in *-tion*	admiration, association, instruction, option, lotion (with different pronunciation)
Any nouns that end in *-tude, -or, -ist, -nce, -ty* in English	altitude, acteur, optimiste, arrogance, université (with slight spelling alterations)

Expert tip: words that are formal in English are more likely to be similar in French. For instance, if you forget how to say 'country' in French, you could say *nation* instead. This is a slightly more formal word that ends in *-tion*, so you can use this cognate to get your point across, without needing to learn a new word!

YOUR TURN: use the hack

1 You'll internalize this #languagehack much better if you try it out yourself now. So let's get you using this technique right away.

01.08 Practise pronouncing the French cognates from the first table and notice how differently they sound from English. Repeat each word to try to mimic the speaker.

2 Go back through Conversations 1 and 2 and find six cognates. Write them in the cheat sheet.

French cognate	English meaning
auteur	author

Now practise guessing three new cognates – using the rules you just learned – and add them to the cheat sheet. Use your French dictionary to check your answers. **Example:** mathematics ⇢ les mathématiques

PRACTICE

1 **01.09** Practise your French accent! Say each of the French cognates below aloud to yourself, then play the audio to see if you got it right. Repeat each word to try to mimic the speaker.

animal *tradition* *statue* *géographie* *machine* *message*

2 Next, cover up the translations in the phrase list, and see if you can remember what the French expressions mean.

GRAMMAR EXPLANATION: combining verbs and nouns

The sentence structure introduced in this conversation is the verb + noun form. It uses action words (verbs) followed by a person, place or thing (noun) – the same way we do it in English.

Because of that, this sentence structure will be simple for you to learn and use. You'll just need to decide which verb you want to use, followed by the thing you want to talk about. So *j'adore le cappuccino* is 'I love cappuccino'. The only difference from English is that French adds the word 'the' (*le*, *la*, or *les*) before the noun. We'll discuss the differences between these three 'the' words later.

Example:

J'adore *le cappuccino.*	***J'aime*** *les croissants.*	***Je déteste*** *les spaghettis.*
I + verb **+ noun**	I + verb **+ noun**	I + verb **+ noun**

GRAMMAR TIP: *understanding the terminology*
In this book, I'll avoid using overly technical grammar terms, but there are a few worth knowing. Here, we talk about nouns – people, places and things (like ***cinéma***, ***étudiants***, ***auteur***, ***France***); and verbs – action words (like ***suis***, ***habite***, ***aime*** that you've seen follow ***je/j'***). These are the building blocks of all sentences.

1 What things do you like, love or dislike? Complete the sentences with the nouns from the box, or use your dictionary to find some 'me-specific' words. Make the sentences true for you!

la pizza *les spaghettis* *le café* *la bière* *la télévision*

a *J'adore* (I love/adore) __________

b *Je déteste* (I hate/detest) __________

c *J'aime* (I like) __________

PUT IT TOGETHER

Now it's time to use this form to talk about your own likes and dislikes. Use your dict ionary to look up new words that describe yourself, then:

- create three new sentences about things you like
- and two sentences about things you don't like.

J'aime les croissants !

____

____

____

Now read your script over and over again until you feel comfortable saying it. Try to memorize it too!

CONVERSATION 3

Why are you learning French?

One question you'll need to learn to answer right away is simply, 'Why are you learning French?' You'll almost definitely get this question when you have your first conversation in French, so let's prepare your answer now.

01.10 Listen to the conversation. Pierre wants to know why Lauren is learning French. Pay attention to the way Lauren forms her answer. How does she say 'because'?

Pierre : Alors, pourquoi tu veux apprendre le français ?

Lauren : Bon, je veux apprendre le français parce que je veux parler une belle langue et je veux comprendre la culture française. Je veux habiter en France et je pense que le français est très intéressant !

FIGURE IT OUT

1 What words do the speakers use to ask a question (why?) and to give a reason (because)? Underline them in the conversation, then write them out.

why? ____________ because ____________

2 What do you think the phrase *la culture française* means?

____

3 Find one word in the conversation that you don't understand and highlight it. Now take a closer look to see if you can infer the word's meaning. When you think you may know what it means, look the word up in a dictionary to see if you're right!

NOTICE

01.11 Listen to the audio and study the table.

CONVERSATION STRATEGY: *smooth out your sentences with connector words*
Speaking in short, simple sentences doesn't sound very natural, but when you're a beginner in French, it gets the job done. You can start smoothing out your French sentences by adding in connector words. Words like *parce que, et, mais* and *ou* ('because', 'and', 'but' and 'or') help you connect your thoughts to sound more natural.

Example:
I want to learn French *because* I want to learn a beautiful language, *and* I want to understand French culture.

Essential phrases for Conversation 3

French	Meaning	Pronunciation
pourquoi	why	pooR-kwa
tu veux apprendre le français ?	do you want to learn French?	tew vuh zah-pRawNd luh fRawN-seh
je veux apprendre	I want to learn	zhuh vuh zahpRawNd
parce que ...	because ...	pahRs kuh
je veux parler une belle langue	I want to speak a beautiful language	zhuh vuh pahr-lay ewn behl lawNg
comprendre la culture française	to understand French culture	kohN-pRawNd lah kewl-tewR fRawN-sehz
habiter en France	to live in France	ah-bee-tay awN fRawNs
je pense que…	I think that…	zhuh pawNs kuh
le français est très intéressant !	French is very interesting!	luh fRawN-seh eh tReh zahN-tay-Ray-sawN

1 What words in French correspond to the following English words?

a well ... bon ______
b so ... ______
c and ... ______
d because ... ______

2 Look at the conversation again. What four verbs follow the expression *je veux*? Underline the verbs and write them out.

______

3 Look for the cognates. What are the French words for the following?

a language ______
b culture ______
c beautiful ______
d interesting ______

GRAMMAR EXPLANATION: combining two verbs

In Conversation 3, you saw a new sentence structure that combines two forms of French verbs – the 'I form' and the 'dictionary form'.

We call this the 'dictionary form' because it's the way the verb looks when you find it in a dictionary. You can also think of it as the 'to-form' (parler is 'to speak'), and language teachers call it the 'infinitive'. This form will always end in **-er**, **-re** or **-ir** in French.

Here are two set phrases that use both of these verb types, and that can help you avoid more complicated phrases in French.

Je veux + **verb** (dictionary form)	*J'aime* + **verb** (dictionary form)
I want + **to** ... (do something)	*I like* + **to** ... (do something)

Examples:

Je veux parler	(I want to speak)
J'aime visiter	(I like to visit / I like visiting)

You can use these combinations in nearly endless ways.

PRACTICE

1 Use Conversation 3 and the verb list to figure out how you'd say in French:

a I love to speak French. ____________

b I hate visiting museums. ____________

c I like learning languages. ____________

d I want to visit France. ____________

In English, you might want to say 'I like visiting museums' instead of 'I like to visit museums'. In French, both are the same. Keep this in mind when using **-ing words** after 'want' or 'like'.

01.12 Listen to the audio and study the table. Pay careful attention to the pronunciation of the words – especially their endings.

Common verbs

dictionary form	*je* form	dictionary form	*je* form
aimer (to like)	j'aime (I like)	apprendre (to learn)	j'apprends (I learn)
adorer (to love)	j'adore (I love)	étudier (to study)	j'étudie (I study)
détester (to hate)	je déteste (I hate)	voyager (to travel)	je voyage (I travel)
vouloir (to want)	je veux (I want)	visiter (to visit)	je visite (I visit)
habiter (to live)	j'habite (I live)	comprendre (to understand)	je comprends (I understand)
penser (to think)	je pense (I think)	aider (to help)	j'aide (I help)
parler (to speak)	je parle (I speak)	espérer (to hope)	j'espère (I hope)

2 Use the prompts given to answer the questions in French.

Pourquoi tu apprends le français ?

a ________________ *cette langue est fascinante.*
(**I think that** this language is fascinating.)

b ________________ *en France* ! (**I want to live** in France!)

c ________________ *des nouvelles langues !*
(**I like learning** new languages!)

d ________________ *la France bientôt.* (**I am visiting** France soon.)

Pourquoi tu es ici en France ?

e ________________ *rencontrer les Français.*
(**I want to** meet French people.)

f ________________ *la cuisine française* ! (**I love** the French cuisine.)

g ________________ *ici.* (**I want to study** here.)

h ________________ *la culture française.*
(**I want to understand** French culture.)

PUT IT TOGETHER

Pourquoi tu veux apprendre le français ? It's time for you to use this sentence structure yourself! Create four sentences in French that combine 'I' forms with dictionary forms of verbs to say things that are true for you. Look up new words in your dictionary to form sentences you think you'll want to use early on.

Example: I hope to understand French. → J'espère comprendre le français.

Je veux apprendre le français parce que...

COMPLETING UNIT 1

Check your understanding

🔊 **01.13** Go back and reread the conversations. Then when you're feeling confident:

- listen to the audio rehearsal, which will ask you questions in French
- pause or replay the audio as often as necessary to understand the questions
- repeat after the speaker until the pronunciation feels and sounds natural
- answer the questions in French (in complete sentences).

Each unit will build on the previous one, helping you to review as you move ahead. Pause or replay the audio as often as necessary to understand the questions. Do your best to answer out loud in complete sentences.

LEARNING STRATEGY:
active listening
When you do a listening exercise, make sure you **actively pay attention** to the audio. A common mistake is to listen to French audio in the background, thinking it will still 'sink in'. The truth is, there's a huge difference between hearing a language and listening to a language. Make sure 100% of your attention is on the audio while it plays!

Show what you know...

Here's what you've just learned. Write or say an example for each item on the list. Then tick off the ones you know.

- [x] Introduce yourself. Je m'appelle Benny !
- [ ] Say where you're from.
- [ ] Give three French–English cognates.
- [ ] Ask the question, 'Why are you learning French?'
- [ ] Give a reason why you're learning French, 'Because...'
- [ ] Give the French connector words for 'and', 'because' and 'but'.
- [ ] Give a phrase you can use to bounce a question back to someone else.
- [ ] Describe your interests using different sentence structures:
  - [ ] I like...
  - [ ] I want to...

COMPLETE YOUR MISSION

It's time to complete your mission: convincing the airport agent to let you through the gates, so your French adventure can begin! To do this, you'll need to prepare your answers to the questions you'll most likely be asked.

STEP 1: build your script

Start your script with the phrases you learned in this unit, combined with 'me-specific' vocabulary, to answer common questions about yourself.

Use connector words along the way to help your sentences flow better!

- say your name and occupation using *je...*
- say where you're from and where you live using *j'habite à...*
- say why you're learning French or visiting France.

Write down your script, then repeat it until you feel confident.

STEP 2: real language hackers speak from day one... *online*

You'll find some **bonus missions** too, for serious French hacking!

If you're feeling good about your script, it's time to complete your mission and share a recording of you speaking your script with the community. Go online, find the mission for Unit 1 and give it your best shot.

STEP 3: learn from other learners

Your task is to ask **a follow-up question in French** to at least three different people.

How well can you understand someone else's introduction? After you've uploaded your clip, check out what others in the community have to say about themselves. Would you let them past security?

STEP 4: reflect on what you've learned

What did you find easy or difficult about this unit? Did you learn any new words or phrases in the community space? After every script you write or conversation you have, you'll gain a lot of insight for what 'gaps' you need to fill in your script. Always write them down!

HEY, LANGUAGE HACKER, LOOK AT YOU GO!

You've only just started on the new path to language hacking, and you've already learned so much. You've taken the first crucial steps, and started to interact with others using French. This is something other students don't do even after years of studying, so you should be truly proud of yourself.

Bon courage !

2 ASKING ABOUT YOU

Mission

Imagine this – your friend brings you to your first *soirée*. You want to blend in and not rely on English.

Your mission is to trick someone into thinking you're a high-level French speaker for at least 30 seconds.

Be prepared to strike up a conversation and talk about **how long you've been** living in your current location, **what you like to do** and the **languages you speak** or want to learn. After the 30 seconds have passed, reveal to the other person how long you've been learning French and dazzle them! To avoid arousing suspicion, keep the other person talking by asking casual questions to show your interest.

This mission will give you the confidence to initiate conversations with new people.

Mission prep

- Use the question and answer words *est-ce que*, *qu'est-ce que*, *depuis* and *depuis quand*
- Ask and respond to questions using the *tu* form
- Negate sentences using *pas*
- Develop a conversation strategy using the filler words *ben*, *alors* and *c'est-à-dire* to create conversational flow
- Pronounce new French sounds (the French *u*; the French *r*).

BUILDING LANGUAGE FOR ASKING QUESTIONS

Let's build on the simple (but effective!) technique of bouncing back a question with *et toi*, and learn to form more specific questions using several new sentence structures.

CONVERSATION 1

Words you need to ask questions

No matter where you live in the world, there are other French learners nearby who want to speak French with you. You can also find native speakers to help you learn. See our Resources for how to connect with other French learners and speakers.

A week into her stay in Paris, Lauren attends a language learners' meet-up near her house. There, she meets Jacques, a Parisian. After the initial introductions, they start to talk about their language skills.

CONVERSATION STRATEGY: *anticipate common questions*
When you start speaking French, a common conversation topic is language learning itself. It makes sense – if you're learning French, people will ask if you speak other languages. Have your answer prepared!

02.01 Notice the different ways Jacques asks questions and how Lauren answers them.

Jacques : Alors, Lauren, est-ce que tu aimes habiter ici, à Paris ?

Lauren : Oui, bien sûr. J'adore. J'adore la ville et les parcs. Surtout le jardin des Tuileries. Et j'apprends beaucoup de français.

Jacques : Bravo ! Tu parles d'autres langues ?

Lauren : Non, je parle seulement anglais et un peu français. Et toi ?

Jacques : Oui ! Je parle bien italien et je parle un peu russe.

Lauren : Vraiment ?

Jacques : Oui, vraiment !

Lauren : Tu parles pas anglais ?

Jacques : Pas encore. J'espère pratiquer un peu mon anglais ici aujourd'hui.

In the film *Pirates of the Caribbean*, Elizabeth Swann invokes the right of 'parlay' and demands to speak to the captain of the Black Pearl. This comes from the French word *parler*, meaning 'to speak' and you can use the association to help you remember the meaning of the word if you like!

FIGURE IT OUT

1 Answer the questions with *oui* (yes) or *non* (no).

a *Est-ce que Lauren aime habiter à Paris ?* *oui / non*

b *Est-ce que Lauren parle trois langues ?* *oui / non*

c *Est-ce que Jacques parle anglais ?* *oui / non*

2 Are the statements about the conversation *vrai* (true) or *faux* (false)?

a Jacques speaks Italian. *vrai / faux*

b Lauren speaks Russian. *vrai / faux*

3 What word makes the difference between saying 'I like' and 'I don't like' in French? Highlight it in the conversation.

4 How would you say 'I don't want' and 'I don't live' in French?

a *je veux* (I want) → ____________________

b *tu habites* (you live) → ____________________

Ici means 'here'. To remember this word, try imagining a mother whose children run out onto an icy road, and their mother yells, *Viens ICI !* (Come HERE!)

NOTICE

02.02 Listen to the audio and study the table.

Essential phrases for Conversation 1

French	Meaning	Pronunciation
est-ce que tu aimes...	do you like...	ehs kuh tew ehm
...habiter ici ?	...living here?	ah-bee-tay ee-see
oui, bien sûr	yes, of course	wee bee-ahN sewR
j'adore	I love it	zhah-doR
j'apprends beaucoup de français	I'm learning a lot of French	zhah-pRawN boh-koo duh fRawN-seh
tu parles d'autres langues ?	do you speak any other languages? (you speak of-other languages?)	tew pahRl doht lawNg
je parle...	I speak...	zhuh pahRl
...seulement anglais	...only English	suhl-mawN awN-gleh
...un peu français	...a little bit of French	ahN puh fRawN-seh
...bien italien	...Italian well	bee-ahN nee-tah-lee-ahN
vraiment ?	really?	vReh-mawN
tu parles pas anglais ?	don't you speak English?	tew pahRl pah zawN-gleh
pas encore	not yet	pah zawN-koR
j'espère pratiquer aujourd'hui	I hope to practise today	zheh-spehR pRah-tee-kay oh-zhooR-dew-wee

VOCAB: *ne...pas*
You may have learned in school French to use both *ne* and *pas* to negate a sentence, as in *je ne parle pas*. This is technically the right way to make a negative sentence, but in casual conversations people often just use *pas*. *Je parle pas* works just fine.

1 What are the two phrases Jacques uses to describe how well he speaks Russian and Italian? Highlight them in the phrase list, then write them out.

_______________ _______________

2 Notice the difference in word order between *Je parle bien italien* in French and 'I speak Italian well' in English. Based on this, how would you say the following in French?

a I speak English well. *Je parle* _______ _______

b I want to speak French well. *Je veux parler* _____ _____ _______

3 How does Jacques ask the question, 'Do you like?'? Highlight it in the phrase list. Using the same question form, how would you ask:

a Do you love (*aimes*)... ? _______________
b Do you want (*veux*)... ? _______________
c Do you live (*habites*)... ? _______________
d Don't you speak (*parles*)... ? _______________

4 What question form does Jacques use to ask if Lauren speaks other languages? Underline it in the phrase list, then write it out.

____

GRAMMAR EXPLANATION: asking questions

There are three ways to ask questions in French with an expected 'yes' or 'no' answer:

- Add *est-ce que* before a statement. ***Est-ce que tu aimes voyager en train ?***
- Simply use a statement, but raise your intonation to show curiosity. ***Tu aimes voyager en train ?*** (vs *Tu aimes voyager en train.*)
- Swap the verb and subject: ***Aimes-tu voyager en train ?*** (This is more formal.)

I like to stick with the first two forms in casual conversations. Just be sure to raise your intonation at the end to make it clear that it's a question – you know what I mean?

PRACTICE

1 Fill in the sentences with the missing word(s) in French.

a *Je parle* ______________ *anglais.* (I speak **only** English.)

b ______________________________ russe.
(I'm **learning a little bit** of Russian.)

c ______________ *! Je parle* ______________________ *!*
(**Really**! I **don't** speak **Italian**!)

d ______________, *j'* ______________ *le français !*
(**Today**, I'm **studying** French!)

e *Je veux parler* ______________ *français,* ______________ *!*
(I want to speak **a lot of** French, **of course**!)

GRAMMAR TIP:
l' before a vowel
Whenever a word starts with a vowel or usually with an *h*, *le* or *la* changes to *l'*. For example: *le anglais → l'anglais; le italien → l'italien; le hôtel → l'hôtel.*

2 02.03 Practise recognizing the difference in sound between questions and statements in French. Listen to the audio and say whether you hear a question or a statement.

a question / statement
b question / statement
c question / statement
d question / statement
e question / statement

3 02.04 Change these statements to questions. Then say them out loud and check your answers against the audio.

a *Alex habite à Paris.* ______________________ (*est-ce que*)
b *Tu parles italien.* ______________________ (invert)
c *Marc apprend le français.* ______________________ (intonation)

GRAMMAR TIP:
'I learn' and 'I'm learning'
Remember, don't be tempted to translate English *-ing* words into a French equivalent. French doesn't work this way. In French, 'I learn French' and 'I am learning French' are said the same way: *j'apprends le français.*

PUT IT TOGETHER

1 Use your dictionary to look up the French translations for the languages given. Then add, in French, two more languages you would like to learn.

a German *l'*______________
b Spanish *l'*______________
c Chinese *le* ______________
d ______________
e ______________

2 How would you answer the questions in French? If you speak other languages, say whether you speak them 'well' or 'a little bit'. If you want to learn other languages, say which ones. Then repeat them out loud.

a *Tu parles d'autres langues ? Non / Oui, je parle* ______________

b *Est-ce que tu veux apprendre d'autres langues ?*
Non / Oui, je veux ______________________

#LANGUAGEHACK: learn vocab faster with memory hooks

The trick I use for remembering vocab is **mnemonics**, or memory hooks.

A mnemonic is a learning tool that helps you remember a lot more words and phrases. I've already given you two mnemonics so far.

- the story about Elizabeth Swann claiming 'parlay'
- the story about the mother yelling *Viens ICI !* to kids on an icy *ici* road.

These associations act like glue for your memory. The key to a good mnemonic is to think about an image or sound that connects the word to its meaning, then try to make it silly, dramatic or shocking – make it memorable! The easiest way to do this is through **sound association**. Simply say the French word out loud until you can think of an English word that sounds like it. It may even be similar in meaning.

Examples:

- the word for 'house', *la maison* [*meh-zohN*], sounds like 'mansion'.
- the word for 'sea', *la mer* [*mehR*], sounds like 'marine' (or submarine).

If you can't think of a similar-sounding word, then try to use a **powerful image** to hook the French word and its meaning to a familiar word in an interesting way.

Examples:

- to remember that *écrivain* [*ay-kRee-vahN*] means 'writer', imagine Keanu 'Reeves' in *The Matrix*, writing a novel while the world falls apart behind him...

I'll occasionally hint at tricks you can use to remember new vocab. For now, you should get used to creating new mnemonics yourself.

YOUR TURN: use the hack

02.05 Listen to the audio to hear the pronunciation of each word. Then use sound association or image association to create your own mnemonics. Repeat the words to mimic the speakers.

a *la lumière* (light)
b *la rue* (street)
c *cher* (expensive)
d *la chose* (thing)
e *le livre* (book)

CONVERSATION 2

How long have you been learning French?

Another 'first question' you can expect when you speak French with someone new is 'How long have you been learning French?' Let's learn to recognize and respond to that question now.

VOCAB: *depuis* for 'since' or 'for'
English uses the phrase 'have been' in expressions like '**I have been** learning French **for** two weeks', whereas the French would say '**I learn** French **since** two weeks'. You 'll use the word ***depuis*** in situations like this. It's a useful word for asking and answering the question 'how long?' In questions, ***depuis quand*** can mean 'since when?' or 'for how long?' In answers, ***depuis*** can mean both 'since' and 'for'.

02.06 Can you identify how Jacques asks Lauren 'how long...?'

Jacques : Depuis quand tu apprends le français ?
Lauren : J'apprends le français depuis deux semaines.
Jacques : Seulement deux semaines ? Tu parles très bien le français !
Lauren : Non, c'est pas vrai ... mais c'est gentil. Merci.
Jacques : De rien.
Lauren : Combien de langues tu veux apprendre encore, Jacques ?
Jacques : Ben, un jour j'espère apprendre trois langues : le japonais, l'arabe et l'anglais.

As in English, the phrase 'it's' in French combines 'it' with 'is' using an apostrophe. So ***ce*** (meaning 'it', 'this' or 'that') with ***est*** becomes ***c'est***.

FIGURE IT OUT

1 Use context along with what you learned in Unit 1 to figure out:

a How long has Lauren been learning French? Select the correct answer, then write it out here in French. one day / only two weeks

____

b How many languages does Jacques hope to learn? Highlight the relevant words in the conversation.

2 Highlight the French forms for:

a only
b true
c languages
d yet
e You speak French very well!
f I hope to learn…

VOCAB: *-ment*
In Conversation 1, you saw the words ***seulement*** ('only') and ***vraiment*** ('really' or 'truly'). In French, the ending ***-ment*** corresponds to the English ending '-ly'. So on its own, ***vrai*** simply means 'true'.

3 Write out the French phrases that are used in Conversation 2 to …

a say 'you're welcome' ______

b ask 'how long' or 'since when'

______

c ask 'how many' ______

NOTICE

02.07 Listen to the audio and study the table.

Essential phrases for Conversation 2

French	Meaning	Pronunciation
depuis quand...	how long… (since when)	duh-pew-wee kawN
tu apprends le français ?	have you been learning French? (you learn the French)	tew ah-pRawN luh fRawN-seh
j'apprends le français…	I've been learning French…	zhah-pRawN luh fRawN-seh
depuis deux semaines	for two weeks (since two weeks)	duh-pew-wee duh suh-mehn
tu parles très bien le français !	you speak French very well!	tew pahRl tReh bee-ahN luh fRawN-seh
non, c'est pas vrai…	no, that's not true…	nohN seh pah vReh
mais c'est gentil	but that's nice	meh seh zhawN-tee
merci	thank you	mehR-see
de rien	you're welcome	duh Ree-ahN
combien de langues… encore ?	how many (how-many of) more languages...?	kohN-bee-ahN duh lawNg awN-koR
un jour j'espère apprendre trois langues	one day I hope to learn three languages	ahN zhooR zhehs-pehR ah-pRawNd tRwa lawNg

CULTURE TIP: *'that's nice'*
Once I was on a train in France when I saw a hat on the ground, picked it up and returned it to its owner. He thanked me by saying, ***c'est gentil***, or 'that's nice'. It sounds weird in English, but in French it's a common way to acknowledge a nice thing someone says or does.

1 Underline the phrase that means '(for) how long' in the phrase list. What does the word *quand* mean on its own? ____________

2 Write out details about the conversation in French:

a How long has Lauren been learning French?
Lauren apprend le français ... ____________

b Which languages does Jacques hope to learn?
Jacques espère ... ____________

3 Notice how the speakers form their answers to questions starting with *Combien* and *Depuis quand*. Fill in the gaps with the corresponding question/answer words.

a ________ *de langues tu apprends ? J'apprends deux langues.*

b *Depuis quand tu apprends l'italien ? J'apprends l'italien* ________ *deux jours.*

c *Combien de langues tu parles ? Je parle deux* ________.

d ________ ________ *tu parles français ? Je parle français depuis deux jours.*

4 The word *encore* was used in Conversation 1 to mean 'yet'. Look at the way *encore* is used in the phrase list. How does the meaning of the word differ in the context of this conversation?

Encore is an extremely versatile word in French. Though it technically means 'yet', you'll see it used in different ways. You may already recognize the word as it is used in English to eagerly request another performance. This is because it also means 'again'.

CONVERSATION STRATEGY: filler words

You'll see some occasional 'filler words' used in French. While they don't add meaning to the conversation, just as we say 'well ...', 'so ...', 'y'know ...' in English, in French you'll hear filler words used in natural conversations. When you need to hesitate, use filler words to make your conversations feel more natural!

02.08 Listen to the audio, which first plays a speaker talking without using filler words. Then you'll hear the phrases repeated, but with filler words added. Notice how the filler words change the flow of the language.

ben	*alors*	*c'est-à-dire*

PRACTICE

Here's some new vocab to help you keep adding to your 'me-specific' script.

02.09 Listen to the audio and study the table.

Numbers (0–10) and time periods

0-5			6-10		
zéro	zero	zay-Ro	six	six	sees
un(e)	one	ahN/ewn	sept	seven	seht
deux	two	duh	huit	eight	ew-weet
trois	three	tRwa	neuf	nine	nuhf
quatre	four	kaht	dix	ten	dees
cinq	five	sahNk			

un jour	a day	ahN zhooR
une semaine	a week	ewn suh-mehn
un mois	a month	ahN mwa
un an	a year	ahN nawN

GRAMMAR TIP:
un / une
The word for 'one' is either *un* or *une*, depending on whether the word is masculine or feminine. (More on this in Unit 3.)

For **jour**, think of a daily journal. For **semaine**, think of the 'same men' you see every **week** on your favourite show. For **mois**, think of the sound people make when they kiss ('mwah!') the money coming out of their account after they get paid every **month**. For **an**, think of the word 'annual'.

GRAMMAR TIP:
plurals
Just like in English, to make a word plural, you'll usually add an s. So we can say *deux semaines, deux ans* and *deux jours*. What if the word already ends in an s? It stays the same: *un mois, deux mois*.

1 Translate the following phrases into French.

a five days ______________

b three years ______________

c eight months ______________

d four weeks ______________

e I have been living in France since my last birthday. (*mon dernier anniversaire*)

____

f I have been learning French for nine weeks.

____

2 Fill in the blanks with the missing French words.

How many days are you here? ______________ *de* ______________ *est-ce que tu es* ______________?

3 Think of some interesting mnemonics for the following words. (Remember: focus on the pronunciation, rather than the spelling.)

a *quatre* b *cinq* c *sept*

PUT IT TOGETHER

Create a cheat sheet with vocab in French that's immediately relevant to you.

Look up other important numbers or dates in your life – the month you were born, the ages of your children, how many cats you have… whatever is meaningful to you – and add them to your cheat sheet.

Numbers and times of year cheat sheet

______________	your phone number
______________	your age
______________	the month you were born
______________	the month you started learning French
______________	
______________	
______________	
______________	

1 *Quel est ton numéro de téléphone ?* Write it into the cheat sheet.

2 *Quel âge as-tu ?* Look up the number in French that corresponds to your age and add it to the cheat sheet. Then use the following phrase to say how old you are.

VOCAB: *j'ai* **'I have'**
In French, to say your age, you literally say 'I have (number) years.' Remember – a lot of the time you can't translate word-for-word from English!

Example: *J'ai* vingt-sept *ans.* (I'm 27 years old.)

J'ai ______________ *ans.*

3 Now look up the month you started learning French, and use *depuis* to answer the question: *Depuis quand tu apprends le français ?*

If someone asked you when you started learning French and this were August, you'd use depuis to say either **depuis mai** 'since May', or **depuis trois mois** 'for three months' … whichever is easier for you to remember!

Example: *J'apprends le français* depuis janvier.

J'apprends le français ______________

HACK IT: *learn vocab strategically*
Remember, you don't need to memorize all of the numbers or other types of vocab in French right away. Start by thinking about **what you'll need** to say most often, and learn that first. The rest will come with time, and conversation!

4 Someone asks you how long you've been learning French. You answer, and then you want to continue the conversation by asking your own question. How would you ask the following in French?

a How long have you been living in France? (*tu habites*)

____

b How long have you been working as a teacher? (*tu travailles comme professeur*)

____

PRONUNCIATION EXPLANATION: *u* and *r*

The French *u*

Remember: the French *u* sound (as in *tu*) sounds similar to the sound in the English word 'dew'. To produce it more accurately, shape your lips as if you were about to say 'oo' (as in 'food'), but actually attempt to say 'ee' (as in 'easy'), without changing your lip position. That's it!

1 🔊 **02.10** Here are some words you've already seen that use the French *u* sound. Listen to the audio and repeat, trying your best to mimic the speaker.

a *tu* (you) b *j'étudie* (I study) c *culture* (culture)

Getting French pronunciation just right takes practice, so don't worry if you don't get it at first. And don't be afraid to really go for it! Go ahead and **purse those lips** out as you're speaking French. It may feel strange (or even mocking), but it's not. That's how French people actually speak! Embrace it.

The French *r*

Remember: the French *r* is nothing like the English 'r', and in fact it comes from another part of your mouth – it's actually closer to an English 'k'!

To produce this sound, position your throat as if you were going to gargle mouthwash, then attempt to say a 'k' sound, but make it softer, and it will sound like a French *r*. Try to get feedback from a native speaker and you will soon get this!

2 🔊 **02.11** Here are some words you've already seen that use the *r* sound. Listen to the audio and repeat, trying your best to mimic the speaker.

a *alors* (so / then) b *après* (after) c *de rien* (you're welcome)

CONVERSATION 3

Sharing your opinions

Lauren and Jacques start to chat about how best to learn a new language.

02.12 Can you understand Lauren's method of learning French?

Jacques : Lauren, qu'est-ce que tu fais pour apprendre le français ?

Lauren : Ben … j'étudie le vocabulaire et je vais en classe chaque semaine.

Jacques : Eh bien … Je pense que c'est une mauvaise idée.

Lauren : Vraiment ?

Jacques : Oui. Pour apprendre l'italien, je préfère aller en classe chaque jour.

Lauren : Oh là là ! Comment tu le fais ?

Jacques : C'est-à-dire … je vais en classe chez moi, sur Internet. C'est simple, tu sais ?

Lauren : Très intéressant. Je dois faire ça !

Jacques : Tu aimes lire beaucoup de livres, non ? Ça aide !

Lauren : Oui, c'est vrai. Je suis d'accord !

CULTURE TIP: ***opinions*** In France you'll find that they are not afraid to be direct when they disagree with you on something, so don't be alarmed if your new French friends start to challenge you on an opinion. It's all in a friendly spirit!

Oh là là ! It sounds cliché, but the French really do say this!

FIGURE IT OUT

1 What does *qu'est-ce que* mean? ______________

2 Find the phrases meaning 'every week' and 'every day' in the conversation.

3 Answer these two questions in French.

a How often does Lauren have a French class? ______________

b How often does Jacques have an Italian class? ______________

4 Highlight three cognates or near cognates in the conversation.

5 *Vrai ou faux ?* Jacques prefers to have his Italian classes at home, on the Internet.

NOTICE

02.13 Listen to the audio and study the table. Pay special attention to the way Jacques pronounces the question *qu'est-ce que tu fais ?*

VOCAB: *vocabulaire technique*
French words about political, technical and scientific topics tend to contain a lot of English cognates. Because of that, you are actually even more likely to come across familiar words in complex conversations than you are in simple conversations!

Essential phrases for Conversation 3

French	Meaning	Pronunciation
qu'est-ce que tu fais...	what are you doing...	kehs kuh tew feh
pour apprendre le français ?	to learn French? (for to-learn the French)	pooR ah-pRawNd luh fRawN-seh
ben... j'étudie le vocabulaire	well... I study vocabulary	bawN zhay-tew-dee luh vo-kah-bew-lehR
je vais en classe...	I go to class...	zhuh veh zawN klahs

chaque semaine	every week	shahk suh-mehn
chaque jour	every day	shahk zhooR
je pense que...	I think that...	zhuh pawNs kuh
je préfère aller...	I prefer to go...	zhuh pRay-fehR ah-lay
comment tu le fais ?	how do you do that?	koh-mawN tew luh feh
c'est-à-dire...	that is to say...	seh-tah-deeR
c'est simple, tu sais ?	it's easy, you know?	seh sahNpluh tew seh
je dois faire ça !	I should do that!	zhuh dwa fehR sah
tu aimes lire beaucoup de livres ?	you like to read a lot of books?	tew ehm leeR boh-koo duh leev
c'est vrai	that's true	seh vReh
je suis d'accord !	I agree!	zhuh sew-wee da-koR

To remember **je pense**, think of the English word 'pensive'.

VOCAB: *que* as 'that'
Here we introduce *que*, which is used as 'that' to connect phrases, such as 'I know that you are French'.

Since you've already learned the word *pas*, you've practically doubled your vocabulary with a shortcut to saying opposites. Imagine that you want to say to your French partner, 'this is hard', but you haven't learned the word 'hard' yet. You can simply say it's 'not easy'. ***C'est pas simple.***

1 Find one new question word and two new filler words in the phrase list and circle them. Then write them here.

a How? ________ b well... ________ c that is to say... ________

2 Write out the five phrases the speakers use to give their opinions.

a I think that ____________________

b I prefer ____________________

c I should ____________________

d I agree ____________________

e That helps! ____________________

Changing a verb from its dictionary form – like 'to like' (**aimer**) – to other forms like 'I like' (**j'aime**) or 'you like' (**tu aimes**) is what language teachers typically refer to as conjugating the verb.

GRAMMAR EXPLANATION: *je* (I) and *tu* (you)

In Conversation 3, you met a lot of new verbs used in different ways. Now you need to know how to change them into different forms.

Let's start with the most common verbs for now: verbs that end in *-er* in the dictionary form.

Dictionary form verbs ending in *-er*

Step 1: Drop the *-er*

Step 2: Add an *-e* for *je*; add *-es* for *tu*

You can see that the rule of changing je to j' doesn't apply to tu.

PRONUNCIATION: *the silent s*

Even though an *-es* is added for verbs with *tu*, the last *-s* is silent. So the pronunciation is exactly the same for *je parle* and *tu parles*.

Examples: *aimer* (to like) → ***j'**aime*, ***tu** aimes*
habiter (to live) → ***j'**habite*, ***tu** habites*
parler (to speak) → ***je** parle*, ***tu** parles*

For other verbs with different endings, just remember for now that most of the time, you'll use the same forms for both *je* and *tu*:

vouloir (to want) → ***je** veux, tu veux*
faire (to do/to make) → ***je** fais, tu fais*

Exceptions

In this course, we don't have a lot of verbs that don't fit these patterns, but one you've seen so far is 'to go', which has the dictionary form *aller*, but the very different *je* form of *je vais* and the non-matching *tu* form of *tu vas*.

Other verbs like these are *savoir* (to know), *devoir* (should), *lire* (to read), *pouvoir* (to be able to) and *dire* (to say). Learn the forms of these top irregular verbs for now:

aller (to go)	savoir (to know)	devoir (should)	lire (to read)	pouvoir (to be able to)	dire (to say)
je vais	je sais	je dois	je lis	je peux	je dis
tu vas	tu sais	tu dois	tu lis	tu peux	tu dis

1 Practise changing these *-er* verbs into the *je* and *tu* forms.

a *étudier* (to study) → *j'* ________________ → *tu* ________________

b *penser* (to think) → *je* ________________ → *tu* ________________

c *demander* (to ask) → *je* ________________ → *tu* ________________

d *commencer* (to start) → *je* ________________ → *tu* ________________

2 Practise changing these other common verbs into the *tu* forms.

a *savoir* (to know) → *je sais* → *tu* ________________

b *devoir* (should) → *je dois* → *tu* ________________

c *lire* (to read) → *je lis* → *tu* ________________

d *pouvoir* (to be able to) → *je peux* → *tu* ________________

e *dire* (to say) → *je dis* → *tu* ________________

PRACTICE

1 Complete the sentences with the missing word(s) in French.

a ________________ *tu aimes* ________________? (**What** do you like **to read**?)

b __________ *beaucoup de* __________ *chez moi.* (I **read** a lot of **books** at my house.)

c *Est-ce que* __________ __________ *que je suis Français ?* (Do **you know** that I'm French?)

d ________________ ________________ ________________ *ça va* ________________ *bien.* (I **know that** things are going **very** well.)

2 Practise what you know by translating these full sentences into French.

a I prefer to speak French. ________________

b You should say that you like pizza. ________________

c You know that I have been learning French for two weeks.

____

d I think that French is simple! ________________

PUT IT TOGETHER

Now it's time for you to use what you've learned to create sentences about yourself in French.

Qu'est-ce que tu penses ? Write four sentences that each do one of the following:

- Use *je veux* to say something you want to do one day.
- Use *je vais* to talk about somewhere you like to go every so often.
- Use *je dois* to say something you should do.
- Use *je pense* que to express an opinion.

COMPLETING UNIT 2

Check your understanding

02.14 Go back and reread the conversations. When you're feeling confident:

- listen to the audio rehearsal, which will ask you questions in French
- pause or replay the audio as often as necessary to understand the questions
- repeat after the speaker until the pronunciation feels and sounds natural to you
- answer the questions in French (in complete sentences).

Show what you know...

Here's what you've just learned. Write or say an example for each item on the list. Then tick off the ones you know.

- [x] Ask a 'yes or no' question. Tu habites à Paris ?
- [ ] Give the *je* and *tu* verb forms (e.g. *apprendre*).
- [ ] Ask the question, 'How long have you been learning French?'
- [ ] Say how long you've been learning French.
- [ ] Say what other languages you speak or want to learn.
- [ ] Negate a sentence using *pas* (e.g. *C'est vrai !*).
- [ ] Give three filler words.
- [ ] Pronounce the French *u* and *r*:
    - [ ] *Tu étudies le français ?*
    - [ ] *Bien sûr ! J'adore la culture !*

COMPLETE YOUR MISSION

It's time to complete your mission: fool someone into thinking you speak French for at least 30 seconds. To do this, you'll need to prepare to initiate a conversation by asking questions and replying with your own answers.

STEP 1: build your script

Keep building your script by writing out some 'me-specific' sentences along with some common questions you might ask someone else. Be sure to:

- ask a question using *depuis quand ?* or *combien ?*
- ask a question using *est-ce que ?* or *qu'est-ce que ?*
- say whether you speak other languages and how well you speak them.
- say how you are learning French.
- say what other languages you want / hope to learn.
- say how long you've been learning French using *depuis*.

Write down your script, then repeat it until you feel confident.

STEP 2: all the cool kids are doing it … *online*

Momentum is a powerful tool. Once you get started, it's so much easier to keep going.

You've put the time into preparing your script; now it's time to complete your mission and share your recording with the community. Go online to find the mission for Unit 2, and use the French you've learned right now!

STEP 3: learn from other learners

How well can you understand someone else's script? **Your task is to listen to at least two clips uploaded by other learners**. How long have they been learning French? Do they speak any other languages? Leave a comment in French saying which words you were able to understand and answering a question they ask at the end of their video. And ask them one of the questions you've prepared.

STEP 4: reflect on what you learned

What new phrases did you learn in the online community? Always write them down!

-
-
-
-

HEY, LANGUAGE HACKER, DO YOU REALIZE HOW MUCH YOU CAN ALREADY SAY?

After only two missions, you've learned so many words and phrases you can use in real conversations. Don't forget that you can mix and match words and sentences to create endless combinations. Get creative!

In the next few units, you'll learn more about how to have conversations in French – even if you have a limited vocabulary or haven't been learning for very long.

Magnifique !

3 SOLVING COMMUNICATION PROBLEMS

Your mission

Imagine this – you're having a great time at your *soirée* when someone decides it's time to play a party game – describe something without saying the word itself!

Your mission is to use your limited language and win the game. Be prepared to **use 'Tarzan French'** and other conversation strategies to **describe a person, place or thing** of your choosing in French.

This mission will help you overcome the fear of imperfection and show you how, with a powerful technique, you can make yourself understood.

Mission prep

- Use phrases for meeting new people: *salut, ça va bien, enchanté(e)*
- Use survival phrases to ask for help with your French: *Tu peux répéter ça ?*
- Talk about what you have and what you need with *j'ai* and *j'ai besoin de*
- Use the French liaison and the CaReFuL mnemonic to improve your pronunciation.
- Develop a new conversation strategy: use 'Tarzan French' to fill the gaps in your vocabulary with *personne, lieu, chose*.

BUILDING LANGUAGE FOR ... MEETING SOMEONE NEW

Practising your French with a tutor or teacher online, especially when you don't live in a French-speaking country, is one of the most effective (and affordable) ways to learn French quickly. In this unit you'll learn strategic survival phrases you can use whenever there's something you don't understand, and you'll use 'Tarzan French' to communicate with limited language or grammar. Strategies like these help you become comfortable making mistakes when speaking, and help you have meaningful conversations despite being a beginner.

#LANGUAGEHACK
power-learn word genders with the word-endings trick

CONVERSATION 1

Having an online chat

It's easy to have conversations with other French speakers online. I've done this for all the languages I've learned. These days I schedule online chats from home to maintain my strongest languages, including French. See our Resources online to learn how!

If you know someone well, a fun way to start a conversation is to say **coucou !** instead. Inspired by the sound of a cuckoo clock, and initially like a 'peekaboo' said to children, it's now used by adults as a casual and fun 'hey!'.

VOCAB: ***question words***
You can use question words at the start or end of a statement. ***Où est-ce que tu es ?*** and ***Tu es où ?*** Both mean 'Where are you?' The second form is more casual.

Lauren has decided to take Jacques' advice and have an online French lesson from home. She's about to have her first online conversation with Antoine, her new teacher. Since this is her first time meeting Antoine, she needs to introduce herself.

03.01 How does Antoine greet Lauren, and how does she reply to *Ça va*?

Antoine : Salut ! Ça va ?
Lauren : Salut ! Tout va bien. Merci beaucoup de m'apprendre le français.
Antoine : De rien ! Pas de problème.
Lauren : Comment tu t'appelles ?
Antoine : Je m'appelle Antoine. Et toi ?
Lauren : Je m'appelle Lauren.
Antoine : Tu as un joli nom ! Enchanté Lauren !
Lauren : Merci, c'est gentil. Enchantée !
Antoine : Alors, où est-ce que tu es aujourd'hui ?
Lauren : Euh, plus lentement, s'il te plait.
Antoine : Aujourd'hui, tu es où ?
Lauren : Ah, oui. Maintenant, je suis à Paris.

FIGURE IT OUT

1 Use context to figure out the gist of the conversation. Which of the following is the false statement?

a Lauren asks Antoine to repeat himself more slowly.
b Antoine wants to know why Lauren is learning French.
c Antoine asks where Lauren is today.

2 How do you say the following in French?

a thank you ____________________

b please ____________________

c you're welcome ____________________

3 How do you ask, 'What's your name?' in French?

____

4 What does *pas de problème* mean in English?

____

5 What question does Antoine ask Lauren at the end of the conversation?

____

NOTICE

03.02 Listen to the audio and study the table.

VOCAB: ***apprendre***
Apprendre is one of those handy words you can use to say two different things. As well as 'to learn', it also means 'to teach' when another person is indicated: *Marie m'apprend la guitare* (Marie is teaching me the guitar).

Essential phrases for Conversation 1

French	Meaning	Pronunciation
salut ! ça va ?	hi! how are you?	sah-lew sah vah
tout va bien	everything's good	too vah bee-ahN
merci beaucoup	thank you very much (thank-you a-lot)	mehR-see boh-koo
... de m'apprendre le français	... for teaching me French (of me-to-learn the French)	duh mah-pRawNd luh fRawN-seh
comment tu t'appelles ?	what's your name? (how you yourself-call?)	koh-mawN tew tah-pehl
pas de problème	not a problem	pah duh pRo-blehm
tu as un joli nom !	you have a pretty name!	tew ah ahN zho-lee nohN
enchanté(e) !	nice to meet you!	awN-shawN-tay
où est-ce que tu es aujourd'hui ?	where are you today?	oo ehs kuh tew eh oh-zhooR-dew-wee
plus lentement	more slowly	plew lawN-tuh-mawN
s'il te plait	please	seel tuh pleh
tu es où ?	where are you?	tew eh oo
maintenant, je suis à Paris	now, I'm in Paris	mahN-tuh-nawN zhuh sew-wee zah pah-Ree

Note that **Comment tu t'appelles ?** isn't exactly the same as 'What's your name?', but more like 'How do you call yourself?'

1 What phrase can you use when someone is speaking too fast?

____

2 Find examples in the phrase list of the different ways you can form the question 'Where are you?'

______________________ ______________________

3 How do you say the following in French?

a Nice to meet you. ____________ b Everything's good. ____________

c I'm in London now. (London = *Londres*) ______________________________

4 Write the English meaning of the French verb forms:

a *je suis* ____________ b *tu as* ____________ c *tu es* ____________

PRACTICE

1 03.03 Look again at the phrase list, and replay the audio to check your pronunciation of these five words and phrases.

beaucoup   *comment*   *aujourd'hui*   *s'il te plait*   *maintenant*

Aujourd'hui is another French word that you should learn as an entire chunk. Don't worry about the apostrophe – think of it as a single word that simply means 'today'.

2 Match the English question with its correct form in French.

a What's your name? 1 *Comment tu apprends le français ?*
b Where are you? 2 *Tu habites en France ?*
c Do you live in France? 3 *Comment tu étudies le français ?*
d How do you study French? 4 *Comment tu t'appelles ?*
e How do you travel? 5 *Je dois parler plus lentement ?*
f How are you learning French? 6 *Où es-tu ?*
g Should I speak more slowly? 7 *Comment tu voyages ?*

The question word 'do' is almost never directly translated to French. Instead of 'Do you like pizza?', simply ask Tu aimes la pizza ? 'You like pizza?'

3 Fill in the blanks with the missing word(s) in French.

a *J'ai* __________ *de travail* __________. (I have **a lot** of work **today**.)

b ____________ ____________ *le temps occupé* ____________ ! (**It's** busy **all** the time **here**!)

c *Tu travailles* ____________ ____________ ? (**Where** are you working **now**?) (lit., You are working **where now**?)

d *Tu* ____________ *m'* ____________ *comment cuisiner.* (You **should teach** me how to cook.)

GRAMMAR EXPLANATION: word order with objects

In Conversation 1, you saw a new French sentence structure in action.

'I love you' in French is *je t'aime*, literally 'I you love'. That's another example of this French sentence structure in use!

When Lauren said, *Merci beaucoup de m'apprendre le français*, you may have noticed that French uses a different word order from how we'd say it in English.

Example: English: You help **me**. French: *Tu m'aides*. (lit., ' You **me** help')

Here's some vocab to help you better understand this sentence structure.

If *me*, *te*, *le* or *la* come before a word starting with a vowel, they shorten to become *m'*, *t'*, *l'*.

03.04 Listen to the audio and study the table.

Word order with objects

Dictionary form	Example	Meaning	Dictionary form	Example	Meaning
aimer	*je t'aime*	I love **you**	*donner*	je te donne	I give **you**
entendre	*je t'entends pas*	I can't hear **you**	*demander*		I ask **you**
voir	*je le vois*	I see **it**	*expliquer*		I explain **it**
dire	*tu me dis*	you tell **me**	*aider*		you help **me**
appeler	*je t'appelle*	I call **you**			

Simply put, the object of a sentence – the person or thing being talked about – will appear *before* the verb in French, instead of after the verb, as in English. These are words like 'me', 'you', 'it', 'him', 'her' and 'them'.

While in English we'd say 'I'm calling you' instead of 'I call you', in French both phrases are translated the same way: *je t'appelle*.

Examples: *je te donne* = I give you
tu me donnes = you give me
je veux te donner = I want to give you
Je peux le donner ? = Can I give it?

1 Complete the sentences with the correct object word in French.

a I'm giving **you** — *je __________ donne*
b I can't see **it**. — *Je __________ vois pas.*
c Can I help **you**? — *Je peux __________ aider ?*

2 Complete these sentences with the correct verb form in French.

Example: Can you help me? *Tu peux m'**aider** ?*

a I hear it. — *Je l'* __________.
b Can you write that? — *Tu peux l'* __________ ?
c (Do) you see me? — *Tu me* __________ ?
d I want to tell you. — *Je veux te* __________.

GRAMMAR TIP:
verb + verb
Remember that when you combine two verbs, the second verb is put into the dictionary form. The same is true when you use this sentence structure. In this sentence structure, the object will always go between two verbs, as you can see in the examples.

3 Now put the words in the correct order to make complete sentences.

a *entends/tu/l'* __________ ? (Do you hear it?)
b *dire/me/tu peux* __________ ? (Can you tell me?)
c *envoyer/l'/je veux* __________. (I want to send it.)

In this situation, the word for 'that' is the same as the French word for 'it'.

4 The table is incomplete! Fill in the empty spaces using the correct object sentence structure.

PUT IT TOGETHER

Où est-ce que tu es aujourd'hui ? Use the words you've just learned to write sentences in French about your life.

- Use *maintenant* to write two sentences about where you are or what you're doing now.
- Use *aujourd'hui* to write two sentences about what you're doing or where you're going today.
- Use your dictionary to look up new words that you need.

There are some exceptions, but most of the time this will be the case. One common exception to keep in mind is dictionary-form verbs which end in -er, like manger. In these verbs, the ending is pronounced 'ay'.

If you're not sure how to pronounce a word, **just guess** and say it anyway! You can't learn French by keeping your mouth shut. Saying a word wrong and getting corrected is much better than saying nothing at all. Don't avoid making mistakes – embrace it. You'll learn French much faster if you do.

Notice that these letters fall outside of the **CaReFuL** mnemonic.

PRONUNCIATION EXPLANATION 1: final consonants

French pronunciation can seem frustrating at first. You'll notice that much of the time, the consonant at the end of a word is silent (as in *Paris*). But other times, it isn't (as in *Tour Eiffel*). Luckily, there's an easy trick for knowing when to pronounce the final consonant – just remember the mnemonic CaReFuL! Usually, the only consonants you pronounce at the end of a word are *C, R, F* and *L*.

03.05 Listen to the audio to hear the way the final consonants are pronounced. Repeat the words to try to mimic the speaker.

petit pour vais parc deux seulement neuf étudiants

1 Say these words aloud. Would you pronounce the last consonant?

a bonjour
b combien
c depuis
d avec
e quand
f avril
g créatif
h manger

PRONUNCIATION EXPLANATION 2: the *liaison*

While you may recognize a word when it's spoken alone, some words when spoken together blur into a *liaison*. Luckily this only happens with specific letters, and you can learn them quickly.

Generally, the letters *s, z, n, d, m, t, x* are silent at the end of words. For example, *les garçons* (lay gahR-sohN), and *chez Pierre* (shay pee-ehR).

But here's how the liaison changes things. If the word *after* begins with a vowel (*a, e, i, o, u*) or a silent *h*, the sound will change.

1 03.06 Listen to the audio to hear how the sound changes. Repeat out loud, trying your best to mimic the speakers.

- s, x, and z all make a 'z' sound

je vais aller	*zhuh vay zah-lay*	I'm going to go
chez eux	*shay zuh*	Their house

- d and t both create a 't' sound

un grand animal	*ahN gRawN tah-nee-mal*	a big animal
un petit ami	*ahN puh-tee tah-mee*	a boyfriend

- m and n create a nasalized sound

mon ami	*mohN nah-mee*	my friend
un an	*ahN nawN*	a year

CONVERSATION 2

I don't understand …

As Lauren continues her online class, she starts having trouble understanding what Antoine is saying, so she needs to ask him for help.

03.07 How does Antoine rephrase his words when Lauren asks for help?

Antoine : Pourquoi tu dis que tu es à Paris 'maintenant'. Tu habites dans une autre ville ?

Lauren : Je suis désolée. Je comprends pas.

Antoine : Pourquoi – pour quelle raison – tu es à Paris ?

Lauren : Ah, je comprends. Je suis ici pour apprendre le français !

Antoine : C'est vrai ? Très intéressant !

Lauren : Et toi ? Tu es où ?

Antoine : Je suis en France, à Toulouse. Je travaille ici.

Lauren : Tu peux répéter ça, s'il te plait ?

Antoine : J'habite à Toulouse, alors, je suis en France.

Lauren : Un instant … Je t'entends pas bien.

Maintenant is an extremely common word that you'll use all the time. Try to think of an association with 'maintaining' something now to help you remember.

The verb 'to work' ***travailler*** is tricky because it sounds so similar to the word 'travel'. I suggest you try to remember it by thinking of your worst morning commute and how **travelling** to work was already lots of **work**.

Remember, you'd only use this in casual situations when talking to a single person. Otherwise, use ***s'il vous plait*** in formal situations or with more than one person.

FIGURE IT OUT

1 Are the following statements *vrai* or *faux*?

a Antoine asks Lauren why she's in Paris. *vrai / faux*

b Lauren says she's in Paris for work. *vrai / faux*

c Antoine lives in Paris. *vrai / faux*

2 03.07 There are five liaisons in this conversation. Can you hear them? Listen to the audio again, then highlight them when you hear them.

3 Several of the French words in the conversation sound similar to their English counterparts. Can you guess their meaning?

a *intéressant* b *répéter* c *raison* d *comprends*

4 What is the meaning of these phrases?

a *Tu habites dans une autre ville ?* ______

b *Tu peux répéter ça ?* ______

c *Un instant … Je t'entends pas bien.* ______

NOTICE

03.08 Listen to the audio and study the table. Repeat the phrases, and pay special attention to *je suis désolée, je comprends* and *je travaille*.

You'll start to notice that sometimes words are written differently depending on whether the speaker is male or female – like **enchanté(e)** and **desolé(e)**. The same applies in English with the word 'fiancé', which is written 'fiancée' if you're speaking about a woman, but 'fiancé' if you're speaking about a man.

Convey whether or not you understand with **je comprends** and **je comprends pas**. Comprendre (to understand) is similar to the more formal word in English 'comprehend'.

Essential phrases for Conversation 2

French	Meaning	Pronunciation
pourquoi tu dis que...	why do you say that...	pooR-kwa tew dee kuh
tu habites dans une autre ville ?	do you live in another city?	tew ah-beet dawN zewn oht veel
je suis désolée	I'm sorry	zhuh sew-wee day-zo-lay
je comprends pas	I don't understand	zhuh kohN-pRawN pah
pour quelle raison tu es à Paris ?	for what reason are you in Paris? (for which reason you are at Paris)	pooR kehl Reh-zohN tew eh zah pah-Ree
j'habite ...	I live ...	zhah-beet
je travaille ici	I work here	zhuh tRah-vay-uh ee-see
Tu peux répéter ça ?	Can you repeat that?	tew puh Ray-pay-tay sah
un instant...	one moment...	ahN nahNs-tawN
je t'entends pas bien	I can't hear you well	zhuh tawN-tawN pah bee-ahN

1 Find examples of the following language in the phrase list, and write them out.

a The *je* and *tu* forms of *habiter* (to live) __________ __________
b The *je* and *tu* forms of *être* (to be) __________ __________
c The *tu* form of *pouvoir* (to be able to/can) and *dire* (to say) __________ __________
d The *je* form of *travailler* (to work) and *entendre* (to hear) __________ __________
e The *je* form of *comprendre* (to understand) and its negative form __________ __________

2 You've seen several 'survival phrases' that Lauren uses to tell Antoine she's having trouble with her French. Write them in the cheat sheet.

Your survival phrases cheat sheet

French	Meaning
Comment dire ... ?	How do you say...?
	More slowly, please.
	I'm sorry.
	I don't understand.
	Can you repeat that?
	One moment.
	I can't hear you well.

Survival phrases are your secret weapon for 'surviving' any conversation in French, even when you're having trouble understanding. Learn these phrases, and you'll never have an excuse to switch back to English.

PRACTICE

1 Combine French words you know in different ways to say:

a Where do you live? ______________________

b What are you saying? ______________________

c Where do you want to live? ______________________

d I understand that you're working. ______________________

Did you notice that most of the 'wh-' question words in English have 'qu-' equivalents in French?

2 You have now seen all of the main question words used in French! Use your dictionary to look up how to ask 'who?' in French, then fill in the French translations in the table.

Question words

French	Meaning	French	Meaning
	Why?		Which?
	What?		When?
	How?		How many?
	Where?	Est-ce que	Do...?
	Who?		Can you?

3 What question words would you ask in French to get the following answers?

a *Samedi.* ____________________
b *14.* ____________________
c *Pierre.* ____________________
d *La gare.* (the train station) ____________________
e *Parce que je veux …* ____________________

GRAMMAR EXPLANATION: how to say 'in' in French

For now, try to recognize the meanings of these words when you see them, but don't worry about getting this right. In truth, you can mix these words up all you like, and French people will still understand you. *Dans* is the most common form, though, so when in doubt, **guess dans.**

The way you say 'in' in French changes depending on what you're describing.

Situation	Word for 'in'	Example
a country (usually ending in e)	en	Je veux voyager en **Italie**. (I want to travel in Italy.)
a city	à	Je suis à **Dublin**. (I'm in Dublin.)
'the'/'a'	dans	Je travaille dans **un** hôpital. (I work in a hospital.)
other places, with no 'the'/'a'	en	Je suis en **classe**. (I'm in class.)

PUT IT TOGETHER

1 Create two of your own survival phrases by combining *tu peux* (can you) with object words like *me, te* and *le*.

Example: Tu peux m'aider, s'il te plait ?

(Can you help me, please?)

____

____

Add these new survival phrases to your survival phrase cheat sheet.

2 Now let's keep building your script. Use what you've learned in Conversations 1 and 2, as well as new 'me-specific' vocabulary to create new sentences that describe:

- Where you're from, but also where you live now (use *mais* and *maintenant*)
- How long you've lived there (use *depuis*)
- Where you work (use *travaille* + *dans un/une*)
- How long you've worked there (use *depuis*)

CONVERSATION 3

Can you hear me now?

I've had wonderful experiences learning French with native speakers. They'll often compliment you for doing such a good job, even if you're a beginner.

The French get an unfair reputation for being impatient with foreign visitors. Outside of the touristy city centres (and sometimes even in them!), you'll find the French to be extremely patient and friendly. Rest assured that you can speak broken French with native speakers and they will be happy to help you. Try it!

03.09 Lauren and Antoine are having Internet connection problems. Which word does Lauren use to tell Antoine that her connection is bad?

Have you noticed that every time we write in French, there's a space before the exclamation and question marks? This isn't a typo – it's how you do it in French! ***C'est vrai ? Oui !***

There are many ways to **sign off or say goodbye** to someone. You could say *salut* (the same word as for 'hi'), *ciao*, *à la prochaine* (until the next time), *à plus* (until later) or just *à* + day/time (like *à demain !* for 'see you tomorrow!'). Any of these are preferable to the overly formal *au revoir*.

Lauren : Je pense que j'ai une mauvaise connexion. Je suis désolée !

Antoine : Pas de problème. Est-ce que tu veux désactiver ta webcam ?

Lauren : C'est pas ma webcam. J'ai un problème avec ... tu sais ... ouf ... j'oublie le mot ! Ma chose Internet !

Antoine : Ton wifi ? Ton ordinateur ?

Lauren : Oui, c'est ça – mon ordinateur ! J'ai besoin de le réinitialiser.

Antoine : Ça marche, si tu penses que c'est une bonne idée.

Lauren : Peut-être ... Tu m'entends maintenant ?

Antoine : Pas bien.

Lauren : Je suis désolée. J'ai un vieil ordinateur. Je peux t'appeler la semaine prochaine ?

Antoine : Pas de souci ! Tu veux reparler quand ? Samedi ?

Lauren : Ça marche ! À bientôt !

Antoine : À la prochaine !

FIGURE IT OUT

1 There are several French words in the conversation that are the same as or similar to their English counterparts. Can you guess their meaning?

a *désactiver* b *réinitialiser* c *connexion*

2 Use words you know along with context to figure out which of the following statements is not true.

a Lauren has a bad connection.

b Lauren and Antoine agree to talk another time.

c The problem is with Lauren's webcam.

d Antoine can't hear Lauren well.

3 Answer the following questions in French.

a What is the phrase Lauren uses when she can't remember the word for 'computer'? ________________

b How do you apologize in French? *Je* ________________

c What are two ways of saying goodbye in French?

________________ ________________

4 Highlight the word meaning 'week'. Is it masculine or feminine? How do you know?

5 What do you think the words *ma* and *mon* mean? *Ta* and *ton*?

________________ ________________

Mistakes are a necessary part of the process – you can't learn French without making lots of them. Mistakes aren't just inevitable, they are important for making progress. In games like chess, players are advised to lose 50 games as soon as possible. Get them out of your system sooner, and you can improve so much faster!

CONVERSATION STRATEGY 1: use 'Tarzan French' to communicate with limited words

As a beginner, you won't always know how to say exactly what you want. Instead of feeling frustrated, focus on getting your point across, rather than speaking eloquently. This means getting comfortable making mistakes.

That's why I recommend you embrace 'Tarzan French'. Find ways to convey your ideas that are understandable, even if your grammar or word choice isn't beautiful. You can still get your meaning across if you know just the key words.

For example, if you want to say 'Could you tell me where the bank is?' you could convey the same meaning with only two words, 'Bank ... where?', just like Tarzan.

Tu peux me dire où est la banque ? → Banque ... où ?

I call the fear of making mistakes **'perfectionist paralysis'**. Perfectionism is your enemy because it will hold you back from actually communicating. If you wait to say everything perfectly, you'll never say anything at all!

Try out your 'Tarzan French'! Look at these sentences. Isolate the key words, then use 'Tarzan French' to convey the same meaning (even if less elegantly).

Example: *Je te comprends pas. Tu peux répéter ça, s'il te plait ?*
→ Répéter, s'il te plait ?

a *Je suis désolée, mais ça te dérange de parler plus lentement ?*

____

b *Peux-tu me dire combien ça coute ?*

____

c *Pardon, tu sais où est le supermarché ?*

____

CONVERSATION STRATEGY 2: use the power nouns *personne, endroit, chose*

These words are power nouns. By definition, they encapsulate pretty much all other nouns, so you can use them in a huge number of situations when you want to describe something but don't know the French word:

personne (person), *endroit* (place), *chose* (thing)

Simply use this formula:

(power noun) + *de* + (any word related to the thing in question)

For example, if you can't remember the words for:

- 'train station' (*la gare*), try 'train place': *endroit de train*
- 'bed' (*le lit*), try 'sleep thing': *chose de dormir*

In Conversation 3, Lauren uses this trick when she forgets the word for 'computer'.

Try it out. How could you convey your meaning using power nouns?

Example: Pen? → ('writing thing') → chose d'écrire

a Library? → ('book place') → __________

b Waitress? → ('restaurant person') → __________

NOTICE

03.10 Listen to the audio and study the table.

Essential phrases for Conversation 3

French	Meaning	Pronunciation
je pense que j'ai…	I think that I have…	zhuh pawNs kuh zhay
pas de problème	no problem	pah duh pRo-blehm
j'ai besoin de …	I need … (I have need of)	zhay buh-zwahN duh
j'oublie le mot !	I forget the word!	zhoo-blee luh mo
ton wifi ? Ton ordinateur ?	your wifi? your computer?	tohN wee-fee tohN noR-dee-nah-tuhR
c'est ça	that's it	say sah
ça marche	that works	sah mahRsh
si tu penses que …	If you think that …	see tew pawNs kuh
c'est une bonne idée.	It's a good idea	seh tewn bon ee-day
peut-être	maybe	puh teht
tu m'entends ?	can you hear me? (do you hear me?)	tew mawN-tawN
je peux t'appeler …	can I call you …	zhuh puh tah-play
… la semaine prochaine ?	… next week?	lah suh-mehn pRo-shehn
pas de souci !	no worries!	pah duh soo-see
à bientôt !	see you later!	ah bee-ahN-toh
à la prochaine !	see you next time!	ah lah pRo-shehn

VOCAB: *avoir besoin de* - ***'to have need of'*** To express 'I need' in French you literally say 'I have need of' then follow this with a noun or a verb, e.g.: *J'ai besoin d'aide* (I need help).

If you need to access someone's **wifi**, just ask for their ***mot de passe*** (password).

You should recognize this phrase, as it's used in French to tell someone your name. But keep in mind that it literally means 'to call you'.

1 Fill in the gaps with the missing verb forms.

a *avoir* (to have) → ____________ (I have) → *tu as* (you have)

b *penser* (to think) → *je pense* (I think) → ____________ (you think)

c *pouvoir* (to be able to) → ____________ (I can) → *tu peux* (you can)

d *entendre* (to hear) → *je t'entends* (I hear you) → ____________ (you hear me)

e ____________ (to call) → *je m'appelle* (I call myself) → *tu t'appelles* (you call yourself)

2 How would you say 'you need' in French? ____________

3 Notice the connector words in the phrase list. If someone says, *je suis désolé(e)*, and you want to tell them 'it's OK', you could use two phrases from the phrase list. One is given here -- find the other.

pas de problème ____________

4 'That works' is an extremely versatile connector phrase. Write it out in French.

____

5 Lauren also uses the new survival phrase 'I forget the word!' Find it in the phrase list, then add it to your survival phrase cheat sheet.

PRACTICE

1 Practise combining new verbs with other words you know.

a I have + a computer ____________
You have + a webcam ____________

b I think that + it works ____________
I think that + you have ____________
You think that + I can ____________

c I can + to say ____________
You can + to have ____________

d I need + another computer ____________
I need + to work ____________
You need + to be ____________

2 Fill in the missing words in French.

a *Tu* ____________ *réinitialiser ton* ____________ ? (**Can** you restart your **computer**?)

b ______ *tu* ______, *je* ______ *t'* ______. (**If** you **want**, I **can help** you.)

c *La* ____________ *fois, j'* ____________ ____________ *une meilleure connexion.*

(**Next** time, I **hope to have** a better connection.)

#LANGUAGEHACK: learn word genders with the word-endings trick

French words are all either masculine or feminine. The gender affects whether the word is prefaced with *le* or *la* (both meaning 'the'), and *un* or *une* (both meaning 'a').

Feminine:	*la conversation* (the conversation)	*une femme* (a woman)
Masculine:	*le train* (the train)	*un homme* (a man)

But why is 'conversation' feminine? At first, it can seem like genders are assigned at random. For instance, *masculinité* is feminine, and *féminisme* is masculine!

Word gender has nothing to do with whether the concept of the word is masculine or feminine. It's actually the *spelling*, in particular the word's ending, that determines its gender – which means you can guess a word's gender from its spelling:

- If a word ends in a consonant in its singular form, it's probably *masculine*.

Examples: *le poulet* (the chicken), *le chocolat* (the chocolate), *un amateur* (an amateur)

- If a word ends in *-e* or *-ion* in its singular form, it's probably *feminine*. Also, guess feminine for the endings *-ée*, *-ité*, *-ie*, *-ue*, *-ance*, *-ence*, *-lle*, *-ule*, *-ure*, *-ette*.

Examples: *une idée* (an idea), *la différence* (the difference), *la culture* (the culture), *la nation* (the nation), *la pollution* (pollution), *une université* (a university)

Exception: the endings *-age*, *-ège*, *-isme*, *-ème* and *-ment* are **usually** masculine.

There are always exceptions, but this trick works most of the time. This is another situation where **guessing is your friend**. Don't avoid using words you know just because you're unsure of the genders. In fact, you could say *le* for everything, and it would almost never cause a communication problem!

English once used word genders, too! We lost them over time, but sailors still refer to the ocean and boats as 'she' – a modern remnant of old English word genders.

YOUR TURN: use the hack

1 So, why is *masculinité* feminine and *féminisme* masculine?

2 *Un* or *une*? Select the correct gender.

a *un/une village*
b *un/une ordinateur*
c *un/une café*
d *un/une baguette*
e *un/une éducation*
f *un/une ville*
g *un/une appartement*
h *un/une privilège*
i *un/une vin* (wine)
j *un/une poème*
k *un/une comédie*
l *un/une différence*
m *un/une famille*
n *un/une camping*
o *un/une action*

The words for 'my' and 'your' also change depending on whether a word is masculine or feminine.

Example:

une maison (f.) (a house) → *ma* maison (my house) → *ta* maison (your house)
un chien (m.) (a dog) → *mon* chien (my dog) → *ton* chien (your dog)

3 Select the correct forms of *mon/ma* and *ton/ta*.

a *un travail* (a job) → *mon/ma travail* (my job) → *ton/ta travail* (your job)
b *une femme* (a wife) → *mon/ma femme* (my wife) → *ton/ta femme* (your wife)

PUT IT TOGETHER

Qu'est-ce que tu as ? Tu as besoin de quoi ? Keep building your script. Look up new 'me-specific' words in your dictionary so that you're practising phrases that you'll use in real conversations. Create three sentences about yourself in French in which you describe:

- your opinion of the newest smartphone on the market (use *je pense que*)
- what technology you have now (use *j'ai*)
- some things you need or would like to buy (use *j'ai besoin de*).

COMPLETING UNIT 3

Check your understanding.

🔊 **03.11** Review the conversations from this unit, and when you're feeling confident:

- listen to the audio and write down what you hear
- feel free to pause or replay the audio as often as you need to

Show what you know...

Here's what you've just learned. Write or say an example for each item in the list. Then tick off the ones you know.

- ☐ Say 'hello' and 'nice to meet you'.
- ☐ Give two phrases for saying goodbye.
- ☐ Say 'I understand' and 'I don't understand'.
- ☐ Say something that you have and something that you need.
- ☐ Use the survival phrases 'Can you repeat that?' and 'More slowly, please'.
- ☐ Use French object words in the right word order, e.g. 'Can you help me?'.
- ☐ Give the French words for 'person', 'place' and 'thing'.
- ☐ Pronounce the French liaison: *je vais aller.*

COMPLETE YOUR MISSION

It's time to complete your mission: use 'Tarzan French' to play (and win!) the word game. To do this, you'll need to prepare phrases for describing a French person, place or thing that other people could guess – without knowing the word itself.

If you get stuck, you're probably struggling with perfectionist paralysis. Take a step back, and remind yourself that your script is supposed to be imperfect today!

STEP 1: build your script

Let's practise embracing 'imperfectionism' with today's script.

Use your 'Tarzan French' and the unit conversation strategies to...

- say whether you're describing a person, place or thing
- for a person, describe him/her with any words you know (What is his/her *travail*? Where is he/she *maintenant*?)
- for a thing, describe whether it's something you have (*j'ai*), need (*j'ai besoin*), like or dislike
- for a place, describe what types of people live there or things associated with it.

For example, you could say:

J'imagine ... une personne célèbre ... travailler ... dans le cinéma ... Pirate ... absurde ... dire beaucoup ... 'où est le rhum ?'

Write down your script, then repeat it until you feel confident.

Really! The more time you spend on a task, the better you will get! (Studies show that you will be **30% better** than your peers who don't practise their speaking regularly.)

STEP 2: practice makes perfect ... *online*

Getting over the embarrassment of 'looking silly' is part of language learning. Use your 'Tarzan French' to help you overcome these fears! Upload your clip to the community area, and you'll be surprised at how much encouragement you get. Go online to find your mission for Unit 3 and see how far you can get with your 'Tarzan French'.

STEP 3: learn from other learners

After you've uploaded your own clip, get inspiration from how others use 'Tarzan French'. **Your task is to play the game and try to guess the words other people describe**. Take note of the clever ways they use the conversation strategies from the unit, and stash them into a mental note to try later on your own.

STEP 4: reflect on what you've learned

Did you learn about new places and people from the community? Write down anything interesting that you might want to look into later – a famous actor you might want to look up, or a film you may want to see. What gaps did you identify in your own language when carrying out your mission? What words do you reach for over and over again? What words do you hear frequently, but don't understand? Note them here!

HACK IT: ***change your search preferences to français***
Did you know that many major websites automatically detect your language from your browser settings, and adjust accordingly? You can change these settings to *français*, and you'll instantly notice your search engine, social networking sites and video searches will automatically change to French! You can also simply go to google.fr (and click *français*) to search French-language websites around the world ... then be sure to type your keywords in French!

HEY, LANGUAGE HACKER, YOU'RE ON A ROLL!

By working around a limited vocabulary, you really can speak French with people quickly. It's not about learning all the words and grammar. It's about communicating – sometimes creatively. By finishing this mission, you've learned valuable skills that you'll use again and again in the real world. Next, you'll learn to talk about your plans for the future.

Fantastique !

4 DESCRIBING YOUR FUTURE PLANS

Your mission

Imagine this – you want to spend a few weeks exploring Europe, but you can only afford the trip if your French-speaking friend comes with you and splits the cost.

Your mission is to make them an offer they can't refuse! **Describe the trip of your dreams** and convince a friend to take the trip with you. Use *on va ...* to draw the person in and say all the wonderful things you'll do together. Be prepared to **explain how you'll get there** and **how you'll spend your time**.

This mission will help you expand your conversation skills by talking about your future plans and combining new sequencing phrases for better French flow.

Mission prep

- Develop a conversation strategy for breaking the ice: *Ça vous dérange si ...*
- Talk about your future travel plans using *je vais* + dictionary form
- Describe your plans in a sequence: *pour commencer, après, ensuite ...*
- Learn essential travel vocabulary: *tu peux prendre un train*
- Use *on* as the informal 'we' form
- Memorize a script that you're likely to say often.

BUILDING LANGUAGE FOR STRIKING UP A CONVERSATION

It takes a bit of courage to get started practising your French. But preparing 'ice breakers' in advance helps a lot! In this unit, you'll build a ready-made script you can use to start any conversation. You'll learn how to make conversations with French speakers more casual, and hopefully even make a new friend or two!

#LANGUAGEHACK
say exponentially more with these five booster verbs

CONVERSATION 1

Excuse me, do you speak French?

CULTURE TIP: ***la Francophonie***
Many people think of France when it comes to the French language, but most people who speak French actually live outside of France. French is spoken in ***Belgique*** (Belgium), ***Suisse*** (Switzerland), ***Luxembourg*** (Luxembourg), 21 ***pays d'Afrique*** (African countries), ***Haïti*** (Haiti) and ***Canada*** (Canada), with about 170 million speakers across five continents, collectively known as ***la Francophonie*** (the French speaking world). Think of French as your passport to an incredibly large pool of fascinating people!

Lauren is back at her local language group. She's been practising her French for a few weeks now and chatting regularly with Jacques, but today, she wants to build up her confidence to approach someone new and strike up a conversation.

04.01 What phrases does Lauren use to approach someone new?

Lauren : Excusez-moi, parlez-vous français ?
Julie : Oui ! Je suis belge.
Lauren : Chouette ! Ça vous dérange si je pratique mon français avec vous ?
Julie : Pas de problème – avec plaisir !
Lauren : Je m'appelle Lauren. On peut se tutoyer ?
Julie : Si tu veux – pourquoi pas ? Je m'appelle Julie.
Lauren : Parfait ! Je suis encore débutante.
Julie : Mais tu peux dire tellement déjà !
Lauren : Merci, mais j'ai besoin de pratiquer encore avec des francophones.
Julie : Je suis très patiente – alors, on parle !

There are many ways to say 'cool' in French. You can actually use the English word **'cool'** if you like (though never to refer to temperature) or **super**, or **génial** which means 'genius-like'. My favourite though is **chouette**, which literally means 'owl'.

FIGURE IT OUT

1 *Vrai ou faux ?*

a Julie is from Belgium. *vrai / faux*
b Lauren asks Julie to go to a café with her. *vrai / faux*
c Lauren thinks Julie is impatient. *vrai / faux*

2 Find and underline the phrases in which:

- a Julie tells Lauren where she's from.
- b Lauren asks Julie if she speaks French.
- c Lauren asks to practise French with Julie.
- d Julie says 'let's talk'.

3 Now find and highlight the words:

a perfect   b patient   c beginner

4 How can you reply to requests? Write out the following phrases.

a If you like ________   c Why not? ________   e Great! ________

b With pleasure! ________   d No problem! ________

NOTICE

04.02 Listen to the audio and study the table. Pay special attention to the way Lauren pronounces *ça vous dérange si* and *on peut se tutoyer*.

Essential phrases for Conversation 1

French	Meaning	Pronunciation
excusez-moi	excuse me (formal)	ehk-skew-zay mwa
parlez-vous français ?	do you speak French? (formal)	pahR-lay voo fRawN-seh
chouette !	cool!	shweht
ça vous dérange si ...	do you mind if ... (formal)	sah voo day-RawN-zh see
...je pratique mon français avec vous ?	...I practise my French with you? (formal)	zhuh pRa-teek mohN fRawN-seh ah-vehk voo
avec plaisir !	with pleasure!	ah-vehk play-zeeR
on peut se tutoyer ?	can we use 'tu'?	ohN puh suh tew-twa-yay
si tu veux	if you like	see tew vuh
je suis encore débutante	I'm still a beginner	zhuh sew-wee zawN-koR day-bew-tawNt
tu peux dire tellement déjà !	you can say so much already!	tew puh deeR tehl-mawN day-zhah
j'ai besoin de pratiquer encore	I need to practise more	zhay buh-zwahN duh pRah-tee-kay awN-koR
alors, on parle !	so let's talk!	ah-loR ohN paRl

To remember that **tellement** means 'so much', think about the different TV shows you like and that there is so much on the 'telly'.

On is also used in expressions like 'let's go' – *on y va*. You can also use the slang, *on y go* !

1 What phrase might you say first to get a French speaker's attention?

____

2 How do you confirm that someone speaks French?

____

3 Which question should you ask when you want to say 'Do you mind if ... '?

____

4 Do you see the difference between formal and casual phrases in French? Match the forms in the box to the correct phrase, formal or casual.

avec toi	*excuse-moi*	*avec vous*
tu parles	*vous parlez*	*excusez-moi*

a you speak formal ______________ casual ______________
b excuse me formal ______________ casual ______________
c with you formal ______________ casual ______________

5 Complete the sentences using *déjà, encore* or *tellement.*

a I'm still speaking *Je parle* __________.
b I'm already speaking *Je parle* __________.
c I'm speaking so much *Je parle* __________.
d I still know *Je sais* __________.
e I already know *Je sais* __________.
f I know so much *Je sais* __________.

CONVERSATION STRATEGY 1: keep it simple with *on* and *tu*

Using *on* instead of *nous*

Your dictionary will tell you that the word for 'we' is *nous*. But there's an easier and more commonly used word in conversational French: *on* (literally 'one', as in 'one is not amused!').

You can use *on* instead of *nous* as a casual way of saying 'we'. This makes life easier for beginners, because you don't need to learn a completely different verb form. You can say *on parle, on pratique, on aime* (we speak, we practise, we like). For *-er* verbs, the *on* form usually looks the same as the *je* form.

Using *tu* instead of *vous*

Likewise, you can keep conversations in the informal *tu* form whenever possible to avoid having to learn the *vous* forms for now. The *vous* form is used in formal situations, as well as when you're addressing more than one person.

Having said that, if you meet a stranger and see an opportunity to practise, it's safer to introduce yourself using the formal (polite) form, *vous*, at first. **But here's a handy tip:** open the discussion with a set phrase like *parlez-vous français ?* Then quickly ask ***on peut se tutoyer ?*** If the other person is about the same age as you and the situation isn't formal, they'll nearly always say *oui*.

In fact, it's such a common transition that French has this special word for using the tu form.

GRAMMAR EXPLANATION: forming verbs with *on*

When the dictionary form of a verb ends in *-er*, then the *on* form is exactly the same as the *je* form. For example:

dictionary form	*je* form	*on* form
parler	je parle	on parle
écouter	j'écoute	on écoute

Otherwise, you can sometimes recognize *on* forms as ending with a *t*. The good news is that even when the spelling changes slightly, *on* forms are still pronounced the same as *je* (and *tu*) forms.

04.03 Listen to the audio and practise the pronunciation.

dictionary form	*je* form	*on* form
savoir (to know)	je sais	on sait
dire (to say)	je dis	on dit
pouvoir (to be able to/can)	je peux	on peut
apprendre (to learn)	j'apprends	on apprend

1 If *je pense* is the *je* form of *penser*, what is the *on* form?

____

2 Translate the following phrases using the *on* form.

a we work ________________ b we study ________________

3 Based on how *je veux* changes to *on veut*, how do you think 'we can' is translated into French, given that 'I can' is *je peux*?

____

PRACTICE

1 The phrase *je suis encore débutant(e)* is a useful phrase that can be modified to say countless other phrases. Use the base of this phrase to create new sentences by replacing *suis* with the given verb.

Example: I am still young. → Je suis encore jeune.

a I'm still living in Europe. (*habite / en Europe*)

____

b Are you still working at the bank? (*travailles / à la banque*)

____

c I am still going to class! (*vais / en classe*)

____

d Can we still practise? (*peut / pratiquer*)

____

2 Fill in the blanks with the missing words in French.

a *J'achète* ______ *mon billet.* (I'm **already** buying my ticket.)

b ______ ______ ______, ______ ______ *utiliser mon téléphone.* (**If you want, you can** use my phone.)

c *Est-ce que tu sais* ______ ______ *'airport' en français ?* (Do you know **how to say** 'airport' in French?)

d *C'est* ______ *d'être* ______ *!* (It's **cool** to be **here**!)

e *J'ai* ______ *tellement à* ______ *avant de voyager.* (I **still** have so much more **to do** before travelling.)

f ______ ______ ______ ______ *je pose une question ?* (**Do you** (formal) **mind if** I ask a question?)

CONVERSATION STRATEGY 2: memorize a regularly used script

A lot of people get nervous speaking to someone new for the first time – especially in another language. But when you plan out what you'll say in advance, you have less to worry about. Luckily, many conversations take a similar pattern, and you can use this to your advantage.

You can ride a bike without understanding aerodynamics, you can use a computer even if you don't know the physics of how circuits work ... and you can use French phrases at the right time, even if you don't understand each word and why they go together the way they do!

Learn set phrases

Just because you don't know the grammar behind a phrase, it doesn't mean you can't use it. You can simply memorize full phrases as chunks, so you can use them whenever you need to – even if you don't fully understand all the individual words.

Try this with the very useful power phrase, *Ça vous dérange si ...* , which can be used in a variety of situations and conversation topics.

Memorize a script

When you learn set phrases that are specific to you and combine them together, you create a personal 'script' you can use over and over again.

While travelling, I'm frequently asked, 'Why are you learning this language?' and about my work as a writer, which isn't easy to explain as a beginner. But because I know these questions are coming, I craft a solid response in advance so I can speak confidently when the question inevitably comes up.

You can even **have a native speaker review your script** and refine your French. It's fine to speak spontaneously with mistakes, but you may as well get it right if you're memorizing it in advance. It's easy and free when you know where to look. See our Resources online to find out how.

You may be asked about your upcoming travels or the personal reasons you're learning French. Ultimately, if you know you'll need to give an explanation or mini-story frequently, memorize it as a well-crafted script to have ready when the subject comes up. Here's how to do this:

- **Decide what you want to say. Make it personal to you.**
- **Then simplify it as much as possible** to remove complicated expressions. If possible, try to do this in French from the start by jotting down key words and phrases – you can fill in the script later. If you find this tricky, start your script in English and then try to translate it into French.
- **Finally, when you have your final script, recite it** as often as you can until you commit it to memory.

PUT IT TOGETHER

1 When might you ask the question *ça vous dérange si ...*? Use this phrase along with your dictionary to create sentences you could imagine yourself using abroad, such as:

- at a social event (e.g. '... if I speak with you?')
- in a park (e.g. '... if I touch your dog?')
- at a café (e.g. '... if I take this seat?')
- at someone's house (e.g. '... if I open a window?').

2 Pick one of the following situations, and prepare a short script you can use without having to think on the spot.

- **Situation 1:** Someone finds out that you're learning French and they also happen to speak French. (For this, I like to prepare some phrases like 'Ah, you speak French!', 'I'm still a beginner' or 'I've only been learning for ...')
- **Situation 2:** Someone asks you to give a mini life story, or asks why you are learning French. (For this you might say something like 'I think the language is beautiful!' or 'One day I hope to go to France.')
- **Situation 3:** You need to interrupt someone on the street to ask a question in French. (Politeness goes a long way here, so be sure to include 'excuse me' or 'I'm sorry', then add something like 'Do you mind if I ask you a question?').

Phrases like these are great to have in your back pocket. You'll use them a ton. You may know a few already, but it's good to have a go-to answer for these questions.

CONVERSATION 2

Where are you going?

Since Lauren and Julie are both visitors to Paris, travel is a natural conversation topic. In fact, as you learn any new language, you'll likely be asked (or want to ask someone else) about travelling to different places.

Pendant means 'during' or 'for' (a certain period of time). Think of a pendulum swinging as time passes.

Several anglicisms have made it into French that you'll recognize, such as **weekend**, cash (for how you pay), OK, brainstorming, email, cool and many others, especially in technology and business. If you hear a French person use these words, try it yourself with a French twang.

VOCAB: *il y a*
The French phrase *il y a* (pronounced eel ee ya) is very useful because it means both 'there is' and 'there are' – it doesn't change. So you could say *il y a un livre* (there is a book), or *il y a trois livres* (there are three books). Learn *il y a* as a chunk.

04.04 What phrase does Julie use to ask 'Do you travel a lot?'

Julie : Alors, tu es à Paris depuis quand ? Tu voyages beaucoup ?

Lauren : Depuis longtemps ... Je suis à Paris **pendant** quelques mois et après je vais au Québec.

Julie : Tu dois visiter mon pays, la Belgique. Tu peux prendre un train pour venir le **weekend**.

Lauren : C'est une bonne idée ! Ce weekend j'ai pas beaucoup d'heures. Peut-être le weekend prochain.

Julie : Tu veux dire que t'as pas 'beaucoup de temps' ?

Lauren : Exactement, oui. Merci !

Julie : Je dois voyager plus, moi-même. Je veux voir les autres villes en France comme Toulouse et Strasbourg. C'est maintenant ou jamais !

Lauren : C'est vrai, mais **il y a** beaucoup à faire ici, à Paris !

FIGURE IT OUT

1 Use context along with words you know to answer the questions.

a Where does Julie suggest that Lauren visit? ____________

b Where is Lauren going after Paris? ____________

2 Highlight the following phrases and write them out here in French.

a since when have you been in Paris? ____________

b for a few months ____________

c exactly ____________

3 Is the word *pays* masculine or feminine? ____________

4 Match the French words with their meanings.

comme jamais alors pendant plus moi-même autre

a more ______

b other ______

c during ______

d then/after ______

e like ______

f myself ______

g never ______

NOTICE

🔊 **04.05** Listen to the audio and study the table.

Essential phrases for Conversation 2

French	Meaning	Pronunciation
tu voyages beaucoup ?	do you travel a lot?	tew vwa-yah-zh boh-koo
pendant quelques mois	for a few months (during some months)	pawN-dawN kehl-kuh mwa
tu dois visiter mon pays	you should visit my country	tew dwa vee-zee-tay mohN pay-ee
tu peux prendre un train pour venir...	you could take a train to come...	tew puh pRawNd ahN tRahN pooR vuh-neeR
tu veux dire que...	you mean... (you want to-say that...)	tew vuh deeR kuh
t'as pas 'beaucoup de temps' ?	you don't have 'a lot of time'?	tah pah boh-koo duh tawN
moi-même	myself (me-same)	mwa mehm
je veux voir les autres villes, comme...	I want to see other towns / cities, like...	zhuh vuh vwaR lay zoht veel kohm
c'est maintenant ou jamais !	it's now or never!	seh mahN-tuh-nawN oo zhah-meh
il y a beaucoup à faire !	there's so much to do!	eel ee ah boh-koo ah fehR

VOCAB: ***you mean ...?***
In French, the way to say 'you mean ...' is ***tu veux dire ...*** (literally 'you want to-say'). You may hear this as you're learning and being corrected by others. You can also say ***je veux dire*** to clarify something you've said.

PRONUNCIATION: ***tu***
If the next word after ***tu*** starts with a vowel (or silent ***h***), in casual conversations you can shorten it to ***t'***. This leads to the much easier-to-pronounce ***t'es*** [*tay*] for 'you are' and ***t'as*** [*tah*] for 'you have', and even ***t'habites*** for '*you live*'. This is akin to 'y'know' in English. Use this trick if you are still working on your ***u*** pronunciation!

VOCAB: *pour* as 'in order to'
Whenever you want to say 'to do' something in French, if you can replace the 'to' in English with 'in order to' – such as 'I'm here (in order) to meet French people' – then remember to put the word *pour* in front of it in French: ***Je suis ici pour rencontrer des Français.***

You saw that *à* can mean 'in' when used before cities. It can also mean 'to' a city, depending on the context. So *Je vais à Dublin* is 'I'm going to Dublin'. When not talking about cities, it almost always means 'to'.

GRAMMAR EXPLANATION: *au, aux, du* and *des*

French has a few ways of shortening ways of saying 'to' and 'of' that you may start to recognize:

Je vais au supermarché.	I'm going **to the** supermarket.
Je donne le jeu aux enfants.	I'm giving the game **to the** children.
une photo du train	a photo **of the** train
le livre des étudiants	the students**'** book (lit., the book of the students)

This doesn't happen with *la*: *je vais à la maison* (I'm going **to the** house).

For now, don't worry about getting these right, but do try to recognize the words *au(x)* and *du/des* when you see them.

1 What phrases could you use to:

a recommend a place someone should visit?

____

b correct yourself in French by saying 'I mean ... '?

____

c ask 'Do you mean ... ?'

____

2 Take a closer look at the literal translations of *pendant* and *moi-même*.

a Now use *pendant* to say in French ...

- during the film ____________ *le* ____________
- for the month ____________ *le* ____________

b How do you think you'd say in French ...

- the same thing *la* ____________ ____________
- yourself ____________ - ____________

3 Match the French phrases with the correct English translations.

a *tu travailles*
b *je vais dire*
c *tu dois visiter*
d *je veux voir*
e *tu voyages*
f *je dois voyager plus*
g *tu peux prendre*

1 you should visit
2 you can take
3 you travel
4 you work
5 I'm going to say
6 I want to see
7 I should travel more

Here's some additional vocabulary you can use to talk about your own travel plans.

Travel vocab

French	Meaning	French	Meaning
prendre...	**to take...**	**aller en...**	**to go by...**
le train	the train	train	train
le bus	the bus	camion	truck
un taxi	a taxi	métro	metro / underground
l'avion	the plane (to fly)	voiture	car (to drive)
l'aéroglisseur	the hovercraft		

PRACTICE

1 Notice the verb meaning 'to take' in French. How would you say 'I take' and 'you take' in French?

a to take ________
b I take ________
c you take ________

2 Now use what you know about different verb forms to practise using this vocab in different ways.

a I'm taking the train ________
b I'm driving ________
c I'm going by car ________
d I'm flying ________

3 **Fill in the correct forms for each of the following phrases.**

a ____________ *weekend* (the weekend)

b ____________ *weekend* (this weekend)

c *le weekend* ____________ (next weekend)

d ____________ *weekend* (each weekend)

4 **Fill in the blanks with the missing words in French.**

a *Tu dois* ____________ *la tour Eiffel* ____________ ____________ *tout Paris.*
(You should **visit** the Eiffel Tower **in order to see** all of Paris.)

b *Tu fais le tour de France* ____________ ____________?
(Are you going around France **by car**?)

c *Je veux* ____________ *dans des villes* ____________ *Antibes* ____________ *Lannion !*
(I want **to go** to towns **like** Antibes **and** Lannion!)

d ____________ ____________ *en Italie,* ____________ ____________ *aller en avion.*
(**In order to go** to Italy, **you should** fly.)

e *Tu peux* ____________ ____________ *mais tu peux aussi* ____________
____________ ____________ .
(You can **fly**, but you can also **take the train**.)

f ____________ ____________ ____________ *tellement de* ____________ *de conduire.*
(**There are** so many **reasons** to drive.)

g *Je reste* ____________ *longtemps dans un seul* ____________ !
(I **never** stay in just one **place** long!)

PUT IT TOGETHER

Read the following questions, then write answers that are true for you.

a *Est-ce que tu voyages beaucoup ? (Ou ... un peu ? Ou ... jamais ?)*

Je voyage ____

b *Tu vas où pour ton prochain voyage ?*

Je vais à/en ____

c *Pour combien de temps tu vas à/en ... ? (Pendant quelques jours/semaines/mois ?)*

Je vais à/en ... ____________ *pendant* ____

d *Tu vas en France quand ? (Cette semaine ? Le mois prochain ? L'an prochain ?)*

Je vais en France ____

e *Comment tu vas voyager ? (Tu prends la voiture, l'avion ou le train ?)*

Je ____

CONVERSATION 3

How are you spending the weekend?

Lauren and Julie start talking about their plans for the weekend.

04.06 Notice how the phrases *je vais* and *tu vas* are used to talk about future plans. How does Julie ask, 'What are you going to do'?

Julie : Alors, qu'est-ce que tu vas faire à Paris ?

Lauren : Ben, pour commencer je vais voir la cathédrale Notre-Dame. Après, je vais au Café les Deux Magots pour boire un verre où Hemingway, Picasso et James Joyce allaient. Ensuite, je vais visiter le troisième arrondissement pour les restaurants spectaculaires. Et je parle français avec tout le monde, bien sûr !

Julie : Incroyable ! Tu vas être occupée ! Je veux faire les mêmes choses – je peux t'accompagner ?

Lauren : Avec plaisir ! Je suis contente de me faire des amis ! On peut découvrir la ville ensemble !

Julie : Je pense que je suis libre demain mais je sais pas encore. Je peux t'envoyer un email ?

Lauren : Oui, voilà mon adresse email. T'as besoin de mon numéro de téléphone aussi ?

Julie : Oui, s'il te plait. Je vais t'appeler ce soir.

Lauren: D'accord. Le voilà !

Julie : Cool. Salut !

Don't worry about understanding the use of **allaient**. We won't be covering it in this course, but Lauren uses it here to show that understanding the grammar of every word isn't important if you can prepare something to say in advance.

The word **même** works both to say 'even' as in *tu peux même aller en voiture* 'you can even go by car', and 'same' as in *la même voiture* – (the same car).

VOCAB: *voilà*
Voilà essentially means 'Here is ...' or 'There is ...' If you say 'Here it is' just keep in mind that the *le* goes first – *le voilà*. You can even say *Me voilà !* for 'Here I am!'

CULTURE EXPLANATION: arrondissements

Paris is divided into 20 *arrondissements* (neighbourhoods). Each one works like a little world of its own.

- The 3rd *arrondissement* is posh and expensive.
- The 5th is the one with famous universities, including La Sorbonne.
- The 13th has a more modern urban landscape.

Every Parisian has their own favourite, so expect to be asked (or plan to ask!) the question, *Quel arrondissement tu préfères ?*

FIGURE IT OUT

1 *Vrai ou faux ?* **Select the correct answer.**

a The first thing Lauren will do is see Notre-Dame. *vrai / faux*

b Then she is going to a café. *vrai / faux*

c Next she is going to visit the third district (*arrondissement*). *vrai / faux*

d Lauren thinks she is free tomorrow, but she is not sure yet. *vrai / faux*

e Julie is going to text Lauren tonight. *vrai / faux*

2 Now answer the following questions in French, starting with the given phrase.

a Why is Lauren going to the café? (In order to ...)

____

b Why is Lauren going to *le troisième arrondissement*? (For ...)

____

3 What is the meaning of the phrase ***T'as besoin de mon numéro de téléphone aussi ?***

____

4 Find and highlight these phrases in the conversation. Then write them out.

a What are you going to do in Paris? ______________________________

b I want to do the same things. ______________________________

NOTICE

04.07 Listen to the audio and study the table.

You may have heard of an **ensuite** bathroom – a bathroom that's attached or next to the main room.

Essential phrases for Conversation 3

French	Meaning	Pronunciation
qu'est-ce que tu vas faire ?	what are you going to do?	[kehs-kuh tew vah fehR]
pour commencer, je vais ...	first, I will go ...	pooR koh-mawN-say zhuh veh
après, je vais voir ...	then / afterwards, I'm going to see ...	ahpReh zhuh veh vwaR
ensuite, je vais visiter ...	next, I'll visit ...	awN-sew-eet zhuh veh vee-zee-tay
pour boire un verre	to drink (a glass)	pooR bwaR ahN vehR
tu vas être occupée !	you will be busy!	tew vah zeht ohk-ew-pay
je veux faire les mêmes choses	I want to do the same things	zhuh vuh fehR lay mehm shohz
je peux t'accompagner ?	can I join you?	zhuh puh tah-kohN-pah-nyay
on peut découvrir la ville ensemble !	we can discover the city together!	ohN puh day-koo-vReeR lah veel awN-sawNb-luh
je suis libre demain	I am free tomorrow	zhuh sew-wee leeb duh-mahN
voilà mon adresse email	here's my email address	vwa-lah mohN nah-dRehs ee-mehl
mon numéro de téléphone	my phone number	mohN new-may-Roh duh tay-lay-fon
je vais t'appeler ce soir	I'll call you tonight	zhuh veh tah-play suh swaR
d'accord	OK	dah-koR

Do you remember **je suis d'accord** (I agree) from Unit 2? The word d'accord also means 'OK'.

1 Find the words or phrases for 'first', 'then' and 'next' and write them.

a first ______ b then ______ c next ______

2 Match the English phrases with their French translations

a Can you email me?
b Can I text you?
c Can I call you?
d Can you call me?

1 *Je peux t'appeler ?*
2 *Je peux t'envoyer un texto ?*
3 *Tu peux m'appeler ?*
4 *Tu peux m'envoyer un email ?*

You can see that saying things right in French means learning how to form verbs differently (*je, tu, on* and so on). And that's even before you start changing from present tense to future or past ... which is when things can really start to get messy!

But don't panic! You will eventually learn to handle even the messiest of those verb forms, but for now, here's a handy trick you can use to press the snooze button on learning conjugations. Learn just these five 'booster' verbs and their forms, and they can do the heavy lifting for you. Simply follow them up with the dictionary form of any other verb you may want to use.

booster verb + **dictionary form**

Aimer for interests

Imagine that you wanted to say 'I go out every weekend' but you didn't know the *je* form of the verb *sortir* (to go out).

Do you remember back in your first mission, when you used *j'aime* + verb to describe your interests?

You could just use *j'aime* as a booster verb. In this case, if you know that 'to go out' in its dictionary form is *sortir*, you can combine it with *j'aime* to express the same idea.

J'aime	+	**sortir**	+	*chaque weekend.*
(I like)	+	(to go out)	+	(every weekend.)
booster verb	+	**dictionary form**		

Aller for future plans

To talk about the near future, you can say as you would in English:

Je vais ... (I am going to ...) *Tu vas ...* (You are going to ...)

To use this 'future' form on your own, again you simply put the dictionary form of the verb after *je vais, tu vas* or *on va.*

When using two verbs one after the other, if you want to negate the sentence using **pas**, put pas just after the first verb.

Examples:

Je vais ***manger.***	(I will **eat.**/I am going to eat.)
Je vais ***comprendre.***	(I will **understand.**/I am going to understand.)
On va ***travailler.***	(We will **work.**/We are going to work.)
Tu vas ***pas étudier.***	(You will **not study.**/You aren't going to study.)

Vouloir for intentions

You can talk about your intentions using *je veux*.

Je veux **voir** le film demain. (I want **to see** the film tomorrow.)

Devoir for obligations

This handy verb can be used to say you 'have to' or 'must' do something. For example, instead of 'I'm working tomorrow', why not say:

Je dois **travailler** demain. (I have to **work** tomorrow.)

Pouvoir for possibility

Use this verb to clarify that you 'can' or 'are able to' do something. For instance, the verb *recevoir* (to receive) can be quite tricky to get right, so you could say:

Je peux **recevoir** la lettre ici. (I can **receive** the letter here.)

YOUR TURN: use the hack

1 Use *je vais* + verb to create these sentences in the future tense.

a I will be busy! ____________________

b I'm going to do a lot. ____________________

c Will you call me tomorrow? ____________________

d Are you going to the restaurant? ____________________

e I'm not going to travel to Lyon. ____________________

2 Combine the booster verbs you've just learned with the verb given in its dictionary form to create French sentences from the English translations provided.

a *Je* __________ __________ *dans la mer.* (*nager* = to swim) (I swim in the sea.)

b *On* __________ __________ *le français ensemble.* (*apprendre*)
(We're learning French together.)

c *Tu* __________ __________ *du café brésilien ?* (*boire* = to drink)
(Do you drink Brazilian coffee?)

PRACTICE

1 Translate the following into French.

a You are not very busy. ____________________

b You are going to be very busy. ____________________

c You will speak French. ____________________

d We are going to travel to Paris. ____________________

e Pierre is going to Ireland. ____________________

f Lauren will not visit Berlin. ____________________

2 Fill in the gaps with the missing French words.

a ________ ________, *je vais* ________ ________ *mon* ________ ________ ________.
(**One moment**, I'm going **to give you** my **phone number**.)

b ________ ________, *je vais* ________ ________ *mais* ________ ________ ________ ________ *!*
(**Tonight** I'm going **to be busy**, but **I am free tomorrow**!)

c *Je le* ________ *pas* ________ *... attends ...* ________ ________ *!* (I don't **see** it **yet** … wait… **here it is**!)

d *Je sais pas* ________ *je vais* ________.
(I don't know **if** I'm going **to be able to**.)

e *Je vais au café* ________ *Nadine* ________ ________ *un verre ! Tu veux m'*________ *?*
(I'm going **with** Nadine to the café **to drink** (a glass)! Do you want **to join (accompany)** me?)

f *On va* ________ *le bus* ________, ________ *?*
(We'll **take** the bus **together**, **OK**?)

PUT IT TOGETHER

1 You've already learned to talk about your travel plans. Now, use what you've learned in Conversation 3 to write about what you're going to do when you get there. Try to include ...

- what you'll do first (*pour commencer, je vais ...*) and next (*Ensuite ...*)
- which sites you are going to visit (*Je vais visiter ...*)
- where you plan to go to eat or to drink (*Pour manger / boire, je vais ...*)
- something you want to see (*Je veux voir ...*)

Voilà ce que je vais faire pendant mon voyage !

2 Now imagine that you've met someone you'd like to hang out with later.

- give them your contact details (*Voilà ...*)
- ask them to call, text or email tomorrow (*Tu peux...*).

COMPLETING UNIT 4

Check your understanding

04.08 You know the drill! Listen to this audio rehearsal, which will ask you questions in French. Use what you've learned to answer the questions in French with details about yourself.

To check that you're understanding the audio, don't forget that you can always look at the transcript online.

Show what you know...

Here's what you've just learned. Write or say an example for each item in the list. Then tick off the ones you know.

- [ ] Give three phrases for politely starting a conversation (using *vous*).
- [ ] Ask a polite question using 'Do you mind if ...'?
- [ ] Use *je vais* + dictionary form to say something you will do tomorrow, this weekend or next year.
- [ ] Use *pendant* to say how long you'll do something for.
- [ ] Give three methods of travel in French.
- [ ] Give the three French words to say 'first', 'then' and 'next'.
- [ ] Give the informal phrase that means 'we can'.

COMPLETE YOUR MISSION

It's time to complete your mission: convince your friend to go with you on your dream holiday. To do this, you'll need to describe the trip of your dreams, using the *on* form to say how you and your friend would spend your time.

Travel is a popular topic among language learners, so this is a script you'll want to make sure you have down solid.

STEP 1: build your script

Qu'est-ce que tu vas faire en France ?

Create a script you can use to tell other language hackers about your travel plans. Incorporate as many new words or phrases from this unit as possible – *déjà*, *encore*, *peut-être*, etc. Be sure to say:

- where you're going and what you plan to do when you get there (for example, you could name popular monuments or tourist attractions, what you will eat or drink, etc.)
- what you want to see first (what are you most excited to explore?)
- when you'd like to go and how long you'd like to be there
- how you will get there and how you'll get around once you're there
- who you plan to travel with.

Give recommendations to other language hackers for things to do at this destination! Write down your script, then repeat it until you feel confident.

CULTURE TIP: *know before you go!* This is a good time to expand on your script with some of your own research! There are many beautiful cities in France, Canada, Belgium, Switzerland, Tunisia, and any of the other French-speaking regions around the world. Look into what sights there are to see and what you can do when you get there. If you can, talk to someone who lives there to get the inside scoop.

STEP 2: feedback promotes learning ... *online*

When the opportunity presents itself in real life, you won't always have notes at the ready, so let's emulate this by having you speak your script from memory. Make sure to revise it well!

This time, when you make your recording, you're not allowed to read your script! Instead, speak your phrases to the camera relying on very brief notes or, even better, say your script from memory.

Give and get feedback from other learners – it will massively improve your French!

STEP 3: learn from other learners

How do other language hackers describe their travel plans and dreams? After you've uploaded your clip, **your task is to listen and choose the holiday you'd most like to go on.** Say why you think the place and plans sound good.

Your language partners can be a great resource for tips and stories on travel and culture! Plus, travel aspirations are a great conversation starter.

STEP 4: reflect on what you've learned

After this mission, you'll have seen and heard so many useful new words and phrases, and you'll know more about new and different places to visit. What would you like to add to your script next? Your travel plans?

HEY, LANGUAGE HACKER, LOOK AT EVERYTHING YOU'VE JUST SAID!

Isn't it so much easier when you already know what you want to say? A lot of language learning involves repeatable and sometimes predictable conversations. If you take advantage of this and prepare answers you typically give often, you can be extremely confident in what you say!

Now, let's build new phrases in your script that you can use to talk about your friends and family.

Superbe !

5 TALKING ABOUT FAMILY AND FRIENDS

Your mission

Imagine this - your good friend develops a serious crush on your French *ami(e)* and asks you to play matchmaker.

Your mission is to casually talk up your friend and spark the interest of your *ami(e) français(e)* to get those two out on a date! Be prepared to **describe your relationship with your friend - how you met, where he or she lives and works,** and the kinds of **things he or she likes to do**.

This mission will get you comfortable talking about other people and using new verb forms as well as descriptive language.

Mission prep

- Talk about 'he' and 'she' using *il/elle* forms
- Talk about 'they' using *ils/elles* forms
- Use phrases to describe things you do with other people: *je passe du temps*, *on*, *ensemble* ...
- Learn essential family vocabulary: *le mari*, *la sœur* ...
- Use the two forms of 'to know': *savoir* and *connaitre*.

BUILDING LANGUAGE FOR DESCRIBING YOUR RELATIONSHIPS

Until now, our conversations have focused mostly on describing *je, tu* and *on*. We'll build on that now with vocabulary you can use to talk about anyone else.

#LANGUAGEHACK

pronounce words you haven't even learned yet

CONVERSATION 1

What do you have planned?

Lauren has been taking online French classes for a few weeks. Today she's practising with Mariam, a French tutor from Tunisia. Lauren is excited to talk about the new friend she made at her language group.

05.01 Notice how Mariam greets Lauren. Which phrase means 'what's new'?

While in English we might say we're happy to hear something, the French say they are **happy 'to learn'** it, or literally 'happy of to-learn'.

Mariam : Salut Lauren, mon étudiante préférée ! Quoi de neuf ?

Lauren : Tout va bien ! En fait, cette semaine, je passe du temps avec une nouvelle amie.

Mariam : C'est formidable ! Je suis contente d'apprendre ça ! Elle s'appelle comment ?

Lauren : Elle s'appelle Julie. Elle est belge. Elle travaille comme ingénieur. Je la connais tout juste.

Mariam : D'accord. Elle est à Paris depuis quand ? Qu'est-ce que vous avez prévu ?

Lauren : Elle est à Paris depuis seulement une semaine. Demain, on prévoit d'aller au restaurant. Après ça, on va passer la semaine ensemble, pour découvrir la ville. Et le weekend prochain, je pense que je vais la voir en Belgique.

Mariam : Mon mari est belge. Il adore – on visite sa ville chaque été.

GRAMMAR TIP: *vous* for 'you two'
Remember that *vous* is not only used in formal situations with strangers, but also for plural 'you', regardless of the level of formality. Similar to 'you two/three' or 'all of you' in English.

VOCAB: *sa ville*
In French, 'his hometown' is translated simply as *sa ville* (his town). ***Où est ta ville ?***

FIGURE IT OUT

1 What is the meaning of the phrase:

Elle s'appelle comment ? ______________________

2 *Vrai ou faux ?* Three of the following statements are *faux*. Select the correct answer and correct the false statements.

a Lauren is spending time with a new friend next week. *vrai / faux*
b Julie works as a lawyer. *vrai / faux*
c Julie has been in Paris for only a week. *vrai / faux*
d Tomorrow, Lauren and Julie are going to a restaurant. *vrai / faux*
e This weekend, Lauren is going to see Julie in Belgium. *vrai / faux*

3 You've learned a lot of words that tell you *when* something is happening. Highlight these words and write the French translations.

a this week ______________
b next weekend ______________
c tomorrow ______________
d after that ______________
e every summer ______________

4 Write the phrases in French.

a What's new? ______________________
b Who? ______________________
c in fact ______________________
d my favourite student ______________________
e I'm happy to ... ______________________

NOTICE

05.02 Listen to the audio and study the table.

Essential phrases for Conversation 1

French	Meaning	Pronunciation
mon étudiante préférée !	my favourite student!	mohN nay-tew-dee-awNt pRay-fay-Ray
quoi de neuf ?	what's new?	kwah duh nuhf
je passe du temps avec une nouvelle amie	I'm spending time with a new friend (f.)	zhuh pahs dew tawN zah-vehk ewn noo-vehl ah-mee
je suis contente d'apprendre ça !	I'm happy to hear that!	zhuh sew-wee kohN-tawNt dah-pRawNd sah
elle s'appelle comment ?	what is her name?	ehl sah-pehl koh-mawN
elle est belge	she's Belgian	ehl eh behlzh
elle travaille comme ...	she works as ...	ehl tRah-vah-ee kohm
je la connais	I know her	zhuh lah koh-neh
qu'est-ce que vous avez prévu ?	what do you (pl.) have planned ?	kehs kuh voo zah-vay pRay-vew
on prévoit d'aller au restaurant	we plan to go to a restaurant	ohN pRay-vwa dah-lay oh Rehs-to-RawN
après ça ...	after that ...	ah-pReh sah
on va passer la semaine ensemble	we'll spend the week together	ohN vah pah-say lah suh-mehn awN-sawN-bluh
je vais la voir	I will see her	zhuh veh lah vwaR
mon mari est ...	my husband is ...	mohN mah-Ree eh
il adore	he loves it (he adores)	eel ah-doR
on visite sa ville chaque été	we visit his hometown every summer	ohN vee-zeet sah veel shahk ay-tay

VOCAB: *who you 'know'*
Connais is another way to say 'know' in French. In this case, it means 'know a person'. More on this in Conversation 2!

1 *Je suis content(e) de* (I am happy to) is another power expression. Use this expression in different ways by combining it with the following verbs.

Example: to know → Je suis content(e) de savoir

a to see ____________

b to be ____________

c to say ____________

2 This conversation introduces forms for talking about 'he' and 'she' in French. Find each of the following in the phrase list and highlight them.

a three instances of 'she' in French
b two instances of 'her' in French
c one instance of 'he' in French

3 Notice the new verb forms used in this conversation. Find the following sets of related verbs and write them out.

a I'm spending time ______
b we'll spend the weekend ______
c he is ______
d she is ______
e we're going ______
f we're planning ______
g we visit ______

4 Match the French with their English equivalents.

a *on prévoit d'aller*
b *on va passer du temps*

1 we are going to spend time
2 we are planning to go

5 Look at the phrases *Je la connais* and *Je vais la voir* in the phrase list and answer these questions.

a How is the word order different from English? ______
b Using the same sentence structure, how would you say 'I see her' in French?

______

GRAMMAR EXPLANATION: using objects *le*, *la* and *les* ('him', 'her' and 'them')

In Unit 3 you learned to use *me* and *te* as objects of a sentence in French. The same works with *le* (him), *la* (her) and *les* (them). So you can say:

Je l'aime.	I love him/her.
Tu le vois dans le parc ?	Do you see him in the park?
Tu aimes la nouvelle actrice ?	Do you like the new actress?
Non, je la déteste !	No, I hate her!
Je vais les voir.	I'm going to see them.

You can see that 'it' depends on the gender of the word being discussed.

Interestingly, the verb **adorer** is a bit of an exception. You'd expect 'I love it' to be je l'adore. To say you love something, simply say J'adore! 'It' is implied.

PRONUNCIATION: ***the silent -re***

You may have noticed that many words ending in *-re* don't have those letters pronounced.
For instance, ***quatre*** (four) is pronounced [kat], ***comprendre*** (to understand) is pronounced [kohN-pRawN], and ***être*** (to be) is pronounced [eht]. In casual French, people tend to skip this sound entirely if it comes after a consonant. This is handy to keep in mind if you are still finding it tricky pronouncing the French *r*.

PRACTICE

1 05.03 Here's some new vocab you can use to talk about your family. Listen to the audio and study the table. Repeat the words as you hear them.

La famille

French	Meaning	French	Meaning
les parents	parents	le fils	son
la mère (maman)	mother (mum)	la fille	daughter
le père (papa)	father (dad)	les enfants	children
le frère	brother	la tante	aunt
la sœur	sister	l'oncle	uncle
le/la meilleur(e) ami(e)	best friend	le cousin	cousin (m)
le mari	husband	la cousine	cousin (f)
la femme	wife	le/la coloc	roommate/ flatmate
le copain	boyfriend	le chien	dog
la copine	girlfriend	le chat	cat
je suis célibataire	I'm single	panda	panda
c'est compliqué	It's complicated		

Notice that grammatical genders (**le** or **la**) for people tend to be the same as the person's gender.

2 What are some other words for family members (or pets!) you have? Add them to the list.

3 Fill in the gaps with the missing words in French.

a *Est-ce que* ________ ________ *des* ________ *ou des* ________ *?*
(Do **you have** any **brothers** or **sisters**?)

b ________ *est mon* ________ ________ *et je* ________ *vois pas assez !*
(**He** is my **favourite nephew**, and I don't see **him** enough!)

c ________ *êtes proches ?* (Are **you (pl.)** close?)

d *Mon* ________ *Jim et moi,* ______ ________ *de monter une affaire* ________.
(My **friend** Jim and I, **we are planning** to start a business **together.**)

e *Ma* ________ *travaille* ________ *médecin.* ________ ________ *à l'hôpital.*
(My **mum** works **as a** doctor. **She works** at a hospital.)

f *J'adore* ________ ________ ________ *avec mes* ________.
(I love **spending time** with my **children**.)

You can see that the plural for 'my' (*mes*) looks similar to the plural for 'the' (*les*).

g *Je parle tout le temps avec* ________ ________ *et je* ________ ________ *souvent.*
(I speak with **my brother** all the time, and I **see him** often.)

h ________ ________ *où ?* (Where does **he study**?)

i ________ ________ *fait du jogging* ________ ________. ________ *adore.*
(**My girlfriend** jogs **every day. She** loves it.)

4 Answer the questions and practise creating sentences about your family members.

a *Ton / ta meilleur(e) ami(e) s'appelle comment ?* ________________________

b *Tu le / la connais depuis quand ?* ________________________

c *Qu'est-ce qu'il / elle fait comme travail ?*

____

5 Describe who you're spending time with this weekend and your plans together. Use the phrases:

- *je passe du temps avec ...* 'I'm spending time with ...'
- *on prévoit de ...* 'we're planning to ...'

a *Avec qui tu passes du temps ce weekend ? Ce weekend, je ...*

____

b *Qu'est-ce que vous avez prévu ? On ...*

____

That's right – *il, elle* and *on* always have the same verb form. This is one reason I prefer to use *on* over *nous* for 'we' – the conjugation is much easier. It's also more commonly heard in casual French!

GRAMMAR TIP: exceptions
Être and ***aller*** are two common verbs that don't follow any patterns we've seen, so learn them independently as *je suis, tu es, il/elle/on est* and *je vais, tu vas, il/elle/on va.*

GRAMMAR EXPLANATION: *il, elle* and *ils / elles*

So far your scripts have relied mostly on the *je* and *tu* forms of verbs. Now let's look at the forms for *il/elle* (he/she), as well as *ils/elles* (they).

il/elle/on – 'he / she / we (informal)'

Good news! You've already seen the verb form for *on,* and it works exactly the same for *il* and *elle,* as well as for people's names.

- For verbs ending in *-er, il/elle/on* forms are the same as the *je* form:

  j'habite à Paris
  elle habite à Paris *Pierre habite à Paris* *on habite à Paris*

- For many verbs (especially those ending in *–ir*), the *il/elle/on* form usually ends with a *t*:

sortir	***lire***	***pouvoir***	***vouloir***
je sors	je lis	je peux	je veux
tu sors	tu lis	tu peux	tu veux
il sort	il lit	il peut	il veut
elle sort	elle lit	elle peut	elle veut
on sort	on lit	on peut	on veut

ils/elles – 'they'

When you want to talk about *François et Marie* and what they are doing, you'll need to use a new form: *ils/elles,* which usually ends in *-ent*:

parler (to speak)	*je parle*	*ils/elles parl**ent***
appeler (to call)	*je m'appelle*	*ils/elles s'appell**ent***

PRONUNCIATION: *silent e*
e isn't always pronounced, such as the first one in ***appeler*** [ahp-lay]. You may notice this whenever there's just one consonant before and after the ***e***. It also works in ***samedi*** [sam-dee] and ***tellement*** [tel-mawN] but not in ***vendredi*** [vawN-druh-dee] because of ***dr*** before the ***e***.

1 Fill in the gaps with the right verb form for the given verb.

a *Ils* ________ *le cinéma. (aimer)*

b *Étienne* ________ *la Belgique chaque été. (visiter)*

c *On* ________ *ici pour pratiquer. (être)*

d *Elles* ________ *dans un hôpital. (travailler)*

e *Julien et Paul* ________ *beaucoup. (danser)*

#LANGUAGEHACK: pronounce words you haven't even learned yet

I know that seeing all these different verb forms may feel overwhelming. So here's some good news for you: even though they look very different, **many of the these forms sound exactly the same.**

This means that in many cases, you *already know how to pronounce* these new verb forms, even if you haven't learned them yet! It also means that you can safely guess how to pronounce these verb forms when you use them in conversation, and you'll have a good chance of guessing correctly!

- ***je/tu/il/elle/on:*** with the exception of *être* and *avoir*, the forms for all verbs **sound exactly the same** for *je*, *tu* and *il/elle/on*. So, even though the spelling may change, as long as you know how to pronounce one of these, you can say the rest!
- ***ils/elles*** (for *-er* verbs): here's a great surprise – the ***-ent*** ending for *ils/elles* is actually **silent for *-er* verbs!** Because of this, the same pronunciation trick applies. Luckily, this includes most of the verbs you've come across so far.

05.04 Carefully listen to the audio to hear how the pronunciation of 'they' (*ils/elles*) verb forms differs from – or is similar to – the other forms. Repeat the words and try to mimic the speakers.

je visite, elle visite, ils visitent, tu passes, on passe, elles passent
je suis, tu es, il est, ils sont, j'ai, tu as, il a, ils ont
je veux, il veut, ils veulent, je peux, tu peux, ils peuvent
je parle, ils parlent, je m'appelle, ils s'appellent
j'aime, ils aiment, je voyage, ils voyagent
j'apprends, tu apprends, il apprend, ils apprennent
je sors, tu sors, il sort, ils sortent, je finis, tu finis, il finit, ils finissent

Pronunciation: *-re/-ir* verbs

While the pronunciation shortcut for *je/tu/il/elle/on* will work fine for these verbs, and *-ent* is also silent for them, there are other sound changes that take place for *ils/elles* with *-re* and *-ir* verbs. The good news is that even if you incorrectly use the *je* pronunciation for these verbs, people will still be able to understand you. This is something you can perfect later.

YOUR TURN: use the hack

🔊 **05.05** Using the pronunciation shortcut, say the following phrases out loud. Then listen to the audio to see if you got them right.

a *Ils volent depuis cinq heures.* (They've been flying for five hours.)
b *Elles dorment à l'hôtel aujourd'hui ?* (Are they (f.) sleeping in the hotel today?)
c *Marc et les enfants arrivent à l'aéroport.* (Marc and the children are arriving at the airport.)

LEARNING STRATEGY: *focus on your key verbs*
Which 'me-specific' verbs would you need to talk about the people close to you? Figure out what they are, then learn those first, in all their conjugations. You might include verbs you can use to talk about where they live, what they do for a living, their age, hobbies, etc. Think about:

- where you or your family live
- what you and your girlfriend/partner like to do or do for a living
- what your friends or children like to do

PUT IT TOGETHER

Qui est ta personne préférée ?
Who do you spend your time with? Describe someone close to you, using your dictionary to look up any new vocabulary you need. Try to answer the following questions:

- What is his/her name?
- Where does he/she live? Who does he/she live with?
- What does he/she do for a living?
- What does he/she like to do?

You might be tempted to talk about where you 'met' someone, but we haven't learned how to talk about things that happened (past tense) yet. It's coming up in Unit 7. In the meantime, practise rephrasing sentences so you can convey the same idea using phrases you know now. This is an invaluable skill in language learning.

CONVERSATION 2

Who do you live with?

The conversation continues as Lauren and Mariam talk about their families.

🔊 **05.06** How does Lauren ask 'how long' Mariam has been married?

Lauren : Tu es mariée ?

Mariam : Oui ! Je suis mariée.

Lauren : Depuis combien de temps vous êtes ensemble ?

Mariam : On est ensemble depuis longtemps. Je connais sa famille depuis vingt ans. Et toi ?

Lauren : Non. Je suis pas mariée. J'ai même pas de copain. Je suis célibataire.

Mariam : Avec qui tu habites ?

Lauren : Tu veux dire aux États-Unis ? À mon retour, je vais habiter dans la maison de ma sœur.

Mariam : Tu es très indépendante.

Lauren : Ma sœur dit toujours que je suis trop indépendante. Elle voyage jamais.

Mariam : Est-ce que vous êtes très différentes ?

Lauren : Pas trop. En fait, on se ressemble beaucoup. Par exemple, elle parle français aussi !

To describe a person's possessions in French, use de ('of'). e.g., **la maison de ma soeur** (the house of my sister).

GRAMMAR TIP: *gender and number*
Add an *s* to the noun when talking about multiple people (*frère – frères*). French also adds an *s* to any adjectives that come before a plural noun (*les jolies sœurs*). You'll also notice an *e* because it's describing a feminine word, as with ***différentes***.

FIGURE IT OUT

1 Find these words in the conversation and highlight them.

a married b single c boyfriend

2 Is the word *famille* masculine or feminine? ____________________

3 What do you think is the meaning of the phrase *Est-ce que vous êtes très différentes ?* ____________________

GRAMMAR TIP:
sa famille
You've already seen how to use ***mon/ton*** for masculine and ***ma/ta*** for feminine nouns. Similarly, you'll use ***son*** for masculine nouns and ***sa*** for feminine nouns – ***son*** and ***sa*** can both mean 'his', 'her' and 'its'. So, ***son père*** can mean 'his father' or 'her father', while ***sa mère*** means 'his mother' or 'her mother'.

4 Complete these sentences in French about the conversation.

a Is Lauren married or single? *Elle* __________ __________.

b At whose house is Lauren planning to live?
Elle va habiter dans __________ __________ __________ __________ __________.

c *Mariam est avec son mari depuis* __________ __________.

d *Lauren va habiter avec sa sœur à son retour aux* __________ __________.

5 How do you say the following in French?

a when I get back ____________________

b Do you mean to say ...? ____________________

c for example ____________________

NOTICE

05.07 Listen to the audio and study the table.

Essential phrases for Conversation 2

French	Meaning	Pronunciation
tu es mariée ?	are you married?	tew eh mah-Ree-ay
depuis combien de temps vous êtes ensemble ?	how long have you been together?	duh-pew-wee kohN-bee-ahN duh tawN voo zeht awN-sawN-bluh
on est ensemble depuis longtemps	we have been together for a long time	ohN neh awN-sawN-bluh duh-pew-wee lohN-tawN
je connais sa famille depuis vingt ans	I have known his family for 20 years	zhuh ko-neh sah fah-mee-yuh duh-pew-wee vahN tawN
j'ai même pas de copain	I don't even have a boyfriend (I've even not of boyfriend)	zhay mehm pah duh ko-pahN

The most common way to say 'boyfriend' is **copain**, which looks similar to companion. 'Girlfriend' is copine. You may also hear petit-ami for 'boyfriend' or petite-amie for 'girlfriend', though these are much less commonly used by adults.

avec qui tu habites ?	who do you live with?	ah-vehk kee tew ah-beet
à mon retour	once I'm back (lit., at my return)	ah mawN ruh-tooR
... je vais habiter dans la maison de ma sœur	... I'll be living at my sister's house	zhuh veh zah-bee-tay dawN lah meh-zohN duh mah suhR
ma sœur dit toujours ...	my sister always says ...	mah suhR dee too-zhooR
elle voyage jamais	she never travels	ehl vwa-yahzh zhah-meh
est-ce que vous êtes très différentes ?	are you (pl.) very different?	ehs kuh voo zeht tReh dee-fay-RawNt
on se ressemble beaucoup	we're a lot alike	ohN suh Ruh-sawN-bluh boh-koo
elle parle le français aussi !	she speaks French too!	ehl pahRl luh fRawN-seh oh-see

1 Find the five *il/elle/on* verb examples in French. Underline them.

2 In Unit 4, you learned to use the French word *même* to mean 'same'. Notice how *même* is used differently here. Write out in French:

a the same thing ____________________

b I don't even have a car. ____________________

3 Notice the phrases used to say what people are doing 'together'. How can you use *depuis* with these phrases to ask and answer questions about 'how long'?

a you're (pl.) together ...? ____________

b we're together ...? ____________

c You've (pl.) been together since ... ____________

d We've been together since ... ____________

4 Using the French phrase for 'my sister's house' as a model, how would you say 'my brother's dog' in French? And 'my friend's father'?

____

____

VOCABULARY EXPLANATION: *savoir* and *connaitre*

French has two ways of saying 'to know'. Most of the time you'll use *savoir*, which implies that you know a piece of information or how to do something. The other form, *connaitre*, implies that you're familiar with something, or that you know a person.

Generally, you'll use *connaitre* instead of *savoir* if you can replace the word 'know' with 'know of' or 'be familiar with'. For example, you can't really say 'I *know of* how to drive', but you can say 'I *am familiar with* Paris' (*Je connais Paris*) or 'I know of him' (*Je le connais*).

Example: ***Je sais*** *que tu es français.* (I know that you are French.)
Je connais *cette chanson !* (I know this song!)

Choose between *savoir* and *connaitre* according to the context.

a *Je connais/sais ce livre.*
b *Tu connais/sais à quelle heure le concert commence ?*
c *On connait/sait Pierre.*
d *Elle connait/sait nager ?* (to swim)

PRACTICE

1 Practise answering questions about your relationships with other people.

a *Est-ce que tu as des frères ou des sœurs ?* *Oui, j'ai... sœurs / frères*
Non, j'ai pas...

____

b *Est-ce que tu es marié(e), célibataire ou tu as un copain/une copine ?*
J'ai / J'ai pas... ______________________________

c *Tu as des enfants ? Combien ?* *Oui, j'ai ... enfants /*
Non, j'ai pas d'enfants.

____

d *Avec qui tu habites ?* *J' habite avec ... / J'habite seul.* (I live alone.)

____

GRAMMAR TIP: ***prepositions at the start***
French sentences can't end in prepositions (words like *à, après, avec, dans, en, à*). But it's easy to change your word order if you imagine a more formal way of saying the sentence in English: *Avec qui tu habites ?* (with whom do you live?)

2 To ask 'who do you live with?' Mariam says *avec qui tu habites ?* which uses a different word order from English. Practise using this word order to form questions.

Example: Who are you giving that **to**? ···> À qui tu donnes ça ?

a Where are you coming from? ______________________

b What (*quoi*) are you writing with? ______________________

c What time (*quelle heure*) does the class start? ______________________

3 A useful phrase to know in French is *je veux dire*, which translates as 'I mean'. Use this phrase to say the following.

a Do you mean ... ? ______________

b he means ______________

c she means ______________

d we mean ______________

4 Fill in the blanks with the missing words in French.

a ________ ________, ________ ________ *et moi*, ________ ________ ________ *pas la télé*. (**In fact, my girlfriend** and I, **we don't** even **watch** TV.)

b Je ________ mon meilleur ____ depuis ________. ________ ________ ________ ________.
(I have **known** my best **friend** for a **long time**. **We're a lot alike**.)

c *Aujourd'hui c'est l'anniversaire* ________ ________ ________.
(Today is **my mother's** birthday.)

d ________ *allez* ________ ________ *avec nous ?*
(Are **you two** going **to Canada** with us?)

GRAMMAR TIP:
'in' and 'to' with countries
In French, there are generally three ways to say 'in' and 'to' with countries. Here's a quick rule of thumb to get it right most of the time:

···> If the country name in French ends in e, use ***en***.

Ex: *Je veux aller **en** Espagn**e**. Tu travailles en Belgiqu**e**. J'habite **en** Irland**e**.*

···> If it ends in an s, use ***aux***.

Ex: *Il habite **aux** États-Uni**s**. On prévoit d'aller aux Pays-Ba**s*** (Netherlands).

···> In all other cases, use ***au***.

Ex: *Elle veut étudier **au** Canada. Je passe les vacances **au** Brésil.*

Use the present tense with the word **depuis** – so you'd say 'I know ...' rather than 'I have known ...'.

PUT IT TOGETHER

Build on the script you wrote from Conversation 1. Write four or five sentences about someone close to you, in which you describe things like ...

···> how long you've known him/her (*connaitre + depuis*)
···> how long you've been together or married (*ensemble + depuis*)
···> what you plan to do together (*on est, on va, on fait, on veut*).

CONVERSATION 3

There are four of us

You can use the phrase **on est** ... or 'we are (number)' to say how many of you there are in a group. It's a useful phrase in a lot of scenarios, from describing your family to telling a waiter in a restaurant how big a table you need.

The conversation gets a bit more detailed now, as Lauren tries to describe the people she has met.

05.08 How do you say 'they are not ...' in French?

Lauren : Est-ce que vous avez des enfants ?

Mariam : Oui, on est quatre. On a deux enfants. Ils s'appellent Sarah et Aziz.

Lauren : Oh, j'adore leurs noms. Ils sont vraiment jolis.

Mariam : Tu penses que tu vas jamais avoir une famille ?

Lauren: J'en suis pas sûre. Peut-être un jour.

Mariam : Et si tu rencontres un Français charmant à Paris ? Alors, vous allez rester en France pour toujours ?

Lauren : Tu es drôle. Je rencontre beaucoup de Français, mais ils sont pas souvent ... comment dire en français ... 'my type'.

Mariam : Ils sont pas ton 'genre'. Oui, je comprends. On sait jamais ! Tout est possible !

CONVERSATION STRATEGY:
substitutions
When you can't think of the word you want, substitute a similar word you already know. For instance, we could use ***peut-être*** (maybe) in place of 'probably' in this conversation.

FIGURE IT OUT

1 Use context to answer the questions, and highlight the relevant words in the conversation.

a How many people are in Mariam's family? __________

b Does Lauren ever want to have a family? __________

c How do you say in French 'they are not "my type"'?

____

2 What do the following phrases mean?

a *On a deux enfants.* ______________________

b *Comment dire en français ... ?* ______________________

c *un Français charmant* ______________________

3 Find and underline these phrases and write them in French.

a Their names are ... ______________________

b I love their names. ______________________

c Anything's possible! ______________________

CONVERSATION STRATEGY: *learn j'en suis pas sûr(e) as a set expression*
This expression means 'I am not sure', or literally, 'I of-that am not sure'. We don't need to get into the technical details of how the ***en*** works like this in this course, but I do recommend you learn this as a set expression. This is the correct form, whereas 'je suis pas sûr' would be incorrect by itself. Don't worry if you don't fully understand the structure of the sentence yet. Some expressions are worth using as soon as possible!

NOTICE

05.09 Listen to the audio and study the table.

Essential phrases for Conversation 3

French	Meaning	Pronunciation
est-ce que vous avez des enfants ?	do you (pl.) have children?	ehs kuh voo zah-vay day zawN-fawN
oui, on est quatre	yes, there are four of us	wee ohN neh kaht
on a deux enfants	we have two children	ohN nah duh zawN-fawN
ils s'appellent ...	their names are ...	eel sah-pehl
ils sont vraiment jolis	they're really pretty	eel sawN vReh-mawN zho-lee
tu vas jamais avoir une famille ?	will you ever have a family? (You go never to-have a family)	tew vah zhah-meh zah-vwaR ewn fah-mee-yuh
j'en suis pas sûre	I'm not sure	zhawN sew-wee pah sewR
vous allez rester en France ... pour toujours?	will you (pl.) stay in France ... forever? (for always)	voo zah-lay Rehs-tay awN frawNs pooR too-zhooR
ils sont pas souvent ...	they are often not ...	eel sohN pah soo-vawN
comment dire en français ...	how do you say in French ...	koh-mawN deeR awN fRawN-seh
on sait jamais !	you never know!	ohN seh zhah-meh

VOCAB: ***on* as 'one' or 'people in general'**
As well as being used commonly for 'we', *on* also means 'one' when used to mean 'people in general'.
On sait jamais (one never knows).

1 How would you ask the following questions in French?

a Do you think you will ever ... ? ______

b Do you (pl.) have ... ? ______

2 How would you say 'I'm sure!' in French? ______

3 Notice the literal translations of the following words, and write them out in French.

a forever ______ b ever ______

4 Match the French phrases with the correct English translations.

1 we are	**2** you (pl.) are	**3** they are	**4** we are going
5 you are (pl.) going	**6** they are going		**7** we know

a _____ *on va*

b _____ *vous allez*

c _____ *ils vont*

d _____ *on est*

e _____ *ils sont*

f _____ *on sait*

g _____ *vous êtes*

PRACTICE

1 Fill in the gaps for each question-answer pair.

a *Martin et Marie, **vous êtes** ensemble depuis longtemps ?*

Non, __________ __________ ensemble depuis seulement quelques jours !

b ***Ton frère est** étudiant ? Non, __________ __________ auteur !*

c ***Tes parents sont** au travail ? Non, __________ __________ en vacances !*

d ***Vous avez** un chien ?*

Marc et moi ? Non, __________ __________ un chat, bien sûr !

e ***Ton amie va** voyager avec toi ?*

Non, __________ __________ voyager avec ma cousine !

f ***Tes sœurs vont** lire un livre ?*

Non, __________ __________ regarder la télé.

PUT IT TOGETHER

You should now have most of the 'me-specific' vocab you need to talk about your family or group of friends!

1 Create a script of four to six sentences to describe people you know. Use the new forms you learned for *il/elle/on* and *ils/elles* to talk about:

- your parents, children or other family members – their names, ages, where they live or what they like
- your friends – how you know them, what they do and what they like
- your co-workers – what they say, what you are working on together
- your pets, people you admire, or anyone else you want to describe!

2 Create four different questions in French using the phrase 'Do you think you will ever ...?' as a base, but change the phrase in each sentence to do the following:

- incorporate at least four of the verbs: *avoir, vouloir, aller, habiter, savoir, parler, rester* or *dire*
- use four different verb conjugations with *tu, il, elle, on, ils* or *elles*

COMPLETING UNIT 5

Check your understanding

05.10 Listen to this audio rehearsal, which asks questions in French, followed by a short answer.

- Combine the answer with the verb in the question to give the full answer.
- Feel free to pause or replay the audio as often as you need.

Example: *Avec qui John habite ? Sa mère.* → Il habite avec sa mère.

Show what you know...

Here's what you've just learned. Write or say an example for each item in the list. Then tick off the ones you know.

- [ ] Give the French phrases for 'my mother' and 'my father', and another family member of your choice.
- [ ] Give two phrases you can use to express how you 'spend time' or what you 'plan' to do.
- [ ] Give one sentence each using:
  - [ ] the *il* verb form to describe what someone (male) you know works as
  - [ ] *the ils/elles* verb form to describe what some friends of yours are doing right now.
- [ ] Say something you plan to do with another person using *on* and *ensemble*.
- [ ] Use *connaitre* to say you 'know' (are familiar with) something or someone.

COMPLETE YOUR MISSION

It's time to complete your mission: talk up your friend to spark an interest in *ton ami(e) français(e)*. To do this, you'll need to prepare a description of your friend and explain the story of how you met and all the good things about him or her.

STEP 1: build your script

Qui est la personne la plus importante dans ta vie ? Use the phrases you've learned so far and 'me-specific' vocabulary to build scripts about your favourite person. Be sure to:

Include **connector words** and other vocab you learned in Units 1–5 as much as possible.

- say who it is (*mon ami(e), mon frère* …)
- explain why the person is so important to you (*il, elle*)
- describe things you do together (*on* and *ensemble*)
- say how long you've known each other (*connaitre* + *depuis*)
- describe their characteristics, jobs, family, etc. (*son, sa*)

Write down your script, then rehearse it until you feel confident!

Use your language to **communicate with real people!** You need to speak and use a language for it to start to take hold in your long-term memory. And it's the best way to see and feel your progress.

STEP 2: keep it real … *online*

This is a script you'll use over and over to talk in French about your nearest and dearest. Start using it right away! Go online, find the mission for Unit 5 and share your recording with the community.

STEP 3: learn from other learners

Your task is to ask a follow-up question in French to at least three different people, to inspire them to build on their scripts just a little bit more.

Remember, your missions help you, but also help others expand their vocabulary.

STEP 4: reflect on what you've learned

What new words or phrases do you need to start filling your gaps?

HEY, LANGUAGE HACKER, YOU'RE OVER HALFWAY THERE!

You have successfully overcome one of the biggest challenges in language learning: getting started and keeping it up. Momentum goes a long way toward learning quickly, so you should feel good about how far you've come. Always focus on what you can do today that you couldn't do yesterday.

Next up: let's get ready for conversations at the French dinner table.

Bravo !

6 HAVE SOME FOOD, DRINK AND CONVERSATION

Your mission

Imagine this – you've discovered an incredible restaurant near your *appartement*, so you invite a new French friend to join you there. You feel *très chic* and *au courant*. But it turns out (to your horror) that your friend has heard bad things about it. Bah, he says, *c'est ennuyeux*!

Your mission is to **convince your friend to come with you** to the restaurant. Be prepared to **give your opinion** and say why you **disagree.** Back it up with details of why the place is so *magnifique* – describe **food you like** and **why you like it**.

This mission will help you become comfortable agreeing or disagreeing and explaining your point of view, as well as talking about food and restaurants – a very important topic.

Mission prep

- Learn phrases and etiquette for dining out: *je prends*, *je voudrais*
- Use food and drink vocabulary: *de l'eau*, *un verre de vin*
- Use expressions for giving opinions and recommendations: *à mon avis*
- Use *du/de la/de l'/des* to mean 'some'
- Make comparisons using *plus*, *moins*, *meilleur*.

BUILDING LANGUAGE FOR FRENCH DINNER CONVERSATION

Having a long meal filled with fun discussion is a key part of French culture – and sharing both agreements and disagreements makes for much more interesting conversations. To blend in, it's important to be able to proudly share your opinions. A lot of your conversations will take place in cafés or restaurants, so let's make sure you also understand the different ways you'll interact with waiters, as well as your dinner companions!

#LANGUAGEHACK
sound more fluent with conversation connectors

CONVERSATION 1

For me...

06.01 Lauren and her friend Julie sit down to eat at a café in Paris. What phrase does the waiter use to ask 'Are you ready to order?'

Lauren : J'ai faim ! Ah, voilà le restaurant !
Waiter : Bonsoir, mesdames. Une table pour deux ?
Julie : Bonsoir, monsieur. Oui, on est deux.
Waiter : Voilà votre table. Et voilà la carte.
Julie : Très bien. On prend une carafe d'eau pour maintenant. Merci beaucoup.
Waiter : Merci à vous !
Waiter : Avez-vous choisi ?
Julie : Oui ! On sait déjà.
Waiter : Je vous écoute.
Lauren : Euh... pour moi, une ratatouille, s'il vous plait.
Julie : Et moi, je prends la salade au chèvre chaud.
Waiter : Et à boire ?
Julie : Tu vas boire quelque chose ?
Lauren : Je voudrais du vin rouge. Et toi, Julie ? Tu vas boire quelque chose ?
Julie : Du vin blanc pour moi, et encore de l'eau.
Waiter : Tout de suite !

You may recognize **ratatouille** as a famous French dish. La salade au chèvre chaud is another common dish that's easy on the wallet (and a personal favourite of mine!).

PRONUNCIATION: *tout de suite !*
While you would expect to pronounce this word [too-duh sew-weet], it's a common phrase with a slight pronunciation change that sounds more like [toot sew-weet].

FIGURE IT OUT

1 Look back at the conversation and answer the questions.

a What does Lauren order to eat? And to drink? Find the words in the conversation and highlight them.
b Which forms in the conversation are formal or plural? Highlight them.

2 What does the phrase *on sait déjà* mean? ____________

3 Find the phrases Sarah and Julia use to order:

a *une ratatouille* ______________________

b *la salade au chèvre chaud* ______________________

c *du vin rouge* ______________________

4 Each of these translations from the conversation is incorrect. Determine what makes each translation wrong and correct it.

a	*bonsoir*	good day	____________
b	*s'il vous plait !*	please (informal)	____________
c	*monsieur*	waiter	____________
d	*mesdames*	madam	____________
e	*Avez vous choisi ?*	Have you eaten? (formal)	____________
f	*Voilà une table.*	Here's your table.	____________

5 Write out the following phrases in French.

a And to drink? ______________________

b Are you going to drink something? ______________________

c we already know ______________________

CULTURE EXPLANATION: *Garçon ! Menu !*

Contrary to what you may have heard, nobody ever calls a waiter over with *Garçon !* You're more likely to get someone's attention with eye contact or by raising your hand subtly and saying *s'il vous plait* or *monsieur/madame*.

When browsing French restaurants, you will see the words *menu* and *entrée* quite often – but be careful! A French *menu* is not the full selection of food to choose from, like you may be used to (that's *la carte*). *Un menu* is a set menu of multiple courses for a *prix fixe* (fixed price). And a French *entrée* is actually a starter or appetizer! For the main course, look for *le plat principal*.

There's a certain way to order in French restaurants that's different from what you might be used to. When interacting with waiters, or any professional in public that you don't know, you'll need to use formal French, with the *vous* form.

NOTICE

🔊 **06.02** Listen to the audio and study the table. Pay special attention to the way the waiter pronounces the phrase *tout de suite* and how Julie says *encore de l'eau.*

Essential phrases for Conversation 1

French	Meaning	Pronunciation
j'ai faim !	I'm hungry! (I-have hunger)	zhay fahN
bonsoir mesdames / monsieur	good evening ladies / sir	bohN-swaR may-dahm muh-see-uhR
voilà la carte	here's the menu	vwah-lah lah kahRt
on prend une carafe d'eau	we'll have (take) a jug of water	ohN pRawN ewn kah-Rahf doh
merci à vous	thank you (pl.)	mehR-see ah voo
avez-vous choisi ?	have you (pl.) decided?	ah-vay voo shwah-zee
On sait déjà.	We know already.	ohN seh day-zhah
je vous écoute.	what would you (pl.) like? (I you (pl.) listen)	zhuh voo zay-koot
pour moi, une ratatouille, s'il vous plait	for me, a ratatouille, please (formal)	pooR mwah ewn Rah-tah-too-ee-uh seel voo pleh
je prends la salade	I'll have (take) the salad	zhuh pRawN lah sah-lahd
et à boire ?	and to drink?	ay ah bwaR
tu vas boire quelque chose ?	are you going to drink something?	tew vah bwaR kehl-kuh shohz
je voudrais...	I would like...	zhuh voo-dReh
du vin rouge / du vin blanc	some red wine / some white wine	dew vahN Roozh/dew vahN blawN
et encore de l'eau	and some more water	ay awN-koR duh loh
tout de suite !	right away!	toot sew-weet

VOCAB: *quelque...*
Given that *chose* means 'thing', and *quelque* is the 'some' in 'something', you can now more easily recognize the following:
quelqu'un (someone)
quelque part (somewhere)
quelquefois (sometimes)

VOCAB: *je voudrais*
You know how to use *je veux* for 'I want', but another, softer option is *je voudrais* for 'I would like', which works better in formal situations.

You've seen the word **encore** used to mean 'again' or, literally, 'yet'. In French, when you want to order more of the same, think of this use of encore de l'eau as either 'water again' or 'yet more water'.

1 Look at the phrase *j'ai faim*. How does English express this feeling differently? ______________________

2 Which phrases from the phrase list are used to do the following?

a order a jug of water ______________________

b order more water ______________________

3 06.02 Find the four phrases used to place an order, and highlight them. Then replay the audio to practise your pronunciation.

a I'll have... b We'll have... c For me... d I would like...

4 Notice which words the speakers use to say 'how much' or 'how many' of something. Do they say 'a' or 'some'? Then write in the missing French word from the phrase list.

a ______ *vin rouge* c ______ *carafe d'eau*

b ______ *table* d ______ *l'eau*

5 What do these phrases and questions mean? Write the English.

a *je sais* ______________

b *je voudrais* ______________

c *je prends* ______________

d *je vais boire* ______________

e *on sait* ______________

f *on a choisi* ______________

g *on prend* ______________

h *Tu sais... ?* ______________

i *Tu prends...?* ______________

j *Tu voudrais...?* ______________

k *Vous avez choisi ?* ______________

l *Tu vas boire...?* ______________

GRAMMAR TIP:
de, d', du **and** ***des*** **for 'some'**

In French, as in English, you'll use *un/une* when you want a defined amount of food or drink (one glass, two bottles). But you'll use *de/d'/du/des* when you want an undefined amount (some water).

CULTURE TIP: *au restaurant*

The French dining experience is a unique one! You'll enjoy it even more if you learn the lingo:

- ***Bonjour/Bonsoir:*** around 6 p.m. in France, everyone's greeting changes from ***bonjour*** (good day) to ***bonsoir*** (good evening).
- ***Mesdames/Messieurs:*** you've learned that the plural of ***mon/ma*** is ***mes***. Similarly, the plural of ***madame*** (lit., 'my-lady') is ***mesdames*** (my-ladies), and ***monsieur*** becomes ***messieurs*** for gentlemen. You'll be greeted with this in many restaurants and other establishments in France.
- ***Une carafe d'eau:*** if you just ask for ***de l'eau*** (water), you may get a pricy bottle that you'd have to pay for. But you can request a ***carafe d'eau***, a (free) jug of tap water, which is very safe to drink in France.
- ***Je vous écoute:*** waiters don't ask the equivalent of 'What would you like?' but say ***Je vous écoute*** (I'm listening (to you)). You can reply with je prends... (I'll take ...) and the waiter will likely respond with ***tout de suite !***

GRAMMAR EXPLANATION: *du / de la / des* (some)

PRONUNCIATION: *how to hear plurals*
Des is also sometimes used as a way to make a plural clear in spoken French, especially since *s* at the end of words is often silent. That way *des voitures* [day vwa-tewR] (some cars), for instance, is clearly distinguished from just *voiture* [vwa-tewR] ('car').

You may have noticed an occasional *du, de la* or *des* appearing in some conversations, as in *Est-ce que vous avez des enfants ?* (Do you have (some) children?). This common feature of French is easiest to understand as a translation of 'some'.

Can you count it?

You'll usually add *des* when you talk about a multiple amount of **something that you can count** (like people, houses, cars), but don't specify the number.

Example: ✔ *Je vois* ***des*** *enfants.* I see (some) children.
✘ ~~Je vois enfants.~~

This is true even when you wouldn't necessarily specify 'some' in English.

Example: ✔ *Je suis ici depuis* ***des*** *heures.* I've been here for (some) hours.
✘ ~~Je suis ici depuis heures.~~

When you *can't* count it...

For things you can't count – especially liquids or intangible things (like *la musique*) – you should use *du* (masculine), *de la* (feminine) or *de l'* (before vowels).

Example: ✔ *Je voudrais* ***de l'****eau.* I would like (some) water.
✘ ~~Je voudrais eau.~~

✔ *Je voudrais* ***de la*** *glace.* I would like (some) ice cream.
✔ *Je voudrais* ***du*** *chocolat.* I would like (some) chocolate.

In English, you cannot count water, ice cream or chocolate, so you say 'some water/ice cream/ chocolate'. It's the same way in French!

1 Imagine you are going through your grocery list, adding each item one by one. Use the appropriate form of *du, de la, de l'* or *des* before each noun in the table (depending on whether or not it is countable or liquid).

French	Meaning	*du/de la/de l'/des*
l'œuf (m)	egg	des œufs
le jambon	ham	
le poisson	fish	
la viande	meat	
le café	coffee	
le lait	milk	
la bière	beer	
le vin	wine	

PRACTICE

1 *Tu vas... quelque chose ?* (Are you going to... something?) is a power phrase. You can modify it in endless ways for different situations. Complete the questions with the appropriate verb. Use the given response to choose the best verb.

a *Tu vas* ______________ *quelque chose ?* *Oui, du café !*

b *Tu vas* ______________ *quelque chose ?* *Oui, du poisson !*

c *Tu vas* ______________ *quelque chose ?* *Oui, des souvenirs !*

2 Fill in the blanks with the missing words in French.

a ______________ ______________ *choisi.* (**We've** decided.)

b __________ *du* __________ *s'il vous plait !* (Some **more wine** please!)

c *Je prends du vin* __________ *et* __________ __________ *du* __________ __________.
(I'll have some **red** wine, and **she'll have** some **white wine**.)

d ________ ________ *ce qu'* ________ ________ *manger.*
(**We know** what **we want** to eat.)

e *Tu as* ______________ ______________ ? (Are you **already hungry**?)

Here's some more important vocab related to eating and drinking to give you a solid base. Before you head to a French restaurant, it's a good idea to learn the names of your favourite dishes in advance.

Eating and drinking vocab

French	Meaning	French	Meaning
le repas	meal	avoir faim (j'ai faim)	to be hungry (I'm hungry)
l'alimentation (f)	food	avoir soif (j'ai soif)	to be thirsty (I'm thirsty)
manger	to eat	prendre (je prends)	to have (to take food) (I'm having)
boire (je bois)	to drink (I drink)	le petit déjeuner	breakfast
cuisiner	to cook / prepare	je prends mon petit déjeuner	I'm having breakfast
avec / sans	with / without	le déjeuner	lunch
le poulet	chicken	déjeuner	to have lunch
le bœuf	beef	le diner	dinner
le porc	pork	diner	to have dinner
le poisson	fish	des fruits	fruit
le légume	vegetable	le verre	glass
je suis végétarien(ne)	I'm a vegetarian	du jus d'orange	orange juice
je suis allergique aux cacahuètes	I'm allergic to peanuts		

3 Add four more food or drink items you would order in French to the table.

I'd suggest you also **bring a pocket dictionary** or use one of the dictionary apps/sites recommended in our Resources on your phone. You may want to try something on the specials board! It's OK to order a dish even if you don't know what it is – be adventurous!

PUT IT TOGETHER

1 Role-play ordering your favourite foods and drinks in French at a restaurant. Take inspiration from what you've learned in this unit (and use your dictionary). You'll order a starter, a main course, two drinks and a dessert.

Tu as faim et soif aujourd'hui !

Luckily, you've already seen **la carte** and it conveniently has all your favourite foods on it.

Alors, qu'est-ce que tu veux cuisiner et qu'est-ce que tu dois acheter pour le faire ?

Le serveur : Alors, avez vous déjà choisi votre entrée ?

Toi : ______________________________

Le serveur : Ah, excellent choix ! Et comme plat principal ?

Toi : ______________________________

Le serveur : Je vois que vous avez faim aujourd'hui ! Et à boire ?

Toi : ____________________ et ____________________.

Le serveur : Tout de suite !

(*30 minutes plus tard.*)

Toi : (Call the waiter over.) ______________________________

Le serveur : Déjà fini ?

Toi : (Say yes, and that you have already chosen your dessert.) ______________________________

Le serveur : Je vous écoute !

Toi : ______________________________

Le serveur : ... Voilà votre dessert ! Bon appétit !

2 Use the vocab you've learned to describe your own upcoming mealtime plans. Try to include:

- what you're planning to eat (*manger, prendre*)
- how you plan to prepare it (*préparer, faire*)
- what you're planning to drink (*boire*).

CONVERSATION 2

In my opinion...

A French friend once said that a dinner without an argument is a dinner wasted.

Dinner conversation is important to the French. A meal is meant to be enjoyed with friends, with interesting discussions and usually with interesting debates.

GRAMMAR NOTE:
***quel/quelle/quels/quelles* (which)**
The French word ***quel*** (which) is used much more frequently than we use its counterpart in English. You'll see it used in ***Quelle heure est-il ?*** (What time is it?). ***Quel*** also changes according to gender and number. Use:

- ***quel*** before masculine words
- ***quelle*** before feminine words
- ***quels*** before plurals (masculine or mixed) and
- ***quelles*** before feminine plurals.

Plus (more) and ***moins*** (less) look a lot like 'plus' and 'minus'.

06.03 Lauren and Julie discover they don't quite see eye to eye on where they should go in Paris. Pay special attention to the way Julie pronounces *il y a*.

Julie: Alors, on va à quel musée demain ?

Lauren: Naturellement, on doit visiter le Louvre.

Julie: Non... il y a tellement de musées à Paris et tu choisis le plus touristique !

Lauren: Je sais qu'il y a beaucoup de touristes, mais il faut le voir !

Julie: Je suis pas d'accord. À mon avis, le Centre Pompidou est mieux. On peut voir de l'art moderne et normalement il y a moins de gens.

Lauren: Oui, il y a moins de gens, mais c'est pas aussi intéressant !

Julie: C'est pas vrai ! Son architecture est incroyable. C'est unique au monde.

Lauren: Je suis d'accord... l'architecture est intéressante, mais je la trouve pas belle.

Julie: Tu sais que beaucoup de Parisiens trouvent la tour Eiffel pas belle et tu veux la visiter quand même.

Lauren: Ben..., on peut faire des compromis. Si tu penses que le Centre Pompidou est mieux que le Louvre, on peut aller à Pompidou demain, pour l'architecture. Et on attend lundi, quand il y a moins de touristes, pour aller au Louvre et voir de l'art !

Julie: Tu as raison – d'accord !

FIGURE IT OUT

1 Find the details in the conversation and write them out.

a What are the names of the two museums being discussed?

____

b Which one does Lauren think they should visit?

____

c What is Lauren's opinion of the Pompidou Centre?

____

d What phrase shows that Lauren and Julie will make a compromise?

____

2 Highlight these phrases.

a the most touristy b if you think that

3 Write the French phrases for:

a I agree ________ b I don't agree ________ c naturally ________

4 Use context to deduce the meaning of the words in bold. *Julie dit que...*

b *le Centre Pompidou est* **mieux que** *le Louvre.* ________

c *le Centre Pompidou a* **moins de** *gens que le Louvre.* ________

d *beaucoup de Parisiens* **trouvent** *la tour Eiffel pas belle.* ________

NOTICE

🔊 **06.04** Listen to the audio and study the table. Pay special attention to the way *tu choisis* and *d'accord* are pronounced.

Essential phrases for Conversation 2

French	Meaning	Pronunciation
naturellement, on doit visiter...	naturally we need to visit...	nah-tew-Rehl-mawN ohN dwa vee-zee-tay
tu choisis le plus touristique !	you choose the most touristy!	tew shwa-zee luh plew too-Rees-teek
il faut le voir !	it has to be seen!	eel foh luh vwaR
je suis pas d'accord !	I disagree!	zhuh sew-wee pah dah-koR
à mon avis...	in my opinion...	ah mohN nah-vee
voir de l'art	to see some art	vwahR duh lahR
il y a moins de gens	there are fewer people	eel ee ah mwahN duh zhawN
c'est unique au monde	there's nothing like it (it's unique to-the world)	say ew-neek oh mawNd
je suis d'accord	I agree	zhuh sew-wee dah-koR
je la trouve...	I find it...	zhuh lah tRoov
ils trouvent...	they think / find...	eel tRoov
quand même	anyway	kawN mehm
on peut faire des compromis	we can compromise	ohN puh fehR day kohN-pRo-mee
si tu penses que...	if you think that...	see tew pawNs kuh
c'est mieux que	it's better than	say mee-uh kuh
tu as raison	you're right (you have reason)	tew ah Reh-zohN
d'accord !	OK!	dah-koR

VOCAB: ***il faut* 'it is necessary'**
Il faut is a useful expression, which means 'it is necessary...'. In this conversation, ***il faut le voir*** means 'It must be seen!' or 'I have to see it!' Since the next verb will be in the dictionary form, you can use it to express anything that 'needs' to happen. For example: ***Il faut boire du vin français !*** (You really should drink French wine!)

Trouver means 'to find' (imagine pirates trying to find a treasure trove). Just like in English, you can use it to discuss finding objects in places (*Tu peux trouver le restaurant ?*), as well as to discuss your opinions (*Je trouve le film fantastique !*)

1 Find the phrase for 'you are right'. How does this phrase translate literally into English? What expression from Conversation 1 also uses *avoir* in French instead of 'to be' as you would in English?

2 Find the words used for comparison and highlight them. Then write them out.

a the most ______ b better ______ c less / fewer ______

3 How would you write the following in French?

a I find it... ______
b I find the Louvre... ______
c They find it... ______
d They find the Louvre... ______
e I know that... ______
f You know that... ______
g We know that there are... ______
h You know that there are... ______
i There is nothing like it... ______

4 Each of these phrases is useful for expressing your opinion in French. Match the French phrase to its English counterpart.

a *à mon avis*
b *je suis pas d'accord*
c *tu as raison*
d *je suis d'accord*
e *je trouve*
f *je voudrais*
g *je pense que*

1 I agree
2 you're right
3 in my opinion
4 I don't agree
5 I would like
6 I think that
7 I find

CULTURE EXPLANATION: debates

French speakers aren't afraid to raise controversial subjects in conversation. No offence is intended, and after a heated debate, people go back to being the best of friends. Know that if a tricky-to-discuss topic comes up, this means that the other person is very interested in hearing your opinion and learning more about you.

If you aren't comfortable talking about the topic, feel free to mention this, but if possible, try to offer at least a basic opinion to get some interesting practice time!

GRAMMAR EXPLANATION: comparisons

French makes it easy to compare things. You can describe something as 'more' or 'less', 'bigger' or 'smaller', plus a range of other comparisons using ***plus*** and ***moins***:

- ***plus*** + adjective for 'more/-er' → *plus grand* (bigger)
- ***moins*** + adjective for 'less' → *moins beau* (less handsome)
- ***le plus*** (or *la/les plus*) + adjective for 'the most/-est' → *le plus grand* (the biggest)
- ***le moins*** (or *la/les moins*) + adjective for 'the least/-est' → *le moins beau* (the least handsome).

Description	Example	*le plus/le moins*	Example
plus + grand (bigger)	Ta ville est plus grande que ma ville. (Your city is bigger than my city.)	le plus + grand (biggest)	Ta ville est la plus grande du pays. (Your city is the biggest in the country.)
plus + intéressant (more interesting)	Je trouve ce musée plus intéressant. (I find this museum more interesting.)	le plus + intéressant (most interesting)	Ce film est le plus intéressant que je connais. (The film is the most interesting (one) that I know.)
moins + cher (less expensive)	Ce resto est moins cher que l'autre. (This restaurant is less expensive than the other one.)	le moins + cher (least expensive)	Voilà le moins cher supermarché de la ville (That's the least expensive supermarket in town.)

You can use *plus* ***que*** 'more than' and *moins* ***que*** 'less than' **to compare people and things**:

Example: *J'aime déjeuner dans le parc* ***plus que*** *dans la brasserie.*
(I like to have lunch in the park **more than** in the brasserie.)

And **to compare amounts**, you can use *plus* ***de*** and *moins* ***de***:

Example: *Je vois* ***moins de*** *touristes aujourd'hui.*
(I see **fewer** tourists today.)

There's one major exception within comparisons:
when you want to talk about '**better**' and '**best**' or '**worse**' and '**worst**'.

adjective/adverb	*-er* form	*-est* form
bon (good) / **bien** (well)	**meilleur(e) / mieux** (better)	**le / la meilleur(e) / mieux** (best)
mauvais (bad) / **mal** (worse)	**pire** (worse)	**le / la pire** (worst)

Example: *Je pense que ce restaurant a* ***le meilleur*** *vin du monde !*
I think that this restaurant has **the best** wine in the world!

Practise using the different forms of *plus, moins, plus de, moins de, meilleur* or *pire* using the given phrases.

Example: a smaller city (*petite ville*) → une plus petite ville

a nicer (*sympa*) ______
b more charming (*charmant*) ______
c more books ______
d most famous (*célèbre*) ______
e the best restaurant ______
f a younger man (*homme*) ______
g less difficult ______
h fewer days ______
i least expensive (*cher*) ______
j the worst film (film) ______

PRACTICE

1 Combine *il y a* with the sentence endings given to form new sentences in French:

Example: There are not... (enough days in the weekend).
→ Il y a pas assez de jours dans le weekend !

a Are there... (only three students here)? ______

b There are some... (books at my house). ______

c I find that there are... (fewer dogs in the park today). ______

2 How would you translate the following into French?

a Paris is bigger than Toulouse. ______
b I find this restaurant too small. ______
c What address do you see? ______
d During the week, you have to work / it's necessary to work.

______

PUT IT TOGETHER

1 Quel est ton endroit préféré à visiter dans le monde ?
Recommend to a friend what to do in a city you know or would like to visit. Try to include:

- the places you would like to visit (*je voudrais*)
- the sites or experiences you think would be the best (*meilleur*)
- what for you is a 'must see' (*il faut le voir*)
- phrases for comparison (*plus, moins*)
- phrases for expressing your opinion (*à mon avis*).

Il y a tellement d'endroits à ________ (ville) que je voudrais visiter...

CONVERSATION 3

What do you recommend?

06.05 Lauren and Julie are sharing their opinions on music and books. What phrase does Lauren use to say 'tell me'?

Lauren : Dis-moi Julie. Je voudrais en savoir plus sur la musique française. Qu'est-ce que tu recommandes ?

Julie : C'est une bonne question ! À mon avis, la meilleure musique en français c'est Jacques Brel. J'aime ça plus que la musique moderne.

Lauren : Ah oui ! Il chante, 'Ne me quitte pas', non ? Je voudrais apprendre les paroles de ses chansons.

Julie : Tu dois en savoir plus sur musique française. Je te donne des chansons à écouter. En échange, tu peux me recommander un bon livre en anglais ?

Lauren : Absolument ! Je lis tout le temps. Demain, je te donne le livre que je lis maintenant. Je suis sûre que tu vas adorer !

Julie : Merci.

Lauren : Merci à toi !

Julie : Alors, le serveur est où ? Je vais demander l'addition. Monsieur ? L'addition, s'il vous plait !

Another important dinner topic in France is culture. You don't need to quote Descartes, but it's good to learn some phrases to contribute to conversations and give your opinion about books, music, art or politics.

PRONUNCIATION:
je suis

06.06 In very casual situations, you can replace the *je* + *s* sound with a 'sh' sound. This gives us [shwee] for *je suis* and [shay pah] for *je sais pas*. This is the French version of 'I dunno'. Listen to the audio to hear the difference between the standard and the casual ways of saying *je suis*.

Literally 'thanks to you,' this is like saying 'no, **thank you!**' as a reply to *merci*.

FIGURE IT OUT

1 Answer the questions with a short phrase in French.

a What does Julie think is the best music in French? ____________

b Which music does she not like as much? ____________

c What is Lauren going to give Julie? ____________

2 Deduce the meaning of the phrases.

a *en échange* ____________ b *absolument* ____________

3 Highlight the French translations of these questions and phrases.

a Where is the waiter?

b The bill, please!

c in my opinion

d I like that more than...

e What do you recommend?

NOTICE

🔊 **06.07** Listen to the audio and study the table.

Essential phrases for Conversation 3

French	Meaning	Pronunciation
dis-moi…	tell me…	dee mwa
je voudrais en savoir plus sur…	I would like to know more about…	zhuh voo-dReh ohN sah-vwaR plews sewR
qu'est-ce que tu recommandes ?	what do you recommend?	kehs kuh tew Ruh-ko-mawNd
c'est une bonne question !	that's a good question!	seh tewn bohNn kehs-tyohN
la meilleure musique c'est…	the best music is…	lah meh-yuhR mew-zeek say
plus que la musique moderne	more than modern music	plews kuh lah mew-zeek mo-dehRn
tu dois en savoir plus sur…	you should know more about…	tew dwah zohN sa-vwaR plews sewR
je te donne des chansons	I'll give you some songs	zhuh tuh don day shawN-sohN
tu peux me recommander…	you can recommend… to me	tew puh muh Ruh-ko-mawN-day
je suis sûr(e) que tu vas adorer	I'm sure you will love it	zhuh sew-wee sewR kuh tew vah zah-do-Ray
je vais demander l'addition	I'm going to ask for the bill	zhuh veh duh-mawN-day lah-dee-see-ohN

You may be tempted to translate 'ask for' as 'demander pour', but the 'for' is implied. No need for it! Think of it as the way we use the word 'request' in English. The same works for attendre, which means both 'to wait' and 'to wait for': **je t'attends** (I'm waiting for you).

Also be aware that in French, you don't 'ask' a question, you 'pose' a question – **poser une question!**

1 Say in French:

a you're going to love it ____________

b I'd like … ____________

c I'll give you … ____________

2 Match the French phrases with the correct English translations.

a *je te donne*	1 I like it more
b *je suis sûr que*	2 I'll give you
c *j'aime ça plus*	3 I'm sure that
d *je voudrais apprendre*	4 I'm going to ask
e *je vais demander*	5 I'd like to learn

3 Notice which phrases can be used to ask for recommendations. Write them out in French.

a Tell me... ____________

b What do you recommend? ______________________

c Can you recommend to me...? ______________________

PRACTICE

1 You can adapt power phrases to use in a variety of different situations.

a Power phrase: *Je vais demander...* (I'm going to ask for...)

... some water ________ ... more time ________

... a taxi ________ ... another drink ________

b Power phrase: *Je voudrais en savoir plus sur... (quelque chose)*

What would you like to know more about? Use this power phrase to write two different sentences referring to your own interests.

____

____

2 Fill in the blanks with the missing words in French.

a *J'adore ______ classique. ______ ______ ______ ______ ______ moderne.*

(I love classic **art. I like that more than** modern **art.**)

b ______ ______ ______, *quel livre* ______ ______ *intéressant ?*

(**In your opinion**, which book **is more** interesting?)

c *Un instant,* ______ ______ ______ ______ ______ *adresse !*

(Hold on a minute, **I should give you our** address!)

#LANGUAGEHACK: sound more fluent with conversation connectors

As a beginner, when you're asked a question in French, you may be tempted to give single word answers. Do you like this book? *Oui.* How is your food? *Bien.*

You can train yourself to give longer replies by learning versatile phrases to use between *oui, non* or other brief answers. **Conversation connectors** are power phrases that you can tack on to nearly anything you say to give your French a bit more weight. Learn them once, and you can use them in countless situations. For example, in Conversation 3, Lauren uses the conversation connector *c'est une bonne question* during her discussion with Julie. Conversation connectors improve your flow and make conversations feel a lot less one-sided.

How to use conversation connectors

Good connectors should be versatile. They don't add extra information to the sentence, but expand it. For example, if someone asks you *Tu aimes ce restaurant ?* you could reply with, *oui, j'aime,* or:

Merci de me poser la question, oui, j'aime ce restaurant, et toi ?

Here are some examples of conversation connectors to get you started.

for adding your opinion

- *franchement* (frankly speaking)
- *à vrai dire* (to tell you the truth)
- *à mon avis* (in my opinion)
- *entre nous* (between us)
- *si je comprends bien* (if I understand correctly)
- *malheureusement* (unfortunately)
- *j'ai l'impression que* (it seems to me that)
- *de plus en plus* (more and more)

for elaborating on an idea

- *c'est-à-dire* (that is to say)
- *c'est pourquoi* (and that is why)

for changing a subject

- *d'autre part* (on the other hand)
- *à propos* (by the way)

- If someone asks, *Tu as quel âge ?* (How old are you?), you could say: *j'ai 41 ans,* or ***Alors... entre nous... malheureusement,*** *j'ai* ***déjà*** *41 ans !*
- If someone asks, *Pourquoi tu apprends le français ?* you could say: *parce que j'aime la culture française,* or ***À vrai dire...*** *j'aime la culture française !* ***Et c'est pourquoi*** *j'apprends le français !*

YOUR TURN: use the hack

1 06.08 Practise getting more familiar with the sound and pronunciation of conversation connectors. Listen to the audio, and repeat each connector phrase to mimic the speaker.

malheureusement	*c'est-à-dire*	*à mon avis*
franchement	*si je comprends bien*	*c'est pourquoi*

2 06.09 Now practise recognizing the phrases. Listen to the audio, and write down the connector phrase you hear in French.

a ____________ c ____________ e ____________

b ____________ d ____________ f ____________

3 Use conversation connectors to give longer replies.

Example: *Est-ce que, cette maison est trop petite ?*

→ À vrai dire, je pense que, franchement, cette maison est pas trop petite !

a *Ton diner est bon ?* ____________

b *Tu habites où ?* ____________

c *Tu veux quelque chose du supermarché ?*

____

d *Est-ce que tu bois du café ?* ____________

As you can see, conversation connectors help you expand on your answers, and give them a much chattier feel! This technique will help you develop a conversational flow even if you have too few words to keep your side of the conversation very interesting for now. For beginners, **momentum helps conversations stay alive** better than more words.

PUT IT TOGETHER

Imagine you have a friend who wants to have a culture-filled weekend and asks you to recommend some worthwhile cultural endeavours. Prepare phrases you could use during French dinner conversations, with culture as a central topic. Create 'me-specific' sentences in which you:

- describe music, art or books that you love
- offer your opinion (*à mon avis, j'aime ça*)
- include power phrases (*je voudrais en savoir plus sur...*)
- use conversation connectors (*franchement, entre nous...*)
- use comparisons (*plus, moins, meilleur*), mieux, pire.

COMPLETING UNIT 6

Check your understanding

🔊 **06.10** Listen to the audio recording, which will play sets of two statements in French. The first statement gives information about someone. The second statement attempts to summarize that information. Based on what you understand, select *vrai* if the summary is correct or *faux* if it's wrong.

Example: *Marie trouve cette ville très jolie.*
Summary: *Elle aime la ville* → *(vrai)/ faux*

a *vrai / faux*
b *vrai / faux*
c *vrai / faux*
d *vrai / faux*
e *vrai / faux*

Show what you know...

Here's what you've just learned. Write or say an example for each item in the list. Then tick off the ones you know.

- ☐ Ask for a specific food item using 'I'll have'.
- ☐ Ask for a specific drink using 'I would like'.
- ☐ Use phrases for formal situations: 'good evening', 'please' (formal), 'thanks' (formal).
- ☐ Talk about unspecified amounts and plurals:
  - ☐ some water
  - ☐ eggs
  - ☐ there are some croissants here
- ☐ Say 'I agree', 'I disagree' and 'in my opinion'.
- ☐ Give one phrase each for giving and asking for recommendations.
- ☐ Give the comparison words 'more than', 'less than', 'most' and 'better than'.
- ☐ Give two examples of conversation connectors.

COMPLETE YOUR MISSION

It's time to complete your mission: convince your friend to try out your favourite restaurant. To do this, you'll need to prepare phrases for giving your opinions and explaining why you agree or disagree. Either describe a restaurant you know and love, or research some restaurants in a French-speaking country you want to visit.

STEP 1: build your script

Keep building your script using opinion phrases:

- describe your favourite restaurant. What type of food and drinks do they serve? Why do you like it so much? Which are your favourites and why?
- convince a friend to try it out by saying what makes it better than other restaurants in town (use comparisons!)
- give or ask for recommendations
- include power phrases and conversation connectors.

Write down your script, then repeat it until you feel confident.

Read restaurant reviews in French online to help you form your argument. You can see how French speakers in real life describe their own favourite (or least favourite) restaurant experiences by reading their own words ... online! Get more details by going online to the #LanguageHacking community.

STEP 2: it's all about me! ... *online*

When you feel good about your script, go online and share your recording with the community. This time, as you're speaking, use conversation connectors between phrases and while you're thinking to help your French flow better. By using these phrases right away, you'll also start burning them into your muscle memory, so they are on the tip of your tongue when you need them!

Yes, it is! **Personalize your language** to talk about yourself and what's important to you! Learning a language is easier when you can talk about things that are meaningful.

STEP 3: learn from other learners

You could use the phrases ***tu recommandes*** ... or ***à ton avis*** ... to let them know that you understand their point of view.

Test out your debating skills with other language hackers! **Your task is to reply in French to at least three different people** to tell them whether you agree or disagree with the argument they made and why.

STEP 4: reflect on what you've learned

What did you find easy or difficult about this unit? Did you learn any new words or phrases in the community space? After every script you write or conversation you have, you'll gain insight into what gaps you need to fill in your script.

HEY, LANGUAGE HACKER, LOOK AT YOU GO!

Now you can share opinions, talk about food, make comparisons and keep the conversation flowing – you've come a long way. Things can only improve from here!

Next, let's make a huge leap forward with the range of conversations you can have – by starting to talk about the past.

Chouette !

7 TALKING ABOUT YESTERDAY ... LAST WEEK ... A LONG TIME AGO

Your mission

Imagine this – you just joined a French meet-up group and you have to introduce yourself by sharing personal stories, but with a twist – your story can be true or completely made up.

Your mission is to tell a true, but possibly unbelievable story or one completely made-up story in as convincing a way as possible so that the others can't guess if it's true or false. Be prepared to **describe a personal story** or a **life lesson you've learned from your past experiences**, whether in learning a new language, moving to a new place or taking a big risk.

This mission will help you expand the range of conversation topics you can confidently contribute to in casual situations and allow you to start using anecdotes to spice up your French *répertoire*!

Mission prep

- Talk about the past in just two steps: *j'ai + parlé*
- Answer questions about the past: *Qu'est-ce que tu as fait hier ?/Je suis allé(e) ...*
- Say how long ago something happened using *il y a*
- Use the past tense to talk about your progress in French: *J'ai bien prononcé ce mot*

BUILDING LANGUAGE FOR RICHER CONVERSATIONS

Until now, your conversations in French have focused on what's happening now or in the future. By the end of this unit, you'll be able to give detailed descriptions of things you did in the past, which will help you have much richer conversations.

#LANGUAGEHACK
time travel – talk about the past and future using the present tense

CONVERSATION 1

What did you do last weekend?

As you speak French with the same people more regularly, a big question is often **'What am I going to talk about?'** Being able to use and understand the French past tense is a great solution to this problem. You can use it to describe personal stories about your life, which makes for endless topics of conversation.

Lauren is talking again with Antoine, one of her tutors, and tells him about her time with her friend Julie.

07.01 How does Antoine ask 'What did you do last weekend?'

Antoine : Coucou Lauren ! Quoi de neuf ? Qu'est-ce que tu as fait le weekend dernier ?

Lauren : Je suis allée au restaurant avec Julie, et on a parlé de nos projets pour le weekend. Puis hier, on est allé au Centre Pompidou et on a visité beaucoup des sites touristiques de Paris !

Antoine : Pourquoi vous avez décidé de visiter Pompidou ? Pourquoi pas le Louvre ?

Lauren : C'est un des musées préférés de Julie. Je me suis amusée ! En fait, on va au Louvre demain !

Antoine : Tu as rencontré Julie il y a juste une semaine, non ?

Lauren : Oui, c'est ça.

Antoine : J'ai visité Pompidou une fois il y a quatre ans.

Lauren : Ça t'a plu ? Comment tu as trouvé ça ?

Antoine : Pas mal. Mais j'ai préféré le café du coin où j'ai mangé une glace délicieuse !

More often than not, you speak 'of' (de) things rather than 'about' them in French.

FIGURE IT OUT

1 What is Antoine's opinion of *le Centre Pompidou*?

a It's fun.
b It's not bad.
c It's one of his favourite museums.

2 Highlight the phrases in the conversation for:

a last weekend
b How did you find it?
c We talked about our plans

3 What do you think the phrase *pourquoi vous avez décidé de visiter* means?

____

4 *Vrai ou faux ?* Select the correct answer.

a Julie read about a restaurant she'd like to go to. *vrai / faux*
b Lauren spoke with Julie. *vrai / faux*
c Yesterday, Lauren went to the Louvre. *vrai / faux*
d Lauren met Julie one week ago. *vrai / faux*

NOTICE

🔊 **07.02** Listen to the audio and study the table. Try to mimic the speakers.

Pay special attention to the way Lauren pronounces the phrases: **je suis allée; on a parlé; on est allé; on a visité.**

Essential phrases for Conversation 1

French	Meaning	Pronunciation
qu'est-ce que tu as fait le weekend dernier ?	what did you do last weekend?	kehs kuh tew ah feh luh week-ehnd dehR-nee-ay
je suis allée / on est allé au ...	I went / we went to the ...	zhuh sew-wee / ohN neh ah-lay oh
on a parlé de nos projets	we talked about our plans	ohN nah pahR-lay duh noh pRoh-zhay
puis hier ...	then yesterday ...	pew-wee ee-yehR
on a visité beaucoup de sites	we visited a lot of sites	ohN nah vee-zee-tay boh-koo day seet
pourquoi vous avez décidé de ... ?	why did you decide to ...?	pooR-kwa voo zah-vay day-see-day duh
c'est un des musées préférés de Julie	it's one of Julie's favourite museums	seh tahN day mew-zay pRay-fay-Ray duh zhew-lee
je me suis amusée !	I had fun! (I am myself amused)	zhuh muh sew-wee zah-mew-say
tu as rencontré ...	you met ...	tew ah RawN-kohN-tRay
il y a une semaine	a week ago	eel ee ah ewn suh-mehn
j'ai visité Pompidou une fois	I visited the Pompidou once	zhay vee-zeetay pohN-pee-doo ewn fwah
ça t'a plu ?	did you like it?	sah tah plew
comment tu as trouvé ça ?	what did you think? (how you have found that)	koh-mawN tew ah tRoo-vay sah
j'ai préféré ...	I preferred ...	zhay pRay-fay-Ray
j'ai mangé ...	I ate ...	zhay mawN-zhay

GRAMMAR TIP:
***de* (of) for possession**
Notice the word order here. This is an example of the possessive ***de*** you saw in Unit 5, and is necessary when someone is referenced like this by name (otherwise we'd use ***ses*** 'her').

VOCAB: *I like it*
While you may expect ***j'aime ça*** for 'I like it', another way to say this is ***ça me plait***, or literally 'that me pleases'. In this conversation, ***plaire*** (to please) is in the past tense. You will recognize this verb from ***s'il te/vous plait*** ('please' or, literally, 'if-it you pleases').

1 Highlight the following phrases in French in the phrase list. Then write them out.

a What did you do?
Qu'est-ce que ______________?

b I preferred *j'* ______________

c I ate *j'* ______________

d I went *je* ______________

e we went *on* ______________

f we talked *on* ______________

g I visited *j'* ______________

h we visited *on* ______________

i you (pl.) decided to *vous* ______________

2 Write the French translations.

a ago ______________

b last (previous) ______________

c once ______________

d the café on the corner ______________

GRAMMAR EXPLANATION: past verb forms

Saying something in the past in French is quite simple. You don't need to learn a unique past form for every verb. You usually just need to make an easy and predictable modification using *avoir* + **past form**.

Step 1: Most verbs in the past start with the present form of the verb *avoir* (to have), which by now you know well:

j'ai *vous* ***avez*** *tu* ***as*** *ils/elles* ***ont*** *il/elle/on* ***a***

Step 2: Add the verb you want to use, but modify it slightly to become **the past form**, which is usually predictable. For most verbs, just replace the last two letters of the dictionary form as follows:

For **-re** verbs, some may use **-u** as their past form ending, but most -re verbs follow other patterns. We'll cover the most important of these shortly.

Dictionary ending	-er verbs	-ir verbs
Past form ending	-é	-i
Example	j'ai mang**é** (I ate)	tu as fin**i** (you finished)

Word-for-word, **j'ai mangé** means 'I've eaten', but this is actually how you say 'I ate' in French.

1 Try it yourself!

a First, write out 'I have'. ______________

b Write out the past form of *parler*. ______________

c Now put them together to form 'I talked'. ______________

Using *être* for movement

The two steps you just learned are all you'll need to use to form the past tense most of the time. But when you say something in the past with a verb **involving movement**, such as:

aller	arriver	entrer	sortir	retourner	venir

then you'll use *être* (to be) instead of *avoir*. Just follow the same two steps to translate 'Marc arrived yesterday': using *être* + **past form**.

(1) Marc *est* ... + (2) arrivé → Marc *est* arrivé hier.

One other difference: you'll see an *e* added for females and an *s* for multiple people when *être* is used (but not when *avoir* is used). That's why Lauren says *je suis allée*. Luckily, for both, the pronunciation is usually the same! *Et voilà !* (That's it!)

GRAMMAR TIP: ***work around the grammar!***
Some verbs don't follow this rule, and there is another kind of past tense in French. But instead of trying to learn even more grammar, we'll find a work-around so that you can use the past form you've already learned in most situations, rather than learning an entirely new form. #languagehacking at its finest!

2 Fill in the gaps using the past form of the given verbs with *avoir*.

a *J'_______ ____________ la télé hier.* (*regarder*)
b *Il _______ ____________ le français ce matin* (*étudier*)
c *Tu _______ ____________ le restaurant ?* (*choisir*)
d *Elle _______ ____________ quelque chose.* (*demander*)

3 Select the correct answer in French to form the past tense:

a *Je suis / J'ai sorti avec mes amis.* (I went out with my friends.)
b *Je suis / J'ai choisi ce musée.* (I chose this museum.)
c *Antoine a regardé / regardi / regardu le film le weekend dernier.* (Antoine watched the film last weekend.)

CONVERSATION STRATEGY: ***guess when you're not sure!***
There are other situations that use **être**, but you can absolutely learn these later. You can always fall back to 'Tarzan French', and just use the **avoir** form – people will understand you. Even though 'j'ai allé' is a mistake, people will recognize that you're learning and know exactly what you mean. For now, just try to be confident with verbs you know you'll use often. If you're ever in doubt, your dictionary will also indicate whether the verb takes **être** or **avoir** in the past tense.

PRACTICE

1 Use *il y a* to say how long ago you met your best friend or partner.

J'ai rencontré mon/ma … ______________________________

2 Now practise creating full sentences in French.

a You should go to the restaurant where I ate two days ago.

____

b We liked the film!

____

c She visited (Hint: she went to see) her brother in Dublin.

____

3 Fill in the gaps, using *avoir* or *être*.

a ________ ________ ________ *trois mois,*

________ ________ ________ *au Canada.*

(Three months **ago, I went** to Canada.)

b ________ ________ *le musée très intéressant !*

(**I found** the museum very interesting.)

c *Ce matin,* ________ ________ ________ *en métro.*

(This morning **I arrived** by *metro*.)

PUT IT TOGETHER

Let's use the past tense forms you've just learned to create 'me-specific' sentences that you could use in real conversations.

1 First, practise answering a common question in the past tense.

Quoi de neuf ? Qu'est-ce que tu as fait hier/le weekend dernier ?

Answer this question with real details about your life. You might include details about:

- where you went
- what you did
- who you talked to
- what you talked about

2 Now use the past tense to describe the details of a trip you took to another city. Draw from your own experiences to create sentences that are true for you, and be sure to answer these questions:

- *Tu es allé(e) où ? (Je suis allé(e) / j'ai visité … une fois …)*
- *Il y a combien de temps ? (Il y a …)*
- *Pourquoi tu as décidé d'aller à … ? (j'ai décidé d'aller à … parce que …)*
- *Ça t'a plu ? Pourquoi ? (Ça m'a plu / ça m'a pas plu, parce que j'ai / je suis …)*
- *Comment tu as trouvé ça ? (J'ai trouvé ça …)*

PRONUNCIATION: ***quoi de neuf ?***
Sound like a native! You will very likely only come across this expression in casual conversations. Because of this, it even has a casual pronunciation. As well as [*kwah duh nuf*], it can be shortened to [*kwahd nuf*].

VOCAB: ***using il y a***
The phrase ***il y a*** means both 'there is / there are' and 'ago' depending on context. When used to mean 'ago', the order is different from English, since it comes before the time – not after.
Il y a trois jours (three days ago).

'To decide to' in French is **décider de**. You've seen that you can follow verbs with prepositions like **à**, **de**, **que** or nothing. You'll get used to this, but for now, don't worry about getting it exactly right.

CONVERSATION 2

Did you study French this week?

People will definitely ask you these questions, so let's prepare you to answer them in French.

Another great way to expand the scope of your French conversations is to learn to talk about your French progress, in French! Now that Lauren and Antoine have caught up, they start discussing what Lauren has been doing to improve her French.

07.03 How does Antoine ask 'Did you have time to study this week?'

Antoine : Alors, est-ce que tu as étudié le français cette semaine ?

Lauren : Oui, j'ai étudié un peu. J'ai appris quelques nouveaux mots et j'ai pratiqué quelques phrases avec Julie.

Antoine : Excellent ! Tu as fait tes **devoirs** ?

Lauren : Oui, je les ais ici.

Antoine : Je dois dire que tu es une étudiante excellente. Quand est-ce que tu as commencé à apprendre le français ?

Lauren : J'ai commencé il y a seulement quelques mois. L'été dernier, j'ai décidé de voyager pendant un an alors j'ai acheté un billet et **j'ai pris l'avion jusqu'à** Paris !

Antoine : C'est vrai, j'ai oublié – tu m'as déjà dit ça !

VOCAB: ***les devoirs***
Remember that *devoir* means 'to have to'. *Devoirs* literally means 'duties / obligations'. This means that the French word for 'homework' is plural. When you refer to it, you'll use *les* (they) rather than *le* (it). You never have a little homework, you always have a lot!

VOCAB: ***'until'***
When you're talking about a long journey like a flight, you have to say 'I flew 'until' Paris', using the word *jusqu'à*: ***J'ai pris l'avion jusqu'à Paris.***
It works the same when you're coming from a long distance – using *depuis* instead of *de*: 'from Rome to Berlin' is ***depuis Rome jusqu'à Berlin.***

FIGURE IT OUT

1 *Vrai ou faux ?* Select the correct answer.

a Lauren studied French this week. *vrai / faux*

b Lauren practised some phrases alone. *vrai / faux*

c Lauren started learning French one year ago. *vrai / faux*

2 Answer the questions in French.

a What did Lauren do with Julie to improve her French this week?

____

b When (how long ago) did Lauren start learning French?

____

3 What is the meaning of the phrase *j'ai oublié – tu m'as déjà dit ça* ?

____

4 There are at least 10 occurrences of the past tense in the conversation. Find them all and circle them.

NOTICE

🔊 **07.04** Listen to the audio and study the table.

Essential phrases for Conversation 2

French	Meaning	Pronunciation
est-ce que tu as étudié le français cette semaine ?	did you study French this week?	ehs kuh tew ah zay-tew-dee-ay luh fRawN-seh seht suh-mehn
j'ai étudié un peu	I studied a little	zhay ay-tew-dee-ay ahN puh
j'ai appris ...	I learned ...	zhay ah-pRee
quelques nouveaux mots	some new words	kehl-kuh noo-voh moh
j'ai pratiqué ...	I practised ...	zhay pRah-tee-kay
quelques phrases	some phrases	kehl-kuh fRahz
excellent !	excellent!	ehk-say-lawN
tu as fait tes devoirs ?	did you do your homework?	tew ah feh tay duh-vwaR
quand est-ce que tu as commencé à ... ?	when did you start ...?	kawN ehs kuh tew ah koh-mawN-say ah
j'ai commencé il y a ...	I started ... ago	zhay koh-mawN-say eel ee ah
j'ai décidé de ...	I decided ...	zhay day-see-day duh
voyager pendant un an	to travel for a year	vwa-yah-zhay pawN-dawN ahN nawN
j'ai acheté ...	I bought ...	zhay ahsh-tay
un billet (d'avion)	a (plane) ticket	ahN bee-yeh (dah-vee-ohN)
je suis arrivée à Paris !	I arrived in Paris!	zhuh sew-wee zah-Ree-vay ah pah-Ree
j'ai oublié !	I forgot!	zhay oo-blee-ay
tu m'as déjà dit ça !	you told me that already!	tew mah day-zhah dee sah

You may notice that these three past forms do not fit the rule you learned after Conversation 1. You'll discover why shortly.

1 Match the English to the correct French phrases.

a I learned
b you did
c you told me

1 *tu as fait*
2 *tu m'as dit*
3 *j'ai appris*

2 Highlight the following past tense phrases in the phrase list. Then fill in the French translations in section 1 of the past tense cheat sheet. Leave the rest of the cheat sheet blank for now.

a I studied
b I learned
c I practised
d I started
e I decided to
f I bought
g I forgot

Past tense cheat sheet

1. Regular verbs	Past form	2. Irregular verbs	Past form	3. 'Me-specific' verbs	All forms
I studied	J'ai	I said			
I practised	J'ai	I learned			
I started	J'ai	I did			
I decided to	J'ai				
I bought	J'ai				
I forgot	J'ai				

GRAMMAR EXPLANATION: three easy patterns for the top 'irregular' past verbs

In Conversation 1 you learned a simple rule for forming past sentences. As you saw in Conversation 2, there are many exceptions to the rule.

Luckily, the vast majority of these exceptions follow patterns. Learn this list of the three main patterns for irregular past verb forms, and then you'll be able to confidently use the most important verbs in the past tense.

1 Change the verb ending *-ire* to *-it*

Dictionary form		Past form	Meaning
d**ire**	→	d**it**	to say – said
f**aire**	→	f**ait**	to make – made / to do – did
tradu**ire**	→	tradu**it**	to translate – translated
écr**ire**	→	écr**it**	to write – written

2 Change the verb endings *-prendre* and *-mettre* to *-pris* and *-mis*

Dictionary form		Past form	Meaning
prendre	→	**pris**	take – taken
ap**prendre**	→	ap**pris**	learn – learned
com**prendre**	→	com**pris**	understand – understood
mettre	→	**mis**	put – put
per**mettre**	→	per**mis**	to allow/permit – allowed/permitted

3 Some single-syllable verbs replace several letters with *-u*

Dictionary form		Past form	Meaning
l**ire**	→	l**u**	read – read
b**oire**	→	b**u**	drink – drunk
v**oir**	→	v**u**	see – seen
pl**aire**	→	pl**u**	please – pleased

While this list may seem intimidating, it is ultimately just three rules that you can learn, to handle almost any other verb in the past tense. I'll point out any important irregular forms that don't fit these rules, but with this small list you have most verbs covered.

1 **Following the three rules you've just learned, complete the table with the missing French translations.**

French	Meaning
	we made / we did
	I read
	he saw
	she understood

2 **Refer back to your past tense cheat sheet, and:**

a fill in the correct past tense forms for the verbs in Section 2 of the cheat sheet

b review the past tense verb forms you've learned to find any 'me-specific' verbs you think you'll need to use. Add them to Section 3 of the cheat sheet.

PRACTICE

1 **Practise rephrasing French sentences using the past tense. The following sentences use *depuis* in the present tense. Change them to the past using *il y a* (ago), while maintaining the same general meaning.**

Example: *Je suis à Paris depuis une semaine.*

→ *Je suis* <u>arrivé</u> *à Paris* <u>il y a</u> *une semaine. (arriver)*

a *Je mange ici depuis neuf mois.*

J'ai ____________ *ce restaurant* ____________ *neuf mois. (trouver)*

b *J'étudie le français depuis trois ans.*

J'ai ________ *à apprendre le français* ______________________________. *(commencer)*

c *Il me connait depuis une semaine.*

Il m'a ______________________________. *(rencontrer)*

2 **How would you say the following in French?**

a I am watching the film. ______________________________

b I'm going to watch the film tomorrow. ______________________________

c I watched the film last week. ______________________________

3 Fill in the blanks with the missing phrases in French.

a *Ça prend* _______ _______ _______ *donc* _______ _______ *d'habiter ici* _______ *l'automne.*
(That takes **too much time**, so **I've decided** to live here **until** autumn).

b _______ _______, *j'ai* _______ _______ *jusqu'au Canada tout seul.*
(**Once, I flew** (took the plane) to Canada by myself.)

c _______ _______, *j'ai pris le train* _______ *l'Espagne* _______ *en Italie.*
(**Last summer**, I took the train **from** Spain **to** Italy.)

d *Est-ce que* _______ _______ _______ *du dictionnaire ?* _______ _______ _______.
(Do **you need** the dictionary? **I have it here.**)

e _______ _______ _______ *que le livre est* _______ _______ *à lire cette fois que la* _______ _______.
(**I have to say** that the book is **easier** to read this time than **last time**.)

PUT IT TOGETHER

Imagine you're having a conversation with someone in French. When you casually mention something you once did or somewhere you went, the other person says, *Chouette ! Qu'est-ce que tu as fait exactement ?* (Cool! What did you do exactly?)

Create sentences in French about somewhere you went, a movie you saw, or anything else – but try to use new verbs you haven't used before. Be as detailed as you can. Include:

- specific details of what happened – who did what? (*Ils ont appris …*)
- specific details of conversations – who said what? (*La fille a dit …*)
- details about where you went, when you returned (*Je suis allé(e) …*)
- several past tense verbs in various forms.

CONVERSATION 3

Did you know ...?

🔊 **07.05** Lauren and Antoine continue discussing Lauren's progress in French. Pay attention to which words and phrases you recognize. What phrase does Lauren use to ask 'Did you know'?

Lauren : En fait, j'ai appris le français à l'école pendant un an. Tu savais ?

Antoine : Vraiment ? Je pensais que tu étais débutante.

Lauren : J'ai oublié tout ce que j'ai appris, donc je pense que je suis toujours débutante.

Antoine : Pourquoi tu as rien appris ?

Lauren : Mon professeur a seulement enseigné la grammaire. On a jamais vraiment parlé français.

Antoine : Je pense qu'il faut parler le plus possible.

Lauren : Je pensais que ma prononciation était si terrible ! J'étais nerveuse de parler.

Antoine : Tu as pas un accent très fort ! Tu parles bien et tu peux dire tellement de choses maintenant !

Lauren : Merci, c'est gentil !

Luckily, you don't have to learn a complicated new structure to say 'as much as possible'. ***Le plus possible*** does the trick!

To avoid overusing *très*, use other intensifiers. An easy one is ***tellement*** (so).

FIGURE IT OUT

1 Highlight the following cognates (and near cognates) in the conversation.

a my pronunciation b accent c grammar

2 *Vrai ou faux ?* Select the correct answer.

a Lauren studied French in school for one year. *vrai / faux*
b They spoke French often in her class. *vrai / faux*
c Lauren's school teacher said her pronunciation was terrible. *vrai / faux*

NOTICE

07.06 Listen to the audio and study the table.

Essential phrases for Conversation 3

French	Meaning	Pronunciation
j'ai appris ...	I learned ...	zhay ah-pRee
tu savais ?	did you know?	tew sah-veh
je pensais que ... tu étais débutante	I thought that ... you were a beginner	zhuh pawN-seh kuh tew ay-teh day-bew-tawNt
j'ai oublié ... tout ce que j'ai appris	I forgot ... everything I learned	zhay oo-blee-yay toos kuh zheh ah-pRee
pourquoi tu as rien appris ?	why didn't you learn anything?	pooR-kwa tew ah Ree-ahN nah-pRee
mon professeur ... a seulement enseigné la grammaire	my teacher ... only taught grammar	mohN pRo-fay-suhR ah suhl-mawN awN-seh-ny-eh lah gRah-mehR
je pensais que ...	I used to think that ...	zhuh pawN-seh kuh
ma prononciation était si terrible !	my pronunciation was so terrible!	mah pRo-nohN-see-ah-see-ohN ay-teh see tay-Reebl
j'étais nerveuse	I was nervous	zhay-teh nehR-vuhz
tu as pas un accent très fort	you don't have a very strong accent	tew ah pah zuhN ahk-sawN tRay foR

The past tense of ***savoir*** (to know) is generally not used in the ***avoir*** past form we learned in this unit. More on that soon!

VOCAB: ***ce que* – *'everything that'***
Tout ce que (everything that) in French has the extra ***ce*** in the sentence. You will see many expressions before a ***que*** require ***ce***, which isn't translated in English. This also happens for phrases like ***C'est ce que j'avais ...*** (It's what I had ...). No need to worry about this for now. Remember this phrase as a word chunk, and now you'll recognize it when you see or hear it.

The following phrases can be adapted for a variety of different conversational situations. Write them out in French.

a Did you know that ___________

b I thought that ___________

c I wanted ___________

GRAMMAR EXPLANATION: the habitual past

As you advance in French, you will learn to use the 'habitual past' in all situations you may need it. This is used to describe something that happened in the past not in a single moment, but over a longer period and is preferred for **states of mind or being**. For instance, 'I thought', 'I knew', 'I wanted', and the like.

penser	*vouloir*	*savoir*	*être*	*avoir*
je/tu pens**ais**	je/tu voul**ais**	je/tu sav**ais**	j'ét**ais**/tu ét**ais**	j'av**ais**/tu av**ais**
il/elle/on pens**ait**	il/elle/on voul**ait**	il/elle/on sav**ait**	il/elle/on ét**ait**	il/elle/on av**ait**

While it is possible to use these verbs in the past form you've already learned with *avoir* or *être*, you are more likely to hear them in the habitual past forms shown above. So I suggest you just try to recognize these forms for now.

Hint: just as French doesn't directly translate 'do' in present tense questions, you also won't directly translate 'did' if there is another main verb.

PRACTICE

1 How would you say the following in French?

a I thought that you were busy.

____

b Did you think that she was here?

____

c Cécile had the book

____

d We didn't know.

____

e I wanted to eat with you.

____

2 Use what you've learned to complete the dialogues in French.

a *Tu peux me dire quelle est la différence entre ces* _______ _______ ?
(Can you tell me what the difference is between these **two words**?)

b _______ _______ _______ _______ *si vite ! Qu'est-ce que ça* _______ _______ ?
(**You said that** so fast! What does that **mean**?)

c *Est-ce que tu* _______ _______ ? (**Did** you **understand**?)

d *Ma* _______ *est* _______ ? _______ *bien* _______ *ce* _______ ?
(**How** is my **pronunciation**? **Did I say** that **word** right?)

e *Je voulais dire l'*_______ _______. (I meant to say the **other word**.)

f *L'autre jour,* _______ _______ *à mon prof, '*_______ _______ _______ _______ *?' et* _______ _______ _______ *'pas mal'.*
(The other day, **I asked** my teacher **'how is my accent**?' and **she said** 'not bad'.)

g _______ _______ *ma* _______ *toute la semaine.*
(**I practised** my **grammar** all week.)

h _______ _______ *quelques* _______. *Tu peux les vérifier et* _______ _______ *si elles sont correctes ?* (**I wrote** some **phrases**. Can you check them and **tell me** if they are correct?)

i _______ _______ *beaucoup* _______. *Merci !*
(**You helped me** a lot. Thank you!)

#LANGUAGEHACK: time travel – talk about the past and future using the present tense

Language learning is a process, and as a beginner French learner, it's important to remember that you don't need to learn everything at once!

For example, you just learned how to form the past tense, and it's a good idea for you to solidly learn the common past tense phrases you'd likely say most often, such as:

je suis allé (I went) *j'ai vu* (I saw)
j'étais (I was) *tu as dit* (you said)

But one of the truly fun aspects of languages is how flexible, fluid and creative they can be! When you come across any exceptions that are tricky to learn, you shouldn't be restricted in the kinds of conversations you can have right now.

For everything else you may want to say in the past tense in French? Hack it!

I like to focus on whatever my main priority is right now. If it's that you don't know enough words, focus on learning new words. If it's that your teacher can't understand your pronunciation, focus on that. Don't worry about solving every problem – just solve the biggest ones first.

Time travel with the present tense

Have you ever told a story that went something like this?

> 'So, the other day, there I am ... minding my own business, when someone comes up to me, and you'll never guess what happens ... '

What's unique about this form of storytelling is although it's clearly an anecdote about something that happened in the past, the entire sentence is actually told in the *present* tense - 'there I **am**', 'someone **comes** up to me'.

You can do the same thing in French! The key to this #languagehack is to use time indicators – words or phrases that specify a particular time period – along with what you're describing in the present tense.

time indicator + **present tense**

Alors, la semaine dernière, je lis au parc, et ...
(So last week, **I'm reading** in the park, and ...)

Time indicators

Past	Future	Specific days (past and future)
hier **(yesterday)**	demain **(tomorrow)**	lundi **(Monday)**
la semaine dernière **(last week)**	la semaine prochaine **(next week)**	mardi **(Tuesday)**
le mois dernier **(last month)**	le mois prochain **(next month)**	mercredi **(Wednesday)**
l'an dernier **(last year)**	l'an prochain **(next year)**	jeudi **(Thursday)**
mercredi / l'été dernier **(last Wednesday/ summer)**	novembre/le weekend prochain **(next November/weekend)**	vendredi **(Friday)**
une fois **(once, one time)**	un jour **(one day)**	samedi **(Saturday)**
il y a deux semaines **(two weeks ago)**	dans deux semaines **(in two weeks)**	dimanche **(Sunday)**

The time indicator is what transports the sentence backwards or even forwards through time. As in English, you could also say something like:

J'appelle mes parents dans deux heures. (I'm calling my parents in two hours.)

Here are a few more examples of how to 'time travel' in your conversations:

*Par exemple, **un matin il y a neuf mois**, je suis chez moi et je vois quelqu'un dehors ...*
(For example, **one morning nine months ago**, I'm at home and see someone outside ...)

*Alors, **un jour**, je décide de devenir enseignant ...*
(So, **one day**, I decide to become a teacher ...)

***Une fois**, il y a longtemps, je suis au Mexique en vacances ...*
(**One time**, I'm in Mexico on holiday ...)

While this hack is very powerful, you only need to use it if you can't think of the past form introduced in this unit. Use it as a crutch until you are confident using these past forms!

YOUR TURN: use the hack

1 Unscramble the sentences and use time indicators to describe past and future actions, while using the present tense.

Example: *Samedi/au cinéma/aller/je* → Samedi, je vais au cinéma.

a *Demain/du ski/faire/je*

____

b *Lundi prochain/une omelette/manger/on*

____

c *La semaine dernière/un chat/chercher/ils*

____

d *Il y a trois jours/un nouveau mot en français/apprendre/je*

____

2 Now create 'me-specific' sentences in which you describe things you did at different time periods. Say what you did:

a a week ago

____

b last Saturday

____

c two years ago

____

d yesterday

____

3 Now say what you are going to do:

a next Wednesday

____

b in one year

____

PUT IT TOGETHER

Think about a time you got nervous trying to speak French with someone. (Maybe you were even nervous before one of your earlier missions!)

Use what you've learned in this unit to describe those moments – what you were thinking, doing, or saying. Use your dictionary and be sure to include:

- at least three of the following verbs: *penser, vouloir, savoir, être, avoir* in the past.
- a specific time indicator (*Lundi dernier, ...*)
- describe what you did to overcome your nerves (*J'ai décidé de parler de mon weekend ...*).

COMPLETING UNIT 7

Check your understanding

1 07.07 Listen to this audio rehearsal first, in which a French speaker describes what he did this morning. Feel free to take notes or listen to it multiple times.

2 07.08 Now listen to the second audio, which will ask you questions about the speaker. Answer them out loud in French.

Show what you know …

Here's what you've just learned. Write or say an example for each item in the list. Then tick off the ones you know.

- ☐ Say the past tense phrases:
  - ☐ 'I thought' and 'I said'
  - ☐ 'I went' and 'I decided to'
  - ☐ 'I was' and 'I learned'.
- ☐ Give a sentence using *il y a* to say how long ago you did something.
- ☐ Give time indicators for:
  - ☐ 'one time' and 'yesterday'
  - ☐ 'last week' and 'tomorrow'.

COMPLETE YOUR MISSION

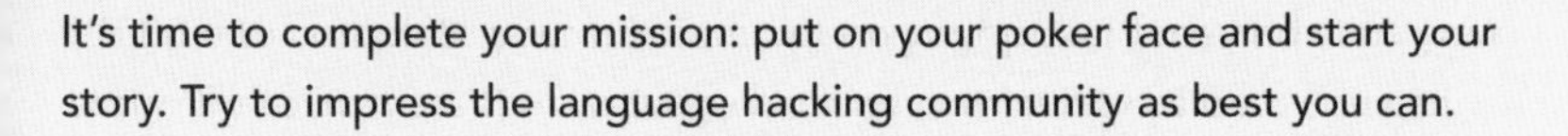

It's time to complete your mission: put on your poker face and start your story. Try to impress the language hacking community as best you can.

STEP 1: build your script

je pensais ... je suis allé ... j'ai appris ...

Expand on your scripts by talking about the past. Use 'me-specific' vocab plus the past tense phrases you've learned to describe an important life lesson you gained from a past experience – perhaps about an embarrassing situation when you used the wrong word in French, or a time when you overcame a personal struggle and felt really encouraged. Be sure to include:

- time indicators to describe when this happened (*il y a ...*)
- several past tense verbs in various forms to describe what you thought, what you wanted, what you've learned and more
- as many details as possible! (use the time travel #languagehack if you get stuck).

Write down your script, then repeat it until you feel confident.

STEP 2: don't be a wallflower! Use language in real social contexts ... *online*

Research in learning emphasizes the importance of **social context** in facilitating language learning.

If you're feeling good about your script, it's time to complete your mission! Go online to find your mission for Unit 7, and share your recording.

STEP 3: learn from other learners

What words of wisdom do the other language hackers have to offer? Which stories are true and which ones are made up?

Your task is to watch at least two video clips uploaded by other hackers. Then ask three follow-up questions in French to see if they can keep the conversation going, to help them fill the gaps in their script and to find out whether what they say is true or false. Make your guess.

STEP 4: reflect on what you've learned

HEY, LANGUAGE HACKER, SEE HOW THINGS HAVE CHANGED?

You've just learned how to talk about anything in the past! Now you can reminisce on the long-forgotten days when you couldn't speak French.

Next, you'll add even more detail to your conversations by describing the specific parts of your daily routine.

Pas mal fait, félicitations!

Your mission

Imagine this: one of your French-speaking friends writes a blog about the daily routines of highly productive people – like you! – and you've been asked to contribute an article.

Your mission is to **prepare your best productivity advice** – in French – for the blog. Be prepared to **describe your daily routine** from your first morning beverage to your bedtime. Talk about **what works well** and **what you'd like to be different**.

This mission will broaden your ability to discuss your daily life, and help you become comfortable with small talk in French.

Mission prep

- Talk about your hobbies, routines and daily life
- Use versatile phrases to express your opinions and perceptions – *c'est important de, je suis content(e) de, je vois que*
- Use phrases for seeing people you know again – *ça fait longtemps!*
- Use expressions with *faire*, like *faire du sport*
- Build upon modes of transport – *prendre le métro*
- Talk about what you would potentially do – *je pourrais.*

BUILDING LANGUAGE FOR DESCRIBING YOUR DAILY LIFE

As a beginner French learner, it's difficult to be detailed when you speak, but you're quickly becoming an *upper-beginner* French learner! So it's time to learn some tricks for adding more detail to your conversations – without a huge amount of new vocab. In this unit, we'll break a typical conversation into its component parts to develop a more complex strategy for helping each part flow well.

#LANGUAGEHACK
the rephrasing technique for talking your way through complicated sentences

CONVERSATION 1

It's been a while!

When a conversation has passed the point of the usual pleasantries, where should you go from there? You don't have to think it up on the spot – instead, prepare for these situations by learning strategic phrases you can use to initiate, warm up and continue any conversation.

08.01 Lauren and Jacques are meeting for lunch at a café. Since they already know each other, they can't rely on the usual meet-and-greet expressions. What phrases do Jacques and Lauren use to 'warm up' the conversation?

Jacques : Bonjour Lauren ! Je suis content de te revoir !

Lauren : Oui, ça fait longtemps !

Jacques : Et je vois que tu fais des progrès en français. Alors, dis-moi, quoi de neuf ?

Lauren : Ben, je suis très occupée en ce moment. Récemment, j'ai commencé à faire la cuisine. Je prends des cours !

Jacques : Vraiment ? Et tu as appris quoi jusqu'à maintenant ?

Lauren : La dernière fois, on a appris à faire le coq au vin. Mais, quand j'essaie de le faire chez moi, ça marche jamais.

Jacques : C'est pas grave, continue comme ça. C'est important de pratiquer.

Lauren : Je sais ! Tu as raison. Je vais vite faire des progrès ! Aujourd'hui, par exemple, j'espère apprendre à faire une mousse au chocolat !

VOCAB: *re-*
French actually uses the prefix *re-* much more than we do in English to imply 'again'. While we can't 're-see' in English, you can ***revoir*** in French (hence ***au revoir*** (goodbye) is more or less 'until-the re-seeing!'). You even see this used as ***reparler*** in unit 3 (to 're-speak' or 'speak again'). Similarly, you can say ***revenir*** (come back), ***rentrer*** (return home – from 're-enter'), and ***rappeler*** (recall or remember).

VOCAB: *quoi* as 'what'
You've seen that question words can appear at the end of a sentence (***Tu vas où ?***). The same is true for ***qu'est-ce que*** (what), but instead of putting ***que*** at the end, you'd use ***quoi***:
Que'est-ce que Jacques étudie ? / Jacques étudie quoi ?

As well as 'to do', **faire** also means 'to make'. Handy!

FIGURE IT OUT

1 Use your understanding of the conversation to fill in the rest of the sentences. Underline the corresponding French phrases.

a Jacques thinks that Lauren's French is ____________________.

b Lauren started taking a cooking class ____________________.

c At her last class, Lauren learned to make ____________________.

2 How do you say 'I'm happy to see you again!' in French?

____

3 Answer these questions in French.

a *Qu'est-ce que Lauren a commencé à faire récemment ?*

____

b *Lauren va faire quoi aujourd'hui ?*

____

4 Highlight the following phrases in French.

a What's new? b It's been a while. c at the moment / these days

5 What does *c'est important de pratiquer* mean in English?

____

NOTICE

08.02 Listen to the audio and study the table.

Essential phrases for Conversation 1

French	Meaning	Pronunciation
je suis content(e) de te revoir !	it's great to see you again!	zhuh sew-wee kohN-tawN(t) duh tuh Ruh-vwaR
oui, ça fait longtemps !	yes, it's been a while!	wee sah feh lohN-tawN
je vois que...	I see that...	zhuh vwa kuh
dis-moi	tell me	dee mwah
je suis très occupée en ce moment	I'm very busy at the moment (in this moment)	zhuh sew-wee tReh zoh-kew-pay awN suh mo-mawN
récemment, j'ai commencé à... prendre des cours de cuisine	recently I started... taking cooking classes	Ray-sah-mawN zhay koh-mawN-say ah pRawNd day kooR duh kew-wee-zeen
tu as appris quoi... jusqu'à maintenant ?	what have you learned... so far? (until now)	tew ah zah-pRee kwah zhews-kah mahN-tuh-nawN
la dernière fois, on a appris à faire...	last time we learned how to make...	lah dehR-nee-ehR fwa ohN nah ah-pRee ah fehR
quand j'essaie de le faire	when I try to make it (when I try of it to-make)	kawN zhay-seh duh luh fehR
c'est pas grave	don't worry about it (it's not serious)	say pah gRahv
continue comme ça !	keep trying! (continue like that!)	kohN-tee-new kohm sah
je vais vite faire des progrès	I will make progress quickly.	zhuh veh veet fehR day pRoh-gReh
j'espère apprendre à faire...	I hope to learn how to make...	zhuh spehR ah-prawNd ah fehR

1 Look at the literal translations of these phrases and notice how they are expressed differently in French. Write them out.

a Keep trying! ______________ b When I try to … ______________

2 Fill in the gaps in each expression.

a ________ ________ *longtemps !* (**It's been** a while!)
b *Tu as appris* ________ ________ ________ ? (**What** have you learned **so far?**)
c *Je vais* ________ *faire des progrès !* (I will make progress **quickly**!)
d *J'espère apprendre* ________ ________ … (I hope to learn **how to make** …)

CONVERSATION STRATEGY: learn set phrases for each 'stage' of a conversation

All typical conversations follow a familiar structure, and when you understand that structure, you can break it down into component parts and prepare phrases to use at each stage to keep the discussion flowing. This way, you're never stuck wondering what to say next.

A lot of people get nervous about what to say during a conversation. If you're meeting someone for the first time, it's easy - just introduce yourself. But if you've talked before, or you've finished your greetings, you'll need to keep the conversation going!

Warm up the conversation

During the first few seconds of a conversation, use some longer pleasantries to give yourself more time to collect your thoughts. For example:

- *Ça fait longtemps !* (It's been a while!)
- *Je suis content(e) de te revoir !* (I'm happy to see you again!)

Get the conversation started

Set a conversation topic into motion! Prepare phrases to get the other person talking for a few minutes:

- *Dis-donc, quoi de neuf ?* (Tell me, what's new with you?)
- *Je vois que ...* (*tu n'as pas changé ...*) (I see that... you haven't changed.)

Lead the conversation yourself

When it's again your turn to talk, think of some phrases you can use to lead the discussion on your own and introduce a new topic of conversation.

- *Ben, récemment, j'ai commencé à ...* (Well, recently I started to ...) (e.g. ... *travailler comme secrétaire / prendre des cours de cuisine*, etc.)
- *Dernièrement, je ...* (Lately I have been ...)

Extend the conversation

You can show your interest with filler words like *intéressant !* or *vraiment ?* But a slightly more detailed question, prepared in advance, will urge the other person to expand on the topic, and therefore extend the conversation. For example:

- *Alors, ça te plait ?* (So, do you like it?)
- *Et tu trouves ça comment ?* (And how do you find it?)

Add detail to your conversation

Remember – you can get more out of a conversation by expanding on a simple topic with details about when, where or how something happened. In Conversation 1, Lauren describes her hobby, cooking: *J'ai commencé à faire la cuisine.* But then she elaborates by adding descriptive details (When? What?):

- *La dernière fois* (when) *j'ai appris ... coq au vin* (what).
- *Quand j'essaie ...* (how) *... chez moi* (where?).
- *Aujourd'hui* (when) *j'espère ... mousse au chocolat* (what).

Study the table and see how a conversation can flow:

Language hacker A	Language hacker B
Conversation warmers	**Conversation warmers**
Ça fait longtemps ! *Je suis content de te revoir !*	*Merci beaucoup pour... !*
Conversation starters	**Conversation leads**
Dis-donc, quoi de neuf ?	*Ben, récemment, j'ai commencé à...*
Je vois que... (tu as pas changé / tu as une copine maintenant...)	*En ce moment, je...*
Parle-moi de toi	*La dernière fois qu'on a parlé ...*
Alors, dis-donc tout !	*... travailler comme secrétaire /... prendre des cours de cuisine*, etc.
Starting replies	**Conversation details**
pas grand-chose	*La dernière fois* (When?) *j'ai appris... coq au vin* (What?)
Je fais... comme d'habitude	*Quand j'essaie...* (How?)... *chez moi* (Where?)
Conversation extensions	*Aujourd'hui* (When?) *j'espère... mousse au chocolat* (What?)
Alors, ça te plait ?	
Et tu ça trouves comment ?	

PRACTICE

1 Look back at the phrase list. Highlight the following conversation components:

a two conversation warmers

b two conversation starters

c two conversation leads

d one conversation extension

2 Create conversation starters using the verbs *savoir*, *connaitre* or *voir* in the correct form.

a I know that … ________________

b Do you know that …? ________________

c Have you seen …? ________________

3 What is your hobby? Pick a hobby that you would likely discuss in a conversation. Then use the phrases *Récemment, j'ai commencé à* … or *En ce moment, je* … to create two conversation leads.

____

____

4 Rephrase the questions to show how they'd sound in casual speech (using the word *quoi*).

Example: *Qu'est-ce que tu apprends ?* → Tu apprends quoi ?
Qu'est-ce que tu dis ? → Tu dis quoi ?

a *Qu'est-ce que tu fais ?* ________________

b *Qu'est-ce que tu vas boire ?* ________________

PUT IT TOGETHER

Create a script in which you describe your hobby to a friend. Start with a conversation lead, but then add details about the same topic. Include:

- details of why / when you started it (*récemment, commencer, il y a*)
- details of what you do (*la dernière fois, quand j'essaie de* …)
- info about what you've learned or achieved so far (*jusqu'à maintenant pour le moment*)
- details about what you hope to learn or achieve (*j'espère*)
- *C'est ... de* or *je suis ... de* (*intéressant / content*, etc.) somewhere in your description.

CONVERSATION 2

Your daily routine

What do you normally do in a day? In a week? Lauren and Jacques talk about the things they do on a regular basis.

08.03 How does Lauren say 'it was strange at first'?

Jacques : Il me semble que tout va bien pour toi à Paris !

Lauren : Oui, merci. C'était bizarre au début mais maintenant, j'ai une routine. Le matin, avant le travail, je me promène à travers la ville.

Jacques : Moi aussi. D'habitude, je promène mon chien le matin dans le quartier. De temps en temps, je fais du vélo.

Lauren : Je fais du vélo partout ! Je prends pas le métro.

Jacques : Moi non plus, ou rarement, car je vais souvent au travail en voiture.

Lauren : Et à midi, je mange toujours au même resto – c'est là qu'on mange la meilleure soupe à l'ognon.

Jacques : Parfois, je viens ici pour déjeuner, mais normalement je fais la cuisine chez moi.

Lauren : Je suis jamais venue dans ce café. Tu veux manger quelque chose ?

VOCAB: *se promener* – ***'to walk oneself'***
In French, you can't just walk ... you have to walk **someone**! The verb ***promener*** always has to have an object. This means that you can walk yourself (***te promener***), or you can walk your dog (***promener ton chien***)... as long as you're walking someone!

VOCAB: *car* – **'because'**
Car is another French word for 'because'. To make things simple, use ***parce que*** most of the time, but try to be aware of *car* and its meaning when you hear it.

CULTURE TIP: ***frigo, resto*** and other shortened words As in English, you can shorten some French words (***frigo*** 'fridge' instead of ***réfrigérateur*** and ***télé*** 'TV' for ***télévision***). This also works for words we wouldn't think to shorten in English, like ***resto*** for ***restaurant***.

FIGURE IT OUT

1 Correct the *faux* statements to make them *vrai*.

  a Lauren prend le métro.

  b Jacques va rarement au travail en voiture.

  c Lauren va au restaurant où on mange la pire soupe à l'ognon.

  d Jacques mange normalement dans un café.

'To drive' can be *conduire* when you talk about driving in general, but when you want to talk about the mode of transport to get you somewhere, you have to say **aller en voiture** (go by car).

2 Is everything going well for Lauren in Paris? Fill in the blanks.

At first it was ________,

but now ____.

3 Which phrase means 'It seems to me that ...'? Highlight it. Would you use this as a conversation lead, a warmer or an extension?

4 Find and highlight each of the following.

  a two sets of opposite phrases:

  me too / me neither   rarely / normally

  b two different modes of transport

NOTICE

🔊 **08.04** Listen to the audio and study the table.

Essential phrases for Conversation 2

French	Meaning	Pronunciation
il me semble que…	it seems (to me that…)	eel muh sawN-bluh kuh
c'était bizarre au début, mais maintenant…	it was strange at first, but now…	say-teh bee-zahR oh day-bew meh mahN-tuh-nawN
avant le travail	before work	ah-vawN luh trah-vah-ee
je me promène	I go for a walk	zhuh muh pRo-mehn
en ville	around the city	awN veel
partout	everywhere	pahR-too
d'habitude je promène mon chien	I usually walk my dog	dah-bee-tewd zhuh pRo-mehn mawN shee-awN
De temps en temps…	From time to time…	duh tawN zawN tawN
je fais du vélo	I ride my bike	zhuh feh dew vay-loh
je prends pas le métro	I don't take the metro	zhuh pRawN pah luh may-tRoh
moi non plus	me neither	mwa nohN plew
rarement	rarely	RahR-mawN
car je vais au travail souvent en voiture	because I often go to work by car	kahR zhuh veh zoh tRah-vah-yuh soo-vawN awN vwa-tewR
l'après-midi / le matin	in the afternoons / mornings	lah-pReh mee-dee / luh mah-tahN
je mange toujours au même resto	I always eat at the same restaurant	zhuh mawNzh too-zhooR oh mehm Rehs-to
je viens ici parfois	sometimes I come here	zhuh vee-ahN ee-see pahR-fwa
je suis jamais venu dans ce café avant	I've never come to this café before	zhuh sew-wee zhah-meh vuh-new dawN suh kah-fay ah-vawN

1 Notice how the phrases in this conversation build on descriptions of routines and activities by *adding details*. Use what you've seen so far, and the following table to help you to provide the requested details in French.

Example: Jacques walks his dog. le matin, d'habitude, dans le quartier
(When?) (How often?) (Where?)

VOCAB: *how often?*
You can express repetition using words like ***chaque*** (each) followed by a singular version of the word, or ***tous / toutes les*** (every) followed by a plural: ***chaque jour*** (each day) and ***toutes les semaines*** (every week).
You can also use any number + ***fois*** (times) to describe 'how often'. Example:
une fois, deux fois, bien souvent (lit., well often)

Conversation details

When ?		How often?	Why? / How?
in the morning 1 le matin	in town 5 ________	10 usually d'habitude	by car 17 ________
before work 2 ________	in the neighbourhood 6 dans le quartier	from time to time 11 ________	for lunch 18 ________
in the afternoon 3 ________	everywhere 7 ________	rarely 12 ________	
before 4 ________	the same (place) 8 ________	often 13 ________	
	at home 9 ________	always 14 ________	
		sometimes 15 ________	
		never 16 ________	

2 Now use the conversation to fill in the table with 'detail phrases' you could use to answer the questions: When? How often? Why / How? Where?

VOCAB EXPLANATION: using *faire* to describe what you do

The verb *faire* means 'to do' or 'to make', and there are many situations in which *faire* works differently from its equivalents in English. This is actually good news – because *faire* is so versatile, you can use *faire* + **noun** to describe a lot of activities, and you'll have fewer new verbs to learn. Here are some common expressions using *faire*:

Activities, hobbies and getting around

French	Meaning	French	Meaning
faire attention	to pay attention	faire du vélo	to go cycling / ride a bike
faire du sport	to play sports	1 ___	to go for a walk
faire le bisou	to kiss hello / goodbye	2 ___	to cook
faire la queue	to queue / stand in line	faire des vidéos	to make videos
faire du shopping	to go shopping		

Fill in the Activities table with missing phrases using *faire*.

PRACTICE

CULTURE TIP: *the 24-hour system*
The 24-hour system is used in most French-speaking countries. If you aren't used to it, just remember these two rules: a) the number is the same as for the 12-hour system in the morning, and b) just add 12 to the number for the afternoon and evening equivalents. The terms a.m., p.m. and o'clock are usually written as *h* and spoken as ***heures***, so ***15h*** is 3 p.m., ***19h*** is 7 p.m., etc.

1 Translate the following to French.

a I play sports often. ___

b Yesterday at 3 p.m. (15h) I went shopping.

___

c Here's my friend, Julie. ___

d The concert starts at 6 p.m. and ends at 8 p.m.

___

2 *Tu aimes faire quoi ?* What hobbies do you have? What activities do you enjoy? Do you build things? Jog every day? Sing, dance, code or do bodybuilding? Look up these 'me-specific' verbs and add them into the Activities table.

a Now choose one or two of your hobbies as a 'base' to add details to.

Example: Je joue du violon. J'ai commencé quand j'avais 10 ans …

___

b Then use the phrase *c'était … au début, mais maintenant …* to describe it.
(*c'était difficile au début, mais maintenant je m'amuse beaucoup !*)

---

c *Ton endroit préféré est où ?* Now write a simple sentence about one of your favourite places.
(*J'aime aller à la bibliothèque.*)

---

d Then use the phrase *Je vais à ... pour ...* to say why you go there and how often.
(*Je vais souvent à la bibliothèque pour lire beaucoup de livres !*)

---

e Now use the phrase *Je suis jamais allé à …* to say somewhere you've never been before, but would like to go one day.
(*Je suis jamais allé au théâtre à Broadway !*)

PUT IT TOGETHER

Write a script describing your normal routine. Think about how you can build on your basic routine by adding details. You might include:

- information about how you get to work / school every day
- a list of what makes up your daily routine
- your hobbies, interests or other activities
- details of how often, when, where, why or how.

CONVERSATION 3

Going out at night

As your conversation comes to an end, you'll want to have phrases prepared to make plans for next time!

08.05 Lauren and Jacques start talking about what they could do this evening. How does Jacques ask 'What are you doing after this?'

Jacques : Tu fais quoi plus tard ? J'espère aller au parc avec des copains pour jouer au foot. Tu veux venir ?

Lauren : J'aimerais bien mais malheureusement, j'ai déjà prévu de faire du shopping avec quelqu'un et puis mon cours de cuisine commence à 16h. J'ai du temps libre après si tu veux !

Jacques : Ça serait génial. Je fais une soirée chez moi. Tu es invitée !

Lauren : Cool ! Qu'est-ce que j'amène ? Et à quelle heure ?

Jacques : À 21h. Un dessert serait parfait. La mousse au chocolat que tu vas préparer cet après-midi, par exemple, non ?

Lauren : Bonne idée ! Et tu habites où ?

Jacques : Mon appartement est à coté de la gare.

Lauren : Tu peux m'écrire l'adresse ?

Jacques : Bien sûr ! Et si tu as ton portable, je peux te montrer sur le plan !

You can say jouer au football, but it's usually shortened to **jouer au foot** in French. It's quite confusing, but foot in French may not be what you initially think!

To play it safe, try to remember to use mon or le before copain for 'boyfriend' (this makes it clear it's a specific person), and un for 'a friend' or des for 'some friends'. The same applies to copine – ma / la copine (my / the girlfriend), une copine (a friend, who happens to be a girl).

LEARNING STRATEGY:
break it down
Whenever you see a word that's quite long, try to see if you understand parts of it. Here you may recognize ***mal*** (badly), ***heureux / heureuse*** (happy) and ***-ment*** (-ly). You could guess this means unhappily, which is quite close, given the context, to its true meaning of 'unfortunately'.

FIGURE IT OUT

1 *Vrai ou faux ?* Select the correct answer.

a After this, Jacques is going to get a drink with his brother. *vrai / faux*

b Jacques invites Lauren to play football with him, and then to a get-together. *vrai / faux*

c Lauren has already planned to go shopping with someone. *vrai / faux*

d Lauren's French class starts at 4 p.m. *vrai / faux*

2 Find the following conversation components.

a First highlight the sentence in which Jacques describes his plans to go to the park.

b Now circle the details (Why? With who?). Write them out.

____________________ ____________________

c Highlight the phrase Lauren gives about going shopping.

d Now circle the detail (With who?). Write it out. ____________________

3 If you know what *je voudrais* means, what do you think *j'aimerais bien* means?

NOTICE

🔊 **08.06** Listen to the audio and study the table.

Essential phrases for Conversation 3

French	Meaning	Pronunciation
tu fais quoi plus tard ?	what are you doing later on?	tew feh kwa plew taR
aller au parc avec des copains… pour jouer au foot	going to the park with some friends … to play football	ah-lay oh pahRk ah-vehk day ko-pahN pooR zhoo-ay oh foot
tu veux venir ?	would you like to come?	tew vuh vuh-neeR
j'aimerais bien, mais malheureusement…	I'd love to, but unfortunately…	zheh-muh-Reh bee-ahN meh mahl-uh-Ruh-zuh-mawN
j'ai déjà prévu de faire du shopping	I already have plans to go shopping	zhay day-zhah pRay-vew duh fehR dew sho-ping
j'ai du temps libre plus tard	I have free time later	zhay dew tawN leeb plew tahR
ça serait génial !	that would be great!	sah suh-Reh zhay-nee-ahl
je fais une soirée	I'm having a get-together	zhuh feh ewn swa-Ray
tu es invitée	you're invited	tew eh zahN-vee-tay
qu'est-ce que j'amène ?	what do I bring?	kehs kuh zhah-mehn
et à quelle heure ?	and at what time?	ay ah kehl uhR
un dessert serait parfait	a dessert would be perfect	ahN day-sehR suh-Reh pahR-feh
mon appartement est à côté de la gare	my apartment is next to the train station	mohN nah-pahR-tuh-mawN eh ah koh-tay duh lah gahR
tu peux m'écrire l'adresse ?	could you write down the address for me?	tew puh may-kReeR lah-dRehs
je peux te montrer sur le plan !	I can show you on the map!	zhuh puh tuh mohN-tRay sewR luh plawN

VOCAB: ***le soir*** **and** ***la soirée***

There are two ways to say 'evening' – *le soir* and *la soirée*. Usually, ***le soir*** means evenings in general, but *la soirée* can be an event that you throw in the evening. You can also say ***Bonne soirée !*** to wish someone a nice evening.

1 Find and highlight the French phrases in the conversation that mean the following:

a What should I bring?
b At what time?
c Can you write the address for me?
d I can show it to you on the map.

CULTURE TIP:
what to bring
If you are invited to a French person's house for dinner or an evening hang-out, bring a gift to show your appreciation! If the event includes a meal or snacks, avoid bringing food or wine (unless requested)– the host may have special plans in mind for the meal. It's always a good idea to get some chocolate, flowers or an interesting gift from home. If all else fails, politely ask your host what they might like you to bring.

GRAMMAR EXPLANATION: conditionals

When talking about a possible future (what you **would** do) in French, you'll see the ending *-**ais*** for *je* / *tu* and *-**ait*** for *on* / *il* / *elle*. To use them yourself, simply add these word endings directly to the dictionary form of *-er* / *-ir* verbs, and to *-re* verbs after removing the *-e*. (Happily, in all these cases, the pronunciation is the same: [eh].) Let's see it in action:

*Je sortir**ais** ce soir, mais je suis fatigué !* (I **would** go out tonight, but I'm tired!)

*On parler**ait** français ou anglais ?* (**Would** we speak French or English?)

*Tu le vendr**ais** pour 50 € ?* (**Would** you sell it for €50?)

There are a few important verbs that don't follow this pattern, and that take a new 'stem' to replace the beginning of the word instead. You'll learn these with time, but here are a few essentials to keep in mind:

Dictionary form → conditional stem → Example		
être	ser-	*je **ser**ais* (I would be)
pouvoir	pourr-	*on **pourr**ait* (we could)
vouloir	voudr-	*je **voudr**ais* (I would like)

CULTURE TIP: €
Currency symbols usually come after the number in French.
As well as this, commas and decimals get swapped, so '€2,200.22' would be *2.200,22* € in French!

Fill in the gaps to form the conditional in the following phrases.

a *J'*________________ *habiter en France ! (adorer)*

b *On* ________________ *content de voir le film. (être)*

c *Elle* ________________ *venir ce soir. (vouloir)*

PRACTICE

1 Now, use these phrases as templates to mix and match vocab to create new sentences in French.

Mettre means both 'to put' and 'to wear' ('to put on').

a What should I wear? (to wear = *mettre*) ______

b What time does it end? (to end = *finir*) ______

c Do you know the address? ______

d Where is the get-together? ______

e When should I arrive? ______

f Can I bring some wine? (*du vin*) ______

2 This conversation is all about making plans. Mix and match the English suggestions given to complete each French sentence in different ways.

Example: *On mange au resto chinois* (this evening) (Monday) (soon) (at 7 p.m.) (next week) ?

→ On mange au resto chinois lundi ?

→ On mange au resto chinois ce soir ?

a *Tu fais quoi* (later) (at 5 p.m.) (tonight) (tomorrow) ?

______

b *J'ai du temps libre* (later) (at 5 p.m.) (tonight) (tomorrow) *pour le concert. Tu viens ?*

______

3 Now mix and match phrases for accepting or turning down an invitation.

a *Ça serait* (cool) (perfect) (impossible) (too late).

______

b *J'aimerais bien mais* (unfortunately…) (I already have plans) (I'm busy).

______

4 How would you say the following in French?

a Could you ask me next time? ______

b I'd go out (*sortir*), but it's too late. ______

5 Practise recognizing the meaning of conditional verbs as you see them. Write the English meaning of the following French phrases.

a *tu préparerais* ______

b *ce serait* ______

c *je voyagerais* ______

d *il dirait* ______

e *tu pourrais* ______

PUT IT TOGETHER

1 A French friend has come to visit you in your hometown, and he's eager to pick your brain. Tell him what an ideal day would look like for him to get the best out of his visit. Try to include:

- the first thing that he would do (*pour commencer tu pourrais ...*)
- places you would visit and why (*moi, je visiterais ...*)
- activities you would do together (*on prendrait un taxi pour aller ...*)
- other insider tips (*le meilleur musée serait ...*).

2 Imagine that someone has invited you to go on an exotic adventure (think kayaking down the Amazon, hiking the Inca trail or climbing Mount Everest). You'd have a lot of questions! Create a French script using phrases and questions to discuss an invitation like this. Use your dictionary as often as you need.

- Say when you'd have free time and when you could go (*Je pourrais aller...*)
- Ask for details of the trip – where it is, when it starts, when it ends (*Le voyage va commencer quand ?*)
- Ask about things you should bring (*Est-ce que je dois amener ...?*)
- Describe how you think it would be (*Je pense que ça serait ...*).

#LANGUAGEHACK: the rephrasing technique for talking your way through complicated sentences

You're used to expressing yourself with a lot of complexity and nuance when you speak in your native language, but when you're learning a new language, you can't do this right away. Getting used to (and comfortable with) this shift is a big part of language learning. So how do you convey your more complex thoughts and feelings when you are still only working with the very basics of the language?

Hope is not lost! Expressing yourself will just require a little rephrasing – putting your ideas into simpler sentences using words and phrases you're more comfortable with.

Here's how to break it down.

- First, **recognize that the rules of expressing yourself as an eloquent native do not (usually) apply to you.** The nuanced language you search for in your head and the desire to convey the right tone and courtesy ... Sometimes, you have to just **let that go.**
  'Excuse me ... I'm sorry ... I just overheard you speaking French ... I've actually been studying it for a while ... do you mind if I practise a few phrases with you? ... I hope I'm not bothering you ...'
- Next, **figure out the one core idea** you're most trying to express.
  'You speak French? Me too! Let's talk.'
- Finally, **'piggy-back' your idea** on to another expression that works just as well.

Example: *Parlez-vous français ? Moi aussi ! On parle ?*

Back to the basics

The gist of what you're trying to say is very often quite simple. For example:

- Instead of trying to say 'Would you like to dance with me?' you can say 'Dance with me!' – *Danse avec moi !*
- Instead of trying to say 'I should avoid eating fish as much as possible due to a medical condition that I have', you can say, 'I can't eat fish because I have an allergy' (or in 'Tarzan French', 'fish... no!' – poisson ... non !).

→ Instead of trying to say 'I'm looking for a flatmate that speaks French and wants to rent the room for at least 12 months', you can say something like *J'ai besoin d'un coloc. 12 mois. On va parler français ensemble !* (I need a flatmate. 12 months. We'll speak French together !)

Phrases you're not sure about

In French, there are a handful of unique phrases that, although common, can be challenging to put into use at first. For example, when getting an invitation somewhere, you may want to say something like 'I'm happy that...' to describe your emotions.

However, this is a more complicated phrase using a verb form you haven't seen yet (*Je suis content que* ... [subjunctive]). Instead of learning this new grammar right now, you could simply use the conditional phrase you've already learned, *Je voudrais bien !* and your friend will surely know you're psyched to tag along!

YOUR TURN: use the hack

1 Practise this rephrasing skill now. For each of the lines given, write an alternative (shorter) translation in French that conveys a similar meaning as the original, but avoids any complicated grammar. There may be a variety of ways to say each one – just try to get the idea across as best and as simply as you can.

Remember, this is a skill, which means that practice is the key to getting better.

Example: I'm probably not going to be able to go out with you.

→ Je peux pas sortir avec toi. (I can't go out with you.)

a I'm not sure if they will be able to win (*gagner*).

____

b I'm so happy that we were able to come to the restaurant together.

____

c I would really love it if you would be willing to dance with me.

____

d I'd rather go to the supermarket later.

____

COMPLETING UNIT 8

Check your understanding

1 🔊 08.07 Listen to the audio rehearsal, in which a French speaker describes her routine as well as things she wishes she could do. Feel free to take notes or listen to it again.

2 🔊 08.08 Now listen to questions about what you've just heard and answer them out loud in French.

Show what you know ...

Here's what you've just learned. Write or say an example for each item in the list. Then tick off the ones you know.

- ☐ Write two short phrases that describe your hobbies using *faire*.
- ☐ Write a sentence that describes a hobby and gives two different details about it.
- ☐ Give three phrases that describe your normal routine using:
  - ☐ 'often'
  - ☐ 'usually'
  - ☐ 'sometimes'
- ☐ Say 'I would be' and 'I could' in French.

COMPLETE YOUR MISSION

It's time to complete your mission: give your best productivity advice to be published on your friend's blog. To do this, you might need to observe yourself and keep track of the things you do regularly. You could even read some French blogs about productivity and mindfulness to help you.

To complete this mission, try searching online for **productivité**, or **être plus productif**. Go online to the #LanguageHacking community for help finding them!

STEP 1: build your script

Keep building your script by using the phrases you've learned in this unit combined with 'me-specific' vocabulary to answer common questions about yourself. Be sure to:

- talk about different parts of your life and weekly routine
- describe where you go, how you get there, what you do
- include details of how often, when, where, why or how
- describe something else you would love to do, but haven't done yet
- describe what you like about your routines, and what could be better.

Write down your script, then repeat it until you feel confident.

STEP 2: learn from your mistakes, and others'… *online*

When learning a new language, mistakes are inevitable. Part of the charm of speaking a second language is realizing that people are much less critical than you imagine!

The key is that if you're making mistakes, you're learning. And if you speak, you can even notice them better and fix them yourself. Added bonus: you can learn from the mistakes of other language hackers too. So look at the corrections and comments people leave – you'll find that your common mistakes are most likely shared.

It's time to complete your mission. Share your productivity advice with the rest of the community! And in return, enjoy some free advice about how you can be more effective in your life. So, go online to find your mission for Unit 8, and use the community space to find out perhaps how you can make learning French part of your daily routine.

STEP 3: learn from other learners

What productivity tips can you gain from other language hackers? After you've uploaded your own clip, check out what the other people in the community have to say about their routines. **Your task is to let at least three different people know what you thought was most useful about their routine.** This time, incorporate conversation starters, leads or extensions to help get the conversation flowing. E.g. *Je vois que tu ...* (I see that you ...)

STEP 4: reflect on what you've learned

HEY, LANGUAGE HACKER, YOU'RE ALMOST THERE!

In this unit we talked a lot about the strategy behind preparing for the kinds of conversations you're likely to have. All the scripts you've been building are preparing you for this ultimate goal.

With the strategies you'll learn next in Missions 9 and 10, you will be amazed at how well your first conversation goes ...

Formidable !

9 DESCRIBE IT!

Your mission

Imagine this ... you're applying to be a tour guide in a French-speaking city. You have to prove your ability to describe a place in detail and give recommendations for where to hang out and what to do.

Your mission is to pass for a local by **describing a city that you know** (or want to know!) well. Be prepared to do your research and give a short description of the highlights of what to do and see. But here's the twist – don't say the name of the city. See if people can *guess*! **Describe the best places**, explain **their characteristics** and say how the city might suit **different personalities**.

This mission will enable you to communicate more creatively by describing the people, places and things in the world around you in more detail.

Mission prep

- Describe places, landscapes and where you live – *j'habite à la campagne*
- Say what you miss using the verb *manquer*
- Describe the weather and environment – *il fait chaud*
- Describe people and their personalities – *elle est aventureuse*
- Describe what someone or something looks like – *avoir l'air de*
- Learn important phrases for shopping – *le moins cher*, *payer en cash*

BUILDING LANGUAGE FOR DESCRIBING THE WORLD AROUND YOU

You're getting closer to your first conversation in French! You know how to say who the important people are in your life and what they do, but now you'll describe their personalities and characteristics as well. With this new vocab, you can express your thoughts more creatively in French – when you can't think of a word you need, just *describe it* instead!

#LANGUAGEHACK
use your hidden moments to get French immersion for the long term

CONVERSATION 1

Describing the city

People from other countries will be interested to hear where you're from, and how it's different from where they're from. Let's prepare you for these conversation topics now by building your script for describing different places.

09.01 Lauren is getting ready to fly back to the United States, and she's thinking about what she misses about home. She describes her hometown to Jacques as they're hanging out by the Seine on a sunny day. What word does Lauren use to say she's 'going back' to the United States?

Lauren : Je vais rentrer aux États-Unis bientôt. C'est ma dernière semaine à Paris, quoi !

Jacques : C'est dommage ! Tu es prête à rentrer ?

Lauren : J'adore Paris mais tu sais que normalement, j'habite à la campagne. **Les montagnes** me manquent, le lac et la forêt proche de chez moi aussi. Mais Paris va me manquer beaucoup aussi !

Jacques : Tu sais ... Pourquoi pas ramener beaucoup de cadeaux pour ta famille et pour te rappeler ton séjour en France ?

Lauren : Très bonne idée ! J'adore faire du shopping ! Hmmm ... je dois les acheter où ?

Jacques : Euh ... ça dépend, quoi. Tu es déjà allée aux Champs-Élysées ? C'est un peu plus sympa que les centres commerciaux. **L'avenue est longue et large** et il y a beaucoup de choses à voir !

Lauren : Je sais pas ... il fait super chaud aujourd'hui. Je vais avoir trop chaud si je passe l'après-midi au soleil.

Jacques : **En fait**, il y a beaucoup d'arbres donc tu peux rester au frais. Et puis tu vas être dans les magasins en tout cas !

Lauren : En ce cas, oui ! On y va !

PRONUNCIATION: ***gn***
In French, *gn* is pronounced like the 'ny' in 'canyon'. Keep this in mind for words like ***campagne***, ***Espagne***, ***montagne***, and ***ognon*** (onion).

VOCAB: ***grand*** **as 'big' and 'tall'**
While the word *grand* usually means 'big' in French, there are cases where its use differs. When you describe people as *grand*, for example, it will always mean 'tall', unless you're referring to your *grand frère* or *grande sœur* (big brother/sister). To avoid confusion, try to use more specific adjectives, as Jacques does here to describe this iconic avenue in Paris.

VOCAB: ***fait*** **as 'fact'**
Fait is not only a form of the verb *faire* – it's also the noun for 'fact'. So, just like in English, *en fait* means 'in fact'.

FIGURE IT OUT

By now you have a great base of French vocabulary, so it's even more important for you to **actively fill in your gaps.** It's a good idea to highlight any new words you come across, and make a note to yourself to add them to your script or your study materials.

1 Each of these sentences is *faux*. Underline the word(s) that make them incorrect, then write the correct word(s) in French.

a It's Lauren's last day in Paris.

____

b Lauren and Jacques are planning to go dancing.

____

c There are a lot of things to eat on the avenue.

____

2 Use context to figure out the meaning of these phrases.

a *Je vais rentrer aux États-Unis bientôt.*

____

b *C'est dommage !*

____

c *Ça dépend, quoi.*

____

3 Write out in French:

a in the countryside ______________________

b the mountains ______________________

c the lake and the forest ______________________

d near my house ______________________

e under the sun ______________________

You will recognize *quoi* in questions, meaning 'what', but it can be put at the end of statements as a filler word too, in order to add emphasis. Listen for this word in casual conversations. It's similar to the way 'y'know' is used in English.

NOTICE

🔊 09.02 Listen to the audio and study the table.

Essential phrases for Conversation 1

French	Meaning	Pronunciation
je vais rentrer aux États-Unis bientôt	I'm going back to the United States soon	zhuh veh RawN-tRay oh zay-tah zew-nee bee-ahN-toh
c'est dommage !	that's a pity!	seh doh-mahzh
tu es prêt(e) à rentrer ?	are you ready to go home?	tew eh pReh(t) ah RawN-tRay
à la campagne	in the countryside	ah lah kawN-pah-nyuh
les montagnes me manquent	I miss the mountains (the mountains to-me are-missing)	lay mohN-tah-nyuh muh mawNk
le lac et la forêt proche de chez moi	the lake and the forest close to my home	luh lahk ay lah fo-Reh pRosh duh shay mwa
Paris va me manquer aussi !	I'll miss Paris too! (Paris goes to-me to-be-missed also!)	pah-Ree vah muh mawN-kay oh-see
ramener beaucoup de cadeaux	to bring back lots of gifts	rah-mehn-ay boh-koo duh kah-doh
pour te rappeler ton séjour	to remind you of your stay	pooR tuh Rah-puh-lay tohN say-zhooR
je dois les acheter où ?	where should I buy them?	zhuh dwa lay zahsh-tay oo
c'est un peu plus sympa que ...	it's a bit nicer than ...	say ahN puh plew sahN-pah kuh
beaucoup de choses à voir	a lot (of things) to see	boh-koo duh shohz ah vwaR
il fait super chaud	It's really hot	eel feh sew-pehR sho
je vais avoir trop chaud	I'll be too hot (I go to-have too hot)	zhuh veh zah-vwaR troh shoh

VOCAB: ***sympa*** **'nice'**
Sympa (nice) can describe enjoyable places and events or friendly and likeable people. It's used mostly in casual situations, as it's the shortened form of *sympathique*. Shortened adjectives like this don't usually change between masculine and feminine.

VOCAB: ***using avoir for describing feelings***
You've seen some cases where French uses *avoir* (to have) when we would say 'to be' in English, like *j'ai faim* and *tu as raison*. Here, ***avoir chaud*** means 'to be hot'. What's the common link? You'll often use avoir to describe how you feel:
- ***j'ai peur*** (I'm scared)
- ***j'ai froid*** (I'm cold)
- ***j'ai mal à la tête*** (I have a headache)

au soleil	in the sun	oh soh-lay-uh
il y a beaucoup d'arbres	there are a lot of trees	eel ee yah boh-koo dahRb
donc tu peux rester au frais	so you can stay cool	dohNk tew puh Rehs-tay oh fReh
en ce cas, oui !	in that case, yes!	awN suh kah wee

1 Review the phrase list to answer questions in French about the conversation.

Example: ***Quelles*** *choses* manquent à Lauren ?

→ Les montagnes, le lac et la forêt manquent à Lauren.

a ***Quand*** *est-ce que Lauren va rentrer aux États-Unis ?*

Lauren va ______________________________

b ***Qu'est-ce que*** *Lauren va ramener pour sa famille ?*

Lauren va ______________________________

c *Lauren va les acheter* ***où*** *?*

Lauren va ______________________________

2 How would you say each of the following in French? Complete each sentence.

a *Tu peux* ____________... ? (Can you remind me... ?)

b *Je vais* ____________ *quelque chose.* (I'm going to remind you about something.)

c *Il* ____________ *mon rendez-vous.* (He reminded me of my appointment.)

3 It's good to know how to rephrase your words to more easily convey your thoughts. Match the French phrases to the English expressions which are closest in meaning.

a *je suis prêt(e)*	1 I'm not sure
b *en ce cas*	2 there are two ways to look at it
c *désolé !*	3 I'm ready
d *j'en suis pas sûr*	4 that's a shame
e *c'est dommage*	5 when you put it that way
f *ça dépend*	6 I'm sorry to hear that

4 A good memory technique is to learn vocabulary in 'clusters' – learning words of a similar category together. Fill in this vocab cluster for words dealing with nature and landscape.

Landscape and nature vocab

French	Meaning	French	Meaning
	the countryside		the forest
	the mountains		the trees
	the lake		the sun
la ville	the city		

5 Conversation 1 also uses a lot of prepositions – words that describe where something is (e.g. 'near', 'on', 'under', 'in'). Use prepositions to answer questions about yourself in French.

a Do you live in the countryside or in a city?
J'habite ______________________

b Do you prefer to stay in the sun or under the trees?
Je préfère rester ______________________

c Is the climate better near the lake, the forest or the mountains?
Le climat est meilleur ______________________

PRACTICE

1 Look up new words you'd need to describe where you live and the landscape in your area. Do you live near the ocean? In the suburbs? In a cramped studio apartment? Add your 'me-specific' vocab to the landscape and nature cheat sheet.

2 Practise describing where you live. Create sentences in French that are true for you.
→ I live ... Near my house, there is/there are ...

____

____

3 Now do the same about a family member or friend.
→ He/She lives ... Near his/her house, there is/are ...

____

____

GRAMMAR EXPLANATION: using *manquer* for 'to miss'

Conversation 1 uses two examples of the verb 'to miss':

Les montagnes me manquent. *Paris va me manquer.*

Notice the word order in these sentences. The French verb for 'to miss' uses a construction that's very different from English. To say 'I miss the mountains' in French, you reverse the subject and the object:

Example:

***Les montagnes** me manquent.* (lit., **'the mountains** to-me are-missed'.)

That's why we use *manquent* with the *-ent* ending ('they' form) in this sentence. It's 'the mountains' that are missed, not 'me'.

***Les montagnes** te manquent.*	(You miss **the mountains.**)
***Les montagnes** nous manquent.*	(We miss **the mountains.**)
***Je** te manque ?*	(Do you miss **me?**)
***Je** manque à Alison.*	(Alison misses **me.**)

GRAMMAR TIP: *the mountains are missed by ...*
When you want to say 'me', 'you' or 'us', use *me*, *te* and *nous*. Otherwise, use *à* followed by a person's name (e.g., *à Lauren*).

Use the verb *manquer* to write each sentence in French.

a I miss you. ______
b I miss them. ______
c We miss her. ______
d Antoine misses me. ______
e I will miss my brother. ______
f Do you miss your girlfriend? ______

VOCAB EXPLANATION: describing the weather

Quel temps fait-il ? (What's the weather like?)

When you want to describe the weather, use the verb *faire*. Most of the time, you'll simply need to say ***il fait*** + description.

Il fait ... (It's ... (lit., it does ...)) *beau* (nice), *mauvais* (bad)
chaud (hot), *froid* (cold), *frais* (cool)
nuageux (cloudy), *du soleil* (sunny), *du vent* (windy)

Two common exceptions are: ***il pleut*** (it's raining) and ***il neige*** (it's snowing).

Comment est le climat ? (What's the climate like?)
When you want to compare general or typical weather patterns, you also use the expression ***il fait .... temps***:

***Il fait** beau **temps** en été.* (The weather is nice in the summer.)
***Il fait** meilleur **temps** à la mer.* (The weather is better by the seaside.)

HACK IT: *recognizable words with ê, î, ô, û*
Whenever you see the ^ accent above a vowel, imagine what the word would look like with an '-s' after that vowel. More often than not, they'll look like the English word! With that in mind, see if you recognize these words: ***forêt, hôpital, côte.***

GRAMMAR TIP: *put grand(e) before the noun*
Grand is one of a few adjectives in French that you'll see before the noun. Others include *petit, jeune* (young), *vieux* (old), *beau* (beautiful) and *nouveau* (new).

1 Practise creating new sentences in French to describe the weather.

a It's nice today. ____________________

b The weather is bad. What a pity! ____________________

c Are you not cold? You know that it's cold on the coast. (*la côte*)

____

2 Use *il fait* or *il* to give two sentences describing the weather where you are right now.

____

____

GRAMMAR EXPLANATION: changing gender and number for adjectives

In French, adjectives tend to 'agree' with the nouns they describe. When the thing being described is feminine (*la montagne*), any accompanying adjectives will also be in their feminine forms (*la grande montagne*). The same is true for plurals (*les grandes montagnes*).

Think of the masculine form of an adjective as being its 'base' form, and from there you can modify it for feminine and plural words as follows:

Adjective endings

Masculine singular	Feminine singular	Masculine or mixed plural	Feminine plural
consonant or -é	-e	-s	-es
vert / fatigué	vert**e** / fatigué**e**	vert**s** / fatigué**s**	vert**es** / fatigué**es**

J'adore son ***vélo vert*** **(m.).** (I love his **green bike**!)
Et regarde – sa ***maison*** *est* ***verte*** **(f.)** *aussi !* (And look – his **house** is **green** too!)
Pourquoi il a tellement de ***choses vertes*** **(f.pl.)***?* (Why does he have so many **green things**?)
Et si on achète des ***t-shirts bleus*** **(m.pl.)** *pour lui ?* (What if we bought him some blue t-shirts?)

Most adjectives follow this process, but sometimes there are a few adjustments. Consider the following examples:

- *gris* (grey) ends in an -*s* already, so its plural (m.) is the same – ***gris***.
  Ex: *un chat gris, des chats gris*, but *une voiture grise, des voitures grises*.
- *rouge* (red) already ends in an -*e*, so its feminine is the same – ***rouge***.
  Ex: *un vin rouge, une tomate rouge*. Any plural would be *rouges*.
- *long* (wide) would change its pronunciation (adding [*zh*]) if an -*e* were added, so to prevent this, -*u* is added as a silent buffer. Ex: *cette avenue est **longue***.

There are of course exceptions to these rules, but if you are ever in doubt, you can look up the word in your dictionary to see both the masculine and feminine forms.

Some important exceptions are: **beau** (m) and **belle** (f), both meaning 'beautiful', **blanc** (m) and **blanche** (f), both meaning 'white', and **nouveau** (m) and **nouvelle** (f), both meaning 'new'.

Write the adjectives in their masculine (singular) and feminine (singular) forms.

a ready ____________ (m) ____________ (f)
b tall ____________ (m) ____________ (f)
c hot ____________ (m) ____________ (f)
d tired ____________ (m) ____________ (f)

PUT IT TOGETHER

You now have a greater ability to talk about your environment, so let's put that into action! Describe where you live, or a place that you love to visit, in as much detail as possible. Include descriptive words (adjectives and nouns) and answer the questions:

- What is the landscape like?
- What is the weather usually like? Sometimes like?
- What would you miss if you were to leave?

Normalement j'habite ...

CONVERSATION 2

Describing personalities

CULTURE TIP: *haggling and street markets*
While the Avenue des Champs-Élysées is gorgeous to visit, my favourite spot for shopping is actually the ***marché aux puces*** (flea market) at Clignancourt. I love to ***marchander*** (haggle) to get a good deal there. It's more fun than when you know the price is standard, and excellent for French practice!

HACK IT: *rewording to fill the gaps in your vocabulary*
There is no easy way to translate 'cheap' into French with a single word, although your dictionary may suggest ***bon marché*** ('good deal'). That phrase works fine, but it's more common to say 'less expensive' (**moins cher/chère**) instead. Rewording can make complex sentences much easier. More on this in this unit's #languagehack.

Now let's focus on a whole new set of descriptive words you can use to talk about people and their personalities.

09.03 Lauren and Jacques have made it to the Avenue des Champs-Élysées to begin shopping, and they discuss what gifts Lauren should get for her family. What words does Lauren use to describe her sister, brother and parents?

Lauren : Cette avenue est impressionnante ! Il y a **tellement de magasins** !

Jacques : Tu sais déjà ce que tu veux acheter ?

Lauren : Je vois beaucoup de choses que je voudrais acheter pour moi mais pour ma famille, je sais pas !

Jacques : Alors raconte, elle est comment ta famille ?

Lauren : C'est pas facile à dire – par exemple, ma sœur est aventureuse et elle veut vraiment venir en France un jour. Peut-être un souvenir typique de Paris pour elle ?

Jacques : Pourquoi pas acheter un béret classique ? Je suis certain qu'elle aimerait ça.

Lauren : Bien sûr ! Ensuite, mon frère. Il est jeune donc je pense qu'il trouverait un souvenir super ennuyeux. Qu'est-ce que je peux acheter pour quelqu'un qui aime seulement les jeux vidéos ?

Jacques : Tu peux trouver un accessoire pour ses jeux ! Tu sais que la technologie est **moins chère** ici.

Lauren : Ah oui, ça me rappelle – il a besoin d'un nouveau casque. Et enfin, mes parents sont plus traditionnels. Ils m'ont déjà demandé de ramener des chocolats français.

Jacques : Ils ont bon gout ! Et moi, je vais t'acheter une deuxième boite de chocolats pour les gouter avant !

FIGURE IT OUT

1 *Vrai ou faux ?* Select the correct answer.

a Lauren finds it easy to think of presents for her family. *vrai / faux*

b Lauren's brother doesn't like souvenirs. *vrai / faux*

c Lauren doesn't like to buy things for herself. *vrai / faux*

2 Answer these questions in French.

a What is Lauren going to get her sister? *Un* __________

b How does Lauren describe her? *Elle est* __________

c How does Lauren describe her brother? *Il est* __________

d How do Lauren and Jacques describe Lauren's parents?
Ils sont __________ *et ils ont* __________

e What does Jacques say about technology in France? *C'est* __________

3 Find the adjectives in the conversation and highlight them.

a impressive
b adventurous
c typical
d classic
e young
f boring
g new
h traditional
i not easy

4 Find the following phrases and highlight them. Write out the bold words in French.

a that **reminds** me __________
b she **really** wants __________
c he **would find** a souvenir __________
d and **finally** __________
e they **already** asked me __________

NOTICE

09.04 Listen to the audio and study the table.

VOCAB: *dur* as 'hard'
As well as *pas facile / difficile*, you can also say something is *dur* to imply that it's hard to do. *Dur* can also describe something physically hard, like a rock.

You may know how to form many masculine and feminine adjectives, but when you're **speaking spontaneously**, you shouldn't stress over getting these forms right. If you use whichever form you remember, the person you're speaking to will understand you.

Essential phrases for Conversation 2

French	Meaning	Pronunciation
cette avenue est impressionante !	this avenue is impressive!	seht ah-vuh-new eh ahN-pRay-syoh-nawNt
il y a tellement de magasins !	there are so many shops!	eel ee ah tehl-mawN duh mah-gah-zahN
Elle est comment ta famille ?	What's your family like?	ehl eh ko-mawN tah famee-yuh
c'est pas facile à dire	it's not easy to say	say pah fa-seel ah deeR
ma sœur est aventureuse	my sister is adventurous	mah suhR eh tah-vawN-tew-Ruhz
un souvenir typique	a typical souvenir	ahN soo-vuh-neeR tee-peek
un béret classique	a classic beret	ahN bay-Reh klah-seek
mon frère est jeune	my brother is young	mohN fRehR eh zhuhn
super ennuyeux	really boring	sew-pehR uh-new-yuh
Qu'est-ce que je peux acheter ?	what can I buy?	kess-kuh zhuh puh ash-tay
un nouveau casque	a new headset	ahN noo-voh kahsk
la technologie est moins chère ici	technology is cheaper here	lah tehk-no-lo-zhee eh mwahN shehR ee-see
ça me rappelle	that reminds me	sah muh Rah-pehl
il a besoin d'un nouveau...	he needs a new... one!	eel ah buh-zwahN dahN noo-voh
et enfin	and finally	ay awN-fahN
mes parents sont plus traditionnels	my parents are more traditional	may pah-rawN sawN plew tRah-dee-see-ohn-ehl
une deuxième boite	a second box	ahN duh-zee-ehm bwat
Ils ont bon gout	They've got good taste.	eel zawN bawN goo

1 Write out the following phrases in French.

a What should I buy? ______________

b My parents are more traditional. ______________

c that reminds me ______________

d really boring ______________

2 Another effective memory technique is to learn words in pairs with their opposites. Use the adjectives from the phrase list, or a dictionary, to complete the sentences.

a *C'est pas* ______________, *c'est* ______________. (It's not **easy**, it's **hard**.)

b *C'est pas* ______________, *c'est* ______________. (It's not **unique**, it's **typical**.)

c *Ils sont pas* ______________, *ils sont* ______________. (They aren't **stupid**, they are **intelligent**.)

d *Ils sont pas* ______________, *ils sont* ______________. (They aren't **modern**, they are **traditional**.)

e *Elle est pas* ______________, *elle est* ______________. (She's not **adventurous**, she is **shy**.)

f *Il est pas* ______________, *il est* ______________. (He's not **old**, he's **young**.)

3 Use the forms below to create phrases describing people and things. Be sure to use the correct word order and gender/plural agreement.

grand	*grande*	*grands*	*grandes*
ouvert	*ouverte*	*ouverts*	*ouvertes*

a my big brother ______________

b my big brothers ______________

c my big sister ______________

d my big sisters ______________

e The shop was open. ______________

f The bakery (*la boulangerie*) was open.

____

g The shops are open. ______________

h The bakeries are open. ______________

PRACTICE

1 How would you say 'it's the cheapest' in French? ______________________________

2 Practise forming adjectives according to gender. The words in the table are grouped according to opposites. Fill in the missing words, including both the masculine and feminine forms (if they are different).

Describing people

French (m. / f .)	Meaning	French (m. / f.)	Meaning
	shy / timid	aventureux / aventureuse	
	ugly	beau / belle	
vieux / vieille			young
bizarre			typical
	unpleasant	sympa	
	pessimistic	optimiste	
	proud	modeste	
	funny	sérieux / sérieuse	

3 Create new sentences with words that are true for you. Be sure to use the correct gender, and look up words in your dictionary if you need to.

a *Je suis* ______________________________.

b *Mon travail est* ______________________________.

c *Mon père/ami/frère est* ______________________________.

d *Sa maison est* ______________________________.

e *Ma mère/cousine/soeur est* ______________________________.

4 Create four phrases that describe different people in your life, using the following word order:

Example: *mon père geek* (my techie father)

Not quite the same as a geek in English, this borrowed word has taken on a new meaning in French, and simply implies '**techie**'. Funny how it can be close, but still not quite the same!

PUT IT TOGETHER

Create a script that describes the personalities of two important people in your life. Look up any new descriptive words you might need now, so you'll have them ready to use during your conversations.

- Use adjectives to describe their personalities.
- Be sure that your adjectives agree with the person in gender and number.
- Use different word orders.

CONVERSATION 3

It looks like ...

By knowing how to describe things in French, you'll have a handy new trick up your sleeve to use in French conversations. When you can't think of a particular word for something, you can just **describe it** instead!

You've learned to describe people and places – now let's build some new vocab you can use to describe things.

09.05 Lauren is looking for a headset for her brother and asks Jacques for advice. Which phrase does Lauren use to ask 'Is this one OK?'

Lauren : Regarde, on vend des casques dans ce magasin et il a l'air pas cher.

Jacques : Ton frère utilise son casque pour quel genre de jeux ?

Lauren : Pour les jeux en ligne ... Comment tu trouves celui-ci, ça va ?

Jacques : Non, ça va pas. – le rouge, c'est bon pour faire du jogging mais pour ton frère, le mieux serait le vert. C'est de la qualité supérieure.

Lauren : Comment tu sais ça ?

Jacques : Je reconnais la marque.

Lauren : C'est un peu cher mais il va l'adorer ! À ce prix-là, je peux pas payer cash – je dois l'acheter avec ma carte de crédit.

Jacques : Pas de problème, on passe à la caisse ? Ton frère va penser que tu es la sœur la plus chouette du monde !

GRAMMAR TIP: *celui-ci – 'this one'*

There are several ways to say 'this' or 'that' in French: use ***ce*** or ***cette*** before masculine/feminine nouns (*ce livre* and *cette fille*) and ***celui*** or ***celle*** when it's just 'this' or 'that' by itself. These words can mean both 'this' or 'that' depending on the context, but when you're pointing or trying to clarify what you're referring to, **add *-ci* for 'this' and *-là* for 'that'**.

FIGURE IT OUT

1 The following statements are *faux*. Highlight the word(s) that make each one incorrect, and write the correct phrase in French.

a Lauren's brother needs a new headset to listen to music.

____

b The headset is not expensive. ______________________________

c Lauren is going to pay in cash. ______________________________

2 Highlight the two possible ways of paying mentioned. What does *à ce prix-là* mean?

3 Answer the questions in French.

a Which headset is better for jogging? *Le* ______________

b Which headset is better for Lauren's brother? *Le* ______________

4 In the context of the conversation, which of the following does *C'est de la qualité supérieure* mean?

a it is a superior quality

b it's better quality

c it's not better quality

5 Find the translation of 'would be' and highlight it.

NOTICE

VOCAB: ***saying what something 'looks like'***
This useful expression in French, 'to have the air of', is how you would describe what something 'seems to be', or what 'it looks like'. The word ***regarder***, on the other hand, is only used when someone is actually looking at someone or something. So, ***cette bouteille de vin a l'air vieille*** (this wine bottle looks old) but ***je regarde cette vieille bouteille de vin*** (I'm looking at this old wine bottle).

The best way to ask if something is 'OK' is to ask 'how it is going' – *celui-ci ça va ?*

Whenever you want to say things like 'the big one', 'the blue one' or 'the small ones' in French you don't need to translate 'one'. Simply use ***le/la/les*** before the adjective: ***le rouge*** (the red one).

🔊 **09.06** Listen to the audio and study the table.

Essential phrases for Conversation 3

French	Meaning	Pronunciation
ce magasin a l'air pas cher	this shop looks like it's inexpensive	suh mah-gah-zahN ah lehR pah shehR
ton frère utilise son casque pour quel genre de jeux ?	what kind of games does your brother use his headset for?	tohN fRehR ew-tee-leez sawN kahsk pooR kehl jawN duh zhuh
pour les jeux en ligne	for online games	pooR lay zhuh zawN lee-nyuh
celui-ci, ça va ?	is this one OK?	suh-lew-wee see sah-vah
le rouge	the red one	luh roozh
c'est de la qualité supérieure	it is better quality	say duh lah kah-lee-tay sew-pay-Ree-uhR
je reconnais la marque	I recognize the brand	zhuh Ruh-ko-neh lah mahRk
c'est un peu cher	it's a little expensive	seh tahN puh shehR
à ce prix	at that price	ah suh pRee
je peux pas payer cash	I can't pay cash	zhuh puh pah peh-yay kahsh
acheter avec ma carte de crédit	to buy with my credit card	ash-tay ah-vehk mah kahRt duh kRay-dee
on passe à la caisse ?	shall we go to the checkout?	ohN pahs ah lah kehs
tu es la sœur la plus chouette	you are the coolest sister	tew ay lah suhR lah plew shweht

1 What phrases could you use to…

a say what something looks like? ______________________

b ask 'what type?' ______________________

2 If you needed to describe an item to a shopkeeper, you could use the following phrases. Write them out here in French.

a this one ______________

b the black one ______________

c the small one ______________

d the new one ______________

3 How would you say the following expressions related to purchases?

a a little expensive ______________

b pay in cash ______________

c a brand ______________

d the checkout ______________

4 If you don't know the word for an item, you could also just say the name of the brand. What international brands could you use to ask the following questions:

a *Vous vendez* __________ ? (shoe brand)

b *Je voudrais un* __________. (tissue brand)

c *Je prends un* __________. (cola brand)

d *Je veux acheter un* __________. (computer brand)

You'll recognize a lot of **familiar brands** in France, and you can use this to your advantage when you're trying to describe what you want.

PRACTICE

1 Fill in the blanks with the word or phrase that works best in the sentence.

a l'air	*dormir*	*a l'air d'être*

a *Aujourd'hui, ton frère* ____________ *fatigué.*

b *Ton chat a l'air de* ____________.

c *Cette voiture* ____________ *vieille !*

2 Create new questions you can use to ask about things in French when shopping.

a How much does this one (f.) cost (*couter*)? ______

b Is it good quality? ______

c Can I use this now? ______

d Do you accept credit cards? ______

e I can only pay in cash. ______

3 Fill in the gaps with the missing words in French.

a *Je peux voir* ______ ______ ? (Can I see **the red ones**?)

b *Je connais pas* ______ ______. (I don't know **the brand**.)

c *Je vais payer* ______ ______ ______. (I'll pay **at the cash register**.)

d *J'aime* ______ ______ *sur la gauche*. (I like **the big one** (f) on the left).

4 Fill in the missing translations in the table.

Describing things

Adjective	Meaning	Colour	Meaning
long(ue)		jaune	yellow
court(e)		rouge	red
	wide	bleu	blue
léger / légère		blanc / blanche	white
lourd(e)		vert(e)	green
		noir	black

CONVERSATION STRATEGY: use the set phrase 'the ... one!'

You can adapt this set phrase in countless ways to communicate what you're describing without saying its name!

09.07 Listen to the audio and repeat the phrases you hear. Write the missing phrases in the table.

The ... one(s)!

French	Meaning	French	Meaning
celui-ci	this one		that one
le noir	the black one		the black ones
le petit	the small one		the big one
le nouveau	the new one		the old ones
le moins cher	the less expensive one		the more expensive ones
l'autre	the other one		not this one, that one!

PUT IT TOGETHER

Qu'est-ce que tu cherches ? (What are you looking for?)

Describe something you want to buy, something you're looking for, or something you've lost -- *without* using the word. You might include:

- what it looks like or what you use it for
- what brand it is
- what colour it is
- 'this one', 'that one' or 'the ... one'
- other descriptive adjectives that you know!

Je cherche quelque chose ...

Add any new adjectives you look up into the Describing things table.

#LANGUAGEHACK: use your hidden moments to get French immersion for the long term

Rather than thinking about how many months or years it may take to learn French, an incredibly effective learning strategy is to focus instead on the *minutes* that it takes.

Don't overlook the value of these short periods of time. They really add up and, more importantly, they're a great way to consistently keep up momentum in your learning.

The minutes you put into your language every day are what truly count. Not everyone has a few hours every day to devote to French. But everyone has a few minutes. Even if you live a busy lifestyle, you can still find **'hidden moments'** throughout your day for French practice. Standing in line in the supermarket, waiting for the lift, sitting on a bus, train or taxi, waiting for a tardy friend ... all of these are wasted moments in our days. These moments are perfect for squeezing French practice into your daily life. Instead of making a distinction between 'study blocks' of French, why not blend it into your life to make language learning a habit?

French immersion – from anywhere

As you've followed Lauren's story, perhaps you thought, 'well she's quite lucky to go to France to improve her French through immersion!' But in fact, thanks to technology, *you* can create a French immersion environment from anywhere in the world, no matter where you live. You can create an at-home immersion environment in lots of different ways:

LEARNING STRATEGY: *study on the go*
When I'm learning a new language, I always use a vocabulary study app and other tools designed for use on-the-go, and pull them out whenever I'm waiting around. Since my smartphone is with me anyway, I use it to learn what I can, when I can, even if it's just a word or two.

- connect with other learners (like you've been doing in our online community!) to get practice through regular video/audio calls
- listen to live streaming radio or watch streaming video from France (or another French-speaking country) online
- play *des jeux vidéos* ! You can change the language settings on your games to French!
- You can also change the language of websites you use often or even your computer and smartphone operating system to French.

You'll see it's not that bad, and you can always change it back if you find it too hard. Usually, you'll just need to look for '**Langues** or **Paramètres linguistiques** under Paramètres'.

YOUR TURN: use the hack

1 Look at the apps and online resources we recommend at (www.teachyourself.com/languagehacking). Pick a few to add to your computer or smartphone so they're ready and waiting during your hidden moments.

2 Look at the websites, apps, games, browsers and even the operating system you use the most, and see if they have an option to change the language to French. Since you're already used to the interface and know where to click or tap, why not go ahead and change the language?

COMPLETING UNIT 9

Check your understanding

1. 🔊 **09.08** Listen to this audio rehearsal, which has someone describing their environment and people around them. Feel free to take notes or listen to it multiple times.
2. 🔊 **09.09** Now listen to the questions about the audio rehearsal you just heard. Answer the questions out loud in French.

Show what you know ...

Here's what you've just learned. Write or say an example for each item in the list. Then tick off the ones you know.

- ☐ Say something you miss using *manquer*.
- ☐ Give two sentences describing where you live.
- ☐ Say 'it's hot', 'it's cold' and 'it's raining'.
- ☐ Give a sentence that uses an adjective to describe a family member's personality. Put the adjective in the right word order and gender.
- ☐ Use three different adjectives to describe your favourite clothes in French. Put the adjectives in the right word order and gender.
- ☐ Ask the questions:
  - ☐ 'Can I pay in cash?'
  - ☐ 'Can I pay with a credit card?'

COMPLETE YOUR MISSION

It's time to complete your mission: pass for a local and use your descriptive language to point out the best places in town to a foreigner. To do this, you'll need to describe the details and characteristics of different places, people and things.

Challenge yourself: make sure you incorporate new verbs you've learned (**manquer, rentrer, acheter, utiliser**) and try to match adjectives to the gender and number of the objects they describe.

STEP 1: build your script

Build a script you can use to give more detailed descriptions of places, people and things. Be sure to:

- say what the weather is usually like or what type of landscape is nearby
- explain what the houses, apartments or neighbourhoods look like
- describe the personalities of the people living there

Write down your script, then repeat it until you feel confident.

This is your last dress rehearsal before you speak one-on-one with a native speaker!

STEP 2: a little goes a long way ... *online*

If you're feeling good about your script, go ahead and give it another go! Go online, find your Unit 9 mission and share your recording with the community for feedback and encouragement.

STEP 3: learn from other learners

How did other language hackers describe their city? After you've uploaded your own clip, check out what the other people in the community have to say. What city are they describing? Would you hire them as a tour guide? **Your task is to ask them two more questions about their city.**

STEP 4: reflect on what you've learned

Did you learn any new words or phrases in the community space? Did you find a new place to add to your bucket list? What did you learn about the gaps in your scripts?

HEY, LANGUAGE HACKER, ARE YOU READY?

You've just learned how to describe pretty much anything, as well as how to work around any gaps you may have in your French. I know you're ready for the ultimate mission – aren't you?

Tu es prêt(e) ? On y va !

10 HAVING YOUR FIRST CONVERSATION

Your mission

You've worked hard. You've kept at it. And now, you're armed with a solid base in the French language. More importantly, you know how to use clever #languagehacks and conversation strategies to make the French phrases you know stretch even further for you.

Your mission is to have a one-on-one conversation – online with video activated – with a native French speaker.

This mission will set you up with the phrases, the confidence and an insider look at how to have your first conversation in French – even if you don't think you're ready.

Mission prep

- Apply what you've learned in the context of a first conversation.
- Prepare the essential phrases you need to have a conversation.
- Develop the mindset: overcome nerves; don't worry about the grammar.
- Find a language partner and schedule your first conversation!

BUILDING LANGUAGE FOR HAVING A CONVERSATION

Here's where all of the vocabulary and – just as importantly – all of the conversation strategies you've learned over the past nine units come into play. You're going to have your first 'face-to-face' conversation with another French speaker!

One-on-one conversations with a native can be intimidating, and that's why I like to cheat – by having my first few conversations in a new language with a partner online. This takes off the pressure, and you have the added luxury of being able to quickly search for words or phrases with online translators and dictionaries. Let's take a look at how you can strategize your own first conversations!

#LANGUAGEHACK
develop a cheat sheet to go into 'autopilot' during your first conversation

YOUR FIRST CONVERSATION

HACK IT: *'groundhog-day' your way to fluency*
Through the beauty of the Internet, you can **have the same 'first conversation' over again** with different language partners until you feel comfortable with it. Then start speaking with the same people again and again to push yourself into new territories.

Listen to this sample 'first' conversation between a language hacker (LH) and his French conversation partner, Cécile.

10.01 As you listen, underline any words or phrases you'd like to use in your own first conversation with a native speaker.

Cécile : Salut !

LH : Salut, **comment tu t'appelles ?**

Cécile : Je m'appelle Cécile. **Et toi ?**

LH : Je m'appelle Benny.

Cécile : Enchantée, Benny. Dis-moi, tu habites où ?

LH : Je suis irlandais mais maintenant j'habite à New York.

Cécile : Ah, très intéressant. L'Irlande. Je suis jamais allée en Ireland mais j'ai visité New York une fois, quand j'avais vingt ans. Tu es déjà venu en France ?

LH : Non … pas encore. Un jour, j'espère …. Je suis désolé – j'ai commencé à apprendre le français seulement il y a quelques semaines. Tu peux parler plus lentement ?

Cécile : Oh, bien sûr ! Pardon.

LH : **Tu es très patiente ! Merci de parler avec moi.** Alors, depuis combien de temps tu enseignes le français … ?

I suggest you **use this phrase even if you already know** the name of your language partner in advance. After all, the point of this conversation is to practise using the phrases you know!

You haven't learned how to say 'Thank you for being patient with me' yet. Notice how this is rephrased by the language hacker.

Put your conversation strategies into action

Every conversation has a certain 'formula' – phrases that you can expect the conversation to include. We've talked a lot about this throughout this book. You can use the expected nature of conversations to your advantage.

🔊 **10.02** Imagine that you're talking with a native French speaker, Cécile, for your own first conversation in French. In this case, the conversation will flow in a slightly different way. Use the prompts given to practise applying the phrases you know, and fill in the gaps in the conversation.

Cécile : Bonjour, enchantée.

Language hacker : ______________________

(Greet your language partner.)

Cécile : Je m'appelle Cécile. Et vous ?

Language hacker : ______________________

(Give your name and ask if you can speak in the *tu* form.)

Cécile : Bien sûr, si tu préfères !

Language hacker : ______________________

(Thank her for talking with you today.)

Cécile : Pas de problème – c'est un plaisir. Alors, pourquoi tu apprends le français ?

Language hacker : ______________________

(Answer her question about why you're learning French.)

Cécile : Très bien ! Tu parles d'autres langues ?

Language hacker : ______________________

(Say whether or not you speak any other languages.)

Cécile : Mon étudiant canadien m'a dit que cette langue est hyper difficile !

Language hacker : ______________________

(Say that you didn't understand and ask her to repeat slowly.)

Cécile : Naturellement. J'ai dit que mon étudiant, Eric – du Canada – il m'a dit que cette langue est très difficile.

CONVERSATION STRATEGY: ***on peut se tutoyer ?***
If your language partner is the same age as you, he or she will likely speak to you in ***tu*** form. If not, don't forget that you can quickly ask ***on peut se tutoyer ?***

Don't take corrections personally. Your language partner knows the reason you're there is to improve your French. By correcting you, they're helping you do that!

Now that you've seen two examples of a first conversation in action, let's start preparing you for the real thing.

#LANGUAGEHACK: develop a cheat sheet to go into 'autopilot' during your first conversation

Here's how I know you can handle this conversation, even if you think you're not ready: because you're going to 'cheat', so to speak.

There is no shame in 'cheating' here. This isn't an exam. This is a conversation. Consider your cheat sheet as stabilizers / training wheels. It will help you make the transition from studying French to speaking French. Using a cheat sheet now gives you momentum so you become experienced at speaking over less time.

The way I like to prepare for my conversations online is to make up a cheat sheet of the words and phrases I plan to use during the conversation – and because I'm having my first conversation online, I can have my cheat sheet right in front of me (on paper, open in another window or on another device) the whole time.

We'll do the same thing for you. You're going to have your own phrases ready, planned out and written out in front of you, so you'll be able to glance at them while you're speaking French. This way, it doesn't matter if your mind goes blank. You'll just take a breath, and look at your cheat sheet.

Let's get to work preparing your cheat sheet. I like to separate mine into four parts:

1. Essential phrases
2. Survival phrases
3. Questions I plan to ask
4. 'Me-specific' phrases

ESSENTIAL PHRASES

My essential phrases are the words and phrases I *know* I'll need to use in every conversation. These are usually greetings and sign-off words, as well as questions I expect to be asked and my planned answers.

I've started you off with some suggestions. Write out the ones you plan to use in French, and then add some new ones of your own.

Essential phrases

(Refer to Units 1–3 for inspiration)

Greetings	Sign offs
Salut ! Ça va ?	À la prochaine !
Merci de parler avec moi !	Alors, je dois finir la leçon.

Don't worry about thinking up every possible word or phrase you might need. **Instead, let the language tell you what you need to learn.** Use the language you know now in natural conversation – however much or little it may be – and you'll quickly learn the 'me-specific' phrases that you haven't (yet!) added to your script.

(Refer to Units 1–6 for inspiration)

Typical questions	Prepared answers
Tu t'appelles comment ?	
Tu viens d'où ?	
Tu habites où ?	
Tu travailles où ?	
Pourquoi tu apprends le français ?	
Tu parles d'autres langues ?	

SURVIVAL PHRASES FOR WHEN I NEED HELP

Don't be afraid of making mistakes in French. Instead, expect them. Prepare for them. Have a plan for dealing with difficult moments. Even if you forget every word you know or can't understand a single word the other person is saying, you can still have a conversation if you've prepared your survival phrases.

I've started you off with some suggestions. Add some new ones of your own.

Survival phrases

(Refer to Unit 6 for inspiration)

In the heat of the moment, there's a lot to think about. Don't worry about saying **single words to get your point across**. You can always add a *s'il te plait* at the end to make sure your partner knows you don't mean to be impolite!

Full phrases	Or shorten them!
Tu peux attendre un moment ?	Un instant.
Tu peux l'écrire ?	Écris ... s'il te plait ?
Tu peux répéter ?	Répéter ?
Plus lentement, s'il te plait.	Lentement.
Je comprends pas.	Pardon ?
Tu peux le dire encore une fois ?	Encore ?

QUESTIONS I PLAN TO ASK

Speaking French with a new person gives you an opportunity to **learn about that person's life**, language and culture! I make sure to prepare in advance if there's anything in particular I'm curious to know.

Plan out a few questions that you can ask the other person. You can use them to take the pressure off you, while the other person talks for a while. And they are great to have ready for when there's a lull in the conversation.

I've started you off with a few good options, but make sure you add more of your own. For example,

- questions about life in the other person's country (*Il fait froid en Suisse maintenant ?*)
- questions about the French language (*Ce mot 'quotidien' – ça veut dire quoi ?*)
- questions about the other person's life, work or hobbies (*Tu aimes faire quoi le weekend ?*)

Prepared questions

(Refer to Units 2–9 for inspiration)

Il fait chaud en …

Comment dire en français … ?

'ME-SPECIFIC' PHRASES I WANT TO PRACTISE

These are the conversation topics specific to me that I want to practise talking about. Things like my interests, what I've been doing lately, what my upcoming plans are and the people in my life.

In your first conversation, if you've practised your essential phrases and your survival phrases, everything from there is just a bonus!

In my online conversations, I like to create a goal of a few new phrases I want to practise during each conversation. But keep it to just a few (between two and five phrases), which is plenty to accomplish in your first conversation. You could prepare to talk about:

- what you're interested in (*J'adore la science-fiction !*)
- what you've been doing today or lately (*J'ai lu un article sur les trains en France.*)
- what your upcoming plans are (*Je veux danser ce weekend.*)
- the people in your life (*Ma copine parle un peu italien.*).

'Me-specific' phrases

J'adore ...

Je veux ...

Mon ami(e) ...

GETTING READY FOR YOUR FIRST CONVERSATION

I strongly suggest having your first few conversations online with video enabled. Technology really is your friend in this situation. In an online chat, you can easily refer to your notes, and you can even look up words on the spot or put phrases you need into an online translator – right in the middle of the conversation.

An automatic translation isn't a replacement for language learning, but it can be used as a crutch at a pinch.

Know this: if all else fails, you can have an entire conversation in French even if you only know these three phrases: *Je comprends pas. Écris-le s'il te plait. Un moment.*

Don't believe me? Envision it. Worst-case scenario:

- Your conversation partner says *bonjour*, you say **bonjour** (success!). But then she says, *@yego^3*8ham#3pt9ane1&* ? And your mind goes blank
- You reply with ***Je comprends pas. Écris-le, s'il te plait***.
- She types out what she said and sends it to you via chat. You select what she wrote, copy it and paste it and quickly find a translation. Ah, you think, I understand! But now it's your turn to respond, and your mind, again, goes blank
- You say, ***Un moment***. She waits patiently while you type what you want to say in English into your online translator. You hit enter and get a translation in French. You read out the words in your best French accent.
- Rinse and repeat.

In fact, you'd be surprised by how much you'd learn even in this worst-case scenario. Even **if you forgot every single phrase you learned** in French except these three, you could have a conversation (of sorts) in French with another person. And you would learn loads of French by the end of it.

Is this scenario ideal? No. But is it better than not having a conversation at all? *Absolutely*.

Luckily, you've already been preparing for this moment for the past nine missions. So you're ready – even if you think you're not. Trust me on this.

Here's how I suggest you set yourself up for your conversation.

- Open up your cheat sheet and keep it within easy view
- Have your translation tool ready (See our Resources!)
- Get ready to connect the call
- Just before your conversation, practise listening to and repeating some French audio (we'll give you a great one in this unit).

This will get your ears and your tongue 'warmed up' for the conversation. I've provided one for you at the end of this unit. Additional audio resources are recommended in our Resources online.

The purpose of your first conversation isn't to prove to your language partner how great at French you are. It's to learn, practise and gain confidence. If you remember that **these are your goals**, there is simply no way to fail! You'll have plenty of time to improve and perfect your skills in later conversations.

What to expect

The first conversation is always the hardest, and it's always the most nerve-racking. But it's a completely crucial first step to becoming comfortable as a beginner French learner. Beginners make mistakes. And as a beginner French learner, you shouldn't expect yourself to know all (or most) of the words. You should expect the opposite.

Don't focus on saying things perfectly, just focus on getting your point across. Being understood – communicating with another human being – is the main goal here. Don't stress about knowing all the grammar, using precisely the right word or having a perfect accent.

Let's review some of the skills you've learned throughout this book. They'll come in handy in your first conversation!

- **Rephrasing** – Remember, you'll need to take many of the phrases you want to say and rephrase them so that they're much more basic (but still convey the same idea). Rephrasing your thoughts into simpler forms is an essential skill for language hackers.
- **'Tarzan French'** – Don't be afraid to speak in 'Tarzan French'! If you know how to say something right, say it right. But if you know how to say something kind-of wrong, then say it wrong! Your language partner will help you figure out the wording you need.
- **Learn from your gaps.** Despite rephrasing, you'll realize that there's still a lot you don't yet know how to say. And as you talk, you'll realize you've been pronouncing some words wrong. Your partner may correct you. Good! This is valuable information. Take note of the phrases you wish you knew. You can learn them for next time.
- **When in doubt, guess!** Finally, if you're not sure what your conversation partner just said, guess! Use context – facial expressions in the video feed and whatever words you do understand – to infer the meaning of the entire phrase.

Talking one-on-one with another person is the best language practice you can get. If there's one secret to #languagehacking, this is it.

Enjoy your first conversation, and the many others to come after that!

CONVERSATION STRATEGY: *handling your nerves*

handling your nerves It's typical for a beginner to expect to be judged by the other speaker. If you find yourself staring at the screen, afraid to push that Call button – and we've all been there – have a friend nearby to boost your confidence (and maybe give you that extra push to get started!). Don't worry! The other person is probably just as nervous as you! If you're doing a language exchange and plan to also help your partner with their English, he or she may be worried more about how their English sounds than how you sound speaking French! And if you are starting with a new teacher, he or she may be hoping to make a good first impression!

COMPLETING UNIT 10

Check your understanding

One mission left to go! Review the phrases and conversation strategies from the unit one more time. When you're feeling confident, listen to the audio rehearsal, which will help you practise your listening, pronunciation and speaking skills.

Don't forget, you can always ask for the help you need – whether it's learning new phrases or improving your pronunciation, it's always OK to ask directly for the help you need!

1 Practise answering common questions.

10.03 Listen to the audio rehearsal, which will ask questions in French.

- Practise answering the questions in French with responses that are true for you.
- Pause or replay the audio as often as you need.

CONVERSATION STRATEGY: *warm up before your first conversation!* Practising with audio is one of the best ways to prepare for a conversation. An hour or two before your French conversation begins, come back to these exercises and replay them to help you get into the flow of French.

2 **10.04** In this audio rehearsal, a French speaker talks casually about herself. Listen to the audio, and after each clip, use what you understand (or can infer) to answer questions about the speaker.

- What is her name? ______
- Where does she live? ______
- How long has she been teaching French? ______
- Does she speak any other languages? If so, which ones? ______
- What does she like to do in her free time? ______

This is exactly what you'll be doing in your first conversation – listening to your partner's end of the conversation and using a combination of your new #languagehacking skills and context to help you even through the tricky parts.

Show what you know ...

Are you ready for your final mission? Before you move on, make sure that you:

- ☐ Write up the essential phrases you'll need into your cheat sheet.
- ☐ Write up survival phrases and add them to your cheat sheet.
- ☐ Prepare two to five 'me-specific' phrases you want to practise. Add them to your cheat sheet.
- ☐ Prepare at least three questions you plan to ask. Add them to your cheat sheet.

My partner Lauren likes to set up a 'conversation bingo' for herself when she's practising a language online. She writes out a few phrases she wants to practise during the call (either by speaking them or hearing them), and tries to cross off as many as she can.

What are your goals?

One more thing. It helps to know before you set up your first chat **what you want to accomplish** or what phrases you'd like to practise. Be realistic but ambitious! And be flexible – you never know where a conversation will take you, and that's a very good thing for language learners.

Write out a few notes on what you want to practise during your first conversation. Then, find your language partner.

COMPLETE YOUR MISSION

It's time to complete your mission: having a one-on-one conversation with a native ... *online*. To do this, you'll need to prepare to:

- say hello and use essential greeting vocab
- say goodbye or set up a time to talk again
- ask at least three questions
- give your answers to commonly asked questions
- use survival phrases when you can't understand or need help.

STEP 1: find your conversation partner and schedule your first conversation

HACK IT: ***time pressure is your friend***
Schedule it for tomorrow or the earliest possible slot. Don't give yourself a long window to get ready – overthinking this step can lead to procrastination later. Make a request for the next time slot, and don't look back!

Follow our Resource guide to find a conversation partner online and schedule your first chat with him or her now.

When you're setting up your first conversation online, send out a few messages to the exchange partners or teachers who look like a good fit for you. Break the ice and send them a message (in French of course!) to set up your first chat. A good icebreaker tells the other person:

- your name
- your language level
- what you'd like to practise or discuss during the conversation.

Example:

Salut ! Je m'appelle Lauren. Je voudrais parler français avec vous. On peut se tutoyer ? Je veux pratiquer des phrases simples. Par exemple, mon nom et mon pays. Je suis débutante – merci d'être patiente avec moi !

Be friendly, and give a short intro to yourself and what you want to practise – but don't say too much. Save some phrases for the conversation! Write out your own icebreaker now.

STEP 2: go all the way ... *online*

Remember, your first conversation is just that – a first conversation. The only way to get to your 50th conversation is to get the first one out of the way, then keep going from there.

The first time might be scary, but it will get easier! So go online and have your first conversation in French for an authentic and good time!

Here's what to do during your conversation:

- Practise rephrasing your thoughts into simple forms.
- Speak 'Tarzan French' if you have to – it's better than nothing!
- Take note of any 'gaps' in your French vocabulary.
- Write down any phrases or words you want to say, but don't know yet.
- Write down new words or phrases you want to review later.

STEP 3: learn from other learners, and share your experience!

Tell the community how it went! (Or, if you're nervous – head over to see how other people's first conversations went.) **Your task is to ask or answer at least three questions from other learners:**

- Were you nervous? How did you handle your nerves?
- What was your teacher or exchange partner like?
- What went well, and what didn't? What would you do differently next time?

STEP 4: reflect on what you've learned

As for those things you didn't know, this is one of the major benefits of having real conversations right away! You learn very quickly where the gaps are in your script, so you can work on filling them.

After your first conversation, it's easy to focus on the words you didn't know or the things you couldn't say. But it's much more productive to focus on your successes instead. Were you 'only' able to give your name, your job and say that you live with your cat? Those are huge wins! Don't overlook those achievements.

- What were your wins? What phrases were you able to say or understand?
- Review the notes you took during your conversation. What words did you need that you didn't know yet? What new words did you learn?

HEY, LANGUAGE HACKER, YOU JUST HAD A CONVERSATION IN FRENCH!

... or at least you should have!

You just broke one of the biggest barriers in language learning! Now that you've crossed that threshold, you are on a fast-track to fluency in French that most people only ever dream about. Enjoy this milestone. And remember – your second conversation will be even better than your first. Your third will be even better than that. Schedule your next spoken lesson now. Don't put it off – that ticking clock is a powerful motivator for language hackers.

Your next mission: ***Continue comme ça !*** Keep it up!

ANSWER KEY

UNIT 1

CONVERSATION 1

Figure it out 1 I am 2 je, j' 3 Et toi ? 4 a auteur b américaine c Paris 5 How are you?/I'm fine.

Pronunciation: questions and answers a Ça va b Et toi ?

Notice 1 an 2 a Je suis b J'habite à (city) c Je suis de Paris. d Je suis de France. 3 a j' b je c j' d je e j' f je

Practice 3 a Je suis de (city/country)/Je suis (nationality) b Je suis (profession) c J'habite à (city).

Put it together Example: Je m'appelle Lauren. Je suis des États-Unis. J'habite à Paris. Je suis auteur.

CONVERSATION 2

Figure it out 1 Qu'est-ce que tu aimes ? 2 but 3 Je déteste les spaghettis. 4 Lauren: her friends, the cinema, travelling, pizza. Pierre: his job as a teacher, visiting museums, tennis. j'aime/j'adore

Notice 1 Qu'est-ce que

Your turn: use the hack 2 américaine, auteur, Paris, France, cinéma, voyager, pizza, spaghettis, musées, tennis

Grammar explanation: Combining verbs and nouns 1 Example: a J'adore les chats. b Je déteste les spaghettis. Je déteste la mayonnaise ! c J'aime les animaux. J'aime la cuisine.

Put it together Example: 1 J'aime le fromage. J'adore mes nouveaux amis français ! J'aime la tour Eiffel. J'aime pas le vin. Je déteste les grèves.

CONVERSATION 3

Figure it out 1 why = pourquoi; because = parce que 2 French culture

Notice 1 a bon b alors c et d parce que 2 apprendre, comprendre, parler, habiter 3 a langue b culture c belle d intéressant

Practice 1 a J'adore parler français. b Je déteste visiter les musées. c J'aime apprendre les langues. d Je veux visiter la France.

Put it together Example: Je veux habiter en France. J'aime parler des languages étrangères. J'espère visiter Paris. Je veux voyager dans le monde entier !

MISSION SCRIPT – MODEL

Salut, je m'appelle John. Ça va ? Bon, je suis canadien mais j'habite à Sydney. Je suis écrivain. J'aime les animaux et j'adore voyager mais je déteste le froid. J'apprends le français parce que je veux visiter la France. Et toi ?

UNIT 2

CONVERSATION 1

Figure it out 1 a oui b non c non 2 a vrai b faux 3 pas 4 a je veux pas (or je ne veux pas) b tu habites pas (or tu n'habites pas)

Notice 1 Je parle bien/Je parle un peu 2 a bien anglais b bien le français 3 a Est-ce que tu aimes ... ? b Est-ce que tu veux ... ? c Est-ce que tu habites ... ? d Est-ce que tu parles pas ... ? 4 Tu parles d'autres langues ?

Practice 1 a seulement b J'apprends un peu de c Vraiment; pas; italien d Aujourd'hui; étudie e beaucoup de; bien sûr 2 a S b S c Q d Q e Q 3 a Est-ce qu'Alex / que Alex habite à Paris ? b Parles-tu italien ? c Marc apprend le français ?

Put it together 1 a l'allemand b l'espagnol c le chinois Examples: d le japonais e le polonais 2 Examples: a Oui, je parle d'autres langues. Je parle bien le portugais et un peu italien./Non, je (ne) parle pas d'autres langues. b Oui, je veux apprendre encore deux langues, le polonais et le russe./Non, je (ne) veux pas apprendre d'autres langues. Seulement le français !

CONVERSATION 2

Figure it out 1 a seulement deux semaines b J'espère apprendre trois langues (le japonais, l'arabe et l'anglais) 2 a seulement b vrai c langues d encore e Tu parles très bien le français ! f J'espère apprendre... 3 a de rien b depuis quand c combien

Notice 1 depuis quand; when 2 a Lauren apprend le français depuis deux semaines. b Jacques espère apprendre le japonais, l'arabe et l'anglais. 3 a Combien b depuis c parles d Depuis quand 4 more

Practice 1 a cinq jours b trois ans c huit mois d quatre semaines e J'habite en France depuis mon dernier anniversaire. f J'apprends le français depuis neuf semaines. 2 Combien; jours; ici

Put it together 4 a Depuis quand tu habites en France ? b Depuis quand tu travailles comme professeur ?

CONVERSATION 3

Figure it out 1 what 2 chaque semaine / chaque jour 3 a (Lauren va en classe) chaque semaine. b (Jacques va en classe) chaque jour. 4 vocabulaire; idée; préfère; simple; Internet 5 vrai

Notice 1 a Comment ? b ben c c'est-à-dire 2 a Je pense que b Je préfère c Je dois d Je suis d'accord e Ça aide !

Grammar explanation: *je* (I) and *tu* (you) verb forms 1 a étudie/étudies b pense/penses c demande/demandes d commence/commences 2 a sais b dois c lis d peux e dis

Practice 1 a Qu'est-ce que, lire ? b Je lis, livres. c tu sais d Je sais que, très bien. 2 a Je préfère parler français. b Tu dois dire que tu aimes la pizza. c Tu sais que j'apprends le français depuis deux semaines. d Je pense que le français est simple !

Put it together Example: Je veux apprendre le chinois un jour. Je vais à la piscine de temps en temps. Je dois apprendre la guitare. Je pense que la France est un beau pays.

MISSION SCRIPT – MODEL

J'apprends le français depuis un mois. J'apprends le vocabulaire et j'étudie chaque semaine. Je parle seulement l'anglais et un peu de français. J'espère apprendre l'allemand un jour. Et toi ? Combien de langues tu parles ? Depuis quand tu enseignes le français ? Qu'est-ce que je dois faire pour apprendre le français ?

UNIT 3

CONVERSATION 1

Figure it out 1 b 2 a merci b s'il te plait c de rien 3 Comment tu t'appelles ? 4 not a problem/ no problem 5 Tu es où ? (Where are you?)

Notice 1 plus lentement (s'il te plait) 2 Où est-ce que tu es ?; Tu es où ? 3 a Enchanté(e). b Tout va bien. c Maintenant, je suis à Londres. 4 a I am b you have c you are

Practice 2 1 f 2 c 3 d 4 a 5 g 6 b 7 e 3 a beaucoup; aujourd'hui b C'est; tout; ici c où; maintenant d dois; apprendre

Grammar explanation: word order with objects 1 a te b le c m' t' 2 a entends b écrire c vois d dire 3 a Tu l'entends ? b Tu peux me dire ? c Je veux l'envoyer. 4 (top to bottom) je te demande, je l'explique, tu m'aides

Put it together Example: Maintenant, je suis à la bibliothèque. Maintenant, j'étudie le français. Aujourd'hui, je vais au restaurant. Aujourd'hui, je regarde la télévision.

Pronunciation explanation 1: final consonants 1 a oui b non c non d oui e non f oui g oui h non

CONVERSATION 2

Figure it out 1 a vrai b faux c faux 2 dans une, suis ici, suis en, un instant, très intéressant 3 a interesting b to repeat c reason d (you) understand 4 a Do you live in another city? b Can you repeat that? c One moment … I can't/ don't hear you well.

Notice 1 a j'habite; tu habites b je suis; tu es c tu peux; tu dis d je travaille; j'entends e je comprends; je comprends pas 2 Comment dire…? Plus lentement, s'il te plait. Je suis désolé. Je comprends pas. (Est-ce que) tu peux répéter ça ? Un moment. Je t'entends pas bien.

Practice 1 a Tu habites où ? b Qu'est-ce que tu dis ? c Tu veux habiter où ? d Je comprends que tu travailles. 2 pourquoi/qu'est-ce que/ comment/où/qui/quel(le)/quand/combien (est-ce que)/ tu peux 3 a Quand ? b Combien ? c Qui ? d Où ? e Pourquoi ?

Put it together 2 Example: Je suis de Londres mais maintenant, j'habite à Liverpool. J'habite ici depuis trois ou quatre mois. Je travaille dans un restaurant. Je suis chef. Je travaille ici depuis février !

CONVERSATION 3

Figure it out 1 a deactivate b reset c connection 2 a vrai b vrai c faux d vrai 3 a J'oublie le mot. b Je suis désolé(e). c À bientôt; À la prochaine 4 semaine; The 'la' before the word tells you that it's feminine. 5 *ma/mon* = my; *ta/ton* = your

Conversation strategy: use 'Tarzan French' to communicate with limited words
a Plus lentement ? b Combien ? c le supermarché, où ?

Conversation strategy: use the power nouns *personne, endroit, chose* a livre ... endroit ? b restaurant ... personne ?

Notice 1 a j'ai b tu penses c je peux d tu m'entends e appeler 2 tu as besoin 3 pas de souci 4 ça marche 5 J'oublie le mot !

Practice 1 a J'ai un ordinateur; Tu as une webcam b Je pense que ça marche; Je pense que tu as; Tu penses que je peux c Je peux dire; Tu peux avoir d J'ai besoin d'un autre ordinateur; J'ai besoin de travailler; Tu as besoin d'être
2 a peux; ordinateur b Si; veux; peux; aider c prochaine; espère; avoir

Your turn: use the hack 1 Because *masculinité* ends in -ité, a feminine ending, and *feminisme* ends in -isme, a masculine ending
2 a un b un c un d une e une f une g un h un i un j un k une l une m une n un o une 3 a mon travail; ton travail b ma femme; ta femme

Put it together Je pense que le nouveau smartphone est fantastique ! J'ai seulement la version 3 mais elle est lente et j'ai besoin d'acheter un chargeur.

MISSION SCRIPT – MODEL

Aujourd'hui, je travaille dans un supermarché. Maintenant, je suis chez moi. J'ai un ordinateur mais j'aime pas. J'ai besoin d'un autre ordinateur.

UNIT 4

CONVERSATION 1

Figure it out 1 a vrai b faux c faux 2 a Je suis belge. b Excusez-moi, parlez-vous français ? c Ça vous dérange si je pratique mon français avec vous ? d On parle ! 3 parfait; patiente; débutante 4 a Si tu veux b Avec plaisir ! c Pourquoi pas ? d Pas de problème ! e Chouette !

Notice 1 Excusez-moi 2 Parlez-vous français ? 3 Ça vous dérange si...? 4 a vous parlez; tu parles b excusez-moi; excuse-moi c avec vous; avec toi 5 a encore b déjà c tellement d encore e déjà f tellement

Grammar explanation: verb forms for *on*
1 on pense 2 a on travaille b on étudie 3 on peut

Practice 1 a J'habite encore en Europe. b Tu travailles encore à la banque ? c Je vais encore en classe ! d On peut encore pratiquer ? 2 a déjà b Si tu veux; tu peux c comment dire d chouette; ici e encore; faire f Ça vous dérange si

Put it together 1 Ça vous dérange si je parle avec vous ? Ça vous dérange si je caresse votre chien ? Ça vous dérange si je m'assieds sur cette chaise ? Ça vous dérange si j'ouvre la fenêtre ? 2 Situation 1 Ah, vous parlez français !; Je suis encore débutant(e).; J'apprends le français depuis quelques semaines seulement.

Situation 2 Je pense que cette langue est très belle.; Un jour, j'irai en France.

Situation 3 Excusez-moi/Je suis désolé(e)...; Ça vous dérange si je vous pose une question ?

CONVERSATION 2

Figure it out 1 a la Belgique/Belgium b au Québec/to Quebec 2 a Tu es à Paris depuis quand ? b pendant quelques mois c exactement 3 masculine 4 a plus b autre c pendant d alors e comme f moi-même g jamais

Notice 1 a Tu dois visiter b Je veux dire que c Tu veux dire que ... ? 2 a pendant le film; pendant le mois b la même chose; toi-même 3 a 4 b 5 c 1 d 6 e 3 f 7 g 2

Practice 1 a prendre b je prends c tu prends 2 a je prends le train b je conduis c je vais en voiture d je prends l'avion 3 a le b ce c prochain d chaque 4 a visiter; pour voir b en voiture c aller; comme; et d Pour aller; tu dois e prendre l'avion; prendre le train f Il y a; raisons g jamais; endroit

Put it together Examples: a Je voyage seulement un peu. b Je vais à Lille/en Irlande. c Je vais à Lille pendant quelques jours. d Je vais en France le mois prochain. e Je vais prendre le train ou la voiture.

CONVERSATION 3

Figure it out 1 a vrai b vrai c vrai d faux e faux 2 a Pour boire un verre (où Hemingway, Picasso et James Joyce allaient) b Pour les restaurants spectaculaires 3 Do you also need my phone number ? 4 a Qu'est-ce que tu vas faire à Paris ? b Je veux faire les mêmes choses.

Notice 1 a pour commencer b après c ensuite 2 a 4 b 2 c 1 d 3

Your turn: use the hack 1 a Je vais être occupé(e) ! b Je vais faire beaucoup. c (Est-ce que) tu vas m'appeler demain ? d (Est-ce que) tu vas au restaurant ? e Je vais pas voyager à Lyon. 2 Examples: a Je peux nager dans la mer. b On va apprendre le français ensemble. c Tu veux boire du café brésilien ?

Practice 1 a Tu es pas très occupé(e). b Tu vas être très occupé(e). c Tu vas parler français. d On va voyager à Paris. e Pierre va aller en Irlande. f Lauren va pas visiter Berlin. 2 a Un moment; te donner; numéro de téléphone b Ce soir; être occupé(e); je suis libre demain c vois; encore; le voilà d si; pouvoir e avec; pour boire; accompagner f prendre; ensemble; d'accord ?

Put it together 1 Example: Je vais cet été pendant trois semaines au Canada. Je sais déjà que je veux aller au Québec. Pour commencer, je vais prendre l'avion pour Montréal où je vais manger de la poutine et je vais aller au musée des Beaux-Arts. Et après, je vais prendre le train pour la ville de Québec. Je veux voir le festival Saint Jean ! 2 Voilà mon numéro et voilà mon adresse email. Tu peux m'appeler ou tu peux m'envoyer un texto demain, si tu veux !

MISSION SCRIPT – MODEL

Je veux aller à Strasbourg en décembre. Je connais déjà ma priorité – les marchés de Noël ! Je vais passer une semaine en ville avec ma copine et on va peut-être réserver un hôtel au centre ville. La ville est très belle et elle est à seulement quelques heures de train.

UNIT 5

CONVERSATION 1

Figure it out 1 What's her name/What's she called? 2 a faux (cette semaine, this weekend) b faux (ingénieur, engineer) c vrai d vrai e faux (le weekend prochain next weekend) 3 a cette semaine b le weekend prochain c demain d après ça e chaque été 4 a Quoi de neuf ? b Qui ? c en fait d mon étudiant(e) préféré(e) e Je suis content(e) de/d' ...

Notice 1 a Je suis content(e) de voir b Je suis content(e) d'être c Je suis content(e) de dire 2 a Elle s'appelle; Elle est belge; Elle travaille comme b Je la connais; Je vais la voir c Il adore. 3 a Je passe du temps b on va passer le weekend c il est d elle est e on va f on prévoit de g on visite 4 a 2 b 1 5 a 'la' comes before the verb in French, but 'her' comes after it in English. b Je la vois.

Practice 2 Examples: le beau père - step father, la belle mère - step mother, les grands-parents - grandparents 3 a tu as; frères; sœurs b Il/C'; neveu préféré; le c Vous d ami; on prévoit; ensemble e mère; comme; Elle travaille f passer du temps; enfants g mon frère; le vois h Il étudie i Ma copine; chaque jour; Elle 4 a Mon/ma meilleur(e) ami(e) s'appelle (Example: Benoît/Florence). b Je le/la connais depuis (Example: dix ans). c Il/elle travaille comme (Example: pilote) 5 Example: Ce weekend, je passe du temps avec mes parents et mon amie Émilie.; b Example: On prévoit d'aller au cinéma.

Grammar explanation : *il, elle* and *ils/elles* 1 a aiment b visite c est d travaillent e dansent

Put it together Example: Je passe la plupart de mon temps avec mon amie, Stephanie. Je la connais depuis toute petite. Elle vient de Baltimore mais elle habite maintenant en Virginie avec son copain, Bill. Bill travaille comme ingénieur chimiste et Stephanie travaille comme infirmière. Le weekend, elle va toujours à des concerts de métal. Elle adore cette musique

CONVERSATION 2

Figure it out 1 a mariée b célibataire c copain 2 feminine 3 Are you (two/plural) very different? 4 a Elle est célibataire. b Elle va habiter dans la maison de sa soeur. c Mariam est avec son mari depuis vingt ans/longtemps. d Lauren va habiter avec sa soeur à son retour aux États-Unis. 5 a À mon retour b Tu veux dire ... ? c par exemple

Notice 1 on est, ma soeur dit, elle voyage, on se ressemble, elle parle 2 a la même chose b J'ai même pas de voiture. 3 a Depuis combien de temps vous êtes ensemble ? b Depuis combien de temps on est ensemble ? c Vous êtes ensemble depuis ... d On est ensemble depuis... 4 le chien de mon frère ; le père de mon ami

Vocabulary explanation: savoir and connaitre a connais b sais c connait d sait

Practice 1 Examples a Oui j'ai deux sœurs. b J'ai pas de copain. c Non, j'ai pas d'enfants. d J'habite seule. 2 a D'où tu viens ? b Avec quoi tu écris ? c À quelle heure commence la classe ? 3 a Tu veux dire ... ? b il veut dire ... c elle veut dire ... d on veut dire ... 4 a En fait, ma copine et moi, on regarde même pas la télé. b Je connais mon meilleur ami depuis longtemps. On se ressemble beaucoup. c Aujourd'hui c'est l'anniversaire de ma mère. d Vous allez au Canada avec nous ?

Put it together Example: J'ai un copain, et on habite ensemble. Je le connais depuis deux ans et on est ensemble depuis deux ans. On prévoit d'être mariés dans quelques mois à Dublin et on veut habiter à New York un jour. On travaille ensemble chez nous, donc naturellement, j'aime notre travail !

CONVERSATION 3

Figure it out **1** a 4 (on est quatre) b She's not sure (J'en suis pas sûre) c Ils sont pas mon genre. **2** a We have two children. b How do you say in French … ? c a charming Frenchman **3** a Ils s'appellent … b J'adore leurs noms. c Tout est possible !

Notice **1** a Tu penses que tu vas jamais … ? b Est-ce que vous avez … ? **2** J'en suis sûr(e) ! **3** a pour toujours, 'for always' b jamais, 'never'. **4** a 4 b 5 c 6 d 1 e 3 f 7 g 2

Practice **1** a Non, on est ensemble depuis seulement quelques jours ! b Non, il est auteur ! c Non, ils sont en vacances ! d Marc et moi ? Non, on a un chat, bien sûr ! e Non, elle va voyager avec ma cousine ! f Non, elles vont regarder la télé.

Put it together **1** Example: J'ai beaucoup de nièces et neveux. Ils habitent partout dans le monde. Mes parents habitent à la montagne, près de ma ville. Je les vois souvent. Mes meilleures amies s'appellent Stephanie et Alexandria. Elles adorent voyager ! **2** Example: Est-ce que tu penses que tu vas jamais habiter en France ?

COMPLETING UNIT 5

1 Ils vont à l'hôpital. Sa fille s'appelle Anna. Jacques arrive à neuf (9) heures. Ils vont rencontrer Mathieu demain. François et Marie vont lire le petit prince. Sa sœur travaille demain. Ses parents aiment pas cette ville. Oui, ils visitent la France chaque été. Son cousin a quatre (4) enfants. Elle connait sa famille depuis toujours.

MISSION SCRIPT – MODEL

Aujourd'hui, je veux parler de mes personnes préférées. Alors, j'habite avec mon copain. Je le connais et on est ensemble depuis deux ans. On travaille ensemble sur Internet. L'an prochain, on prévoit de se marier à Dublin. Toute sa famille va être là. Dans quelques mois, mon copain et moi, on va voir mes parents chez eux, à la montagne. Ils vont faire une soirée avec mes frères, ma soeur, ma famille et beaucoup de mes amis. Je vais être contente de les voir. Surtout mes meilleures amies, Stephanie et Alex. Je les connais depuis notre enfance. Mais maintenant, elles habitent trop loin.

UNIT 6

CONVERSATION 1

Figure it out **1** a Ratatouille and red wine (du vin rouge) b votre table. Merci à vous ! Avez-vous choisi ? Je vous écoute. s'il vous plait. **2** We already know. **3** a Pour moi … s'il vous plait. b Je prends … c Je voudrais … **4** a good evening b please (formal) c sir d ladies e Have you decided/ chosen? (formal) f Here's a table. **5** a Et à boire ? b Tu vas boire quelque chose ? c on sait déjà

Notice 1 I'm hungry (French uses avoir, 'I have hunger', whereas, and English uses 'to be' , 'I am hungry'.) 2 a On prend une carafe d'eau. b Je voudrais encore de l'eau 3 a je prends b on prend c pour moi d je voudrais ... 4 a du vin rouge b une table c une carafe d'eau d de l'eau 5 a I know b I would like c I'll have (lit., 'I take') d I'm going to drink / I will drink e We know f We have decided (lit., 'we have chosen') g We'll have / take (lit., 'We take') h (Do) you know...? i You'll take...? (lit., 'you take?') j Would you like... ? k Have you (pl./formal) decided? (lit., 'you (pl./formal) have chosen') l Are you going to drink...? / Will you drink...?

Grammar explanation : *du/de la/des (some)*

1 des œufs, du jambon, du poisson, de la viande, du café, du lait, de la bière, du vin

Practice 1 a boire b manger c acheter 2 a On a choisi. b Encore du vin, s'il vous plait ! c Je prends du vin rouge et elle prend du vin blanc. d On sait ce qu'on veut manger. e Tu as déjà faim ?

Put it together 1 Example: Oui, je vais prendre les oeufs mayonnaise. En plat principal, je choisis le boeuf bourguignon. Je voudrais boire du vin rouge et de l'eau. Monsieur, s'il vous plait. Oui, j'ai déjà choisi mon dessert. Alors, en dessert, je vais manger une salade de fruits. 2 Example: J'adore l'omelette espagnole ! J'apprends comment la faire avec des amis espagnols quand je vais chez eux et on on mange souvent au déjeuner, comme ce weekend par exemple ! Pour la préparer, je vais acheter des pommes de terre et des œufs. On va boire de la sangria avec l'omelette !

CONVERSATION 2

Figure it out 1 a le Louvre and le Pompidou (*Centre*) b the Louvre c it's not as interesting d on peut faire des compromis 2 a le plus touristique b si tu penses que 3 a je suis d'accord b je suis pas d'accord c naturellement 4 a better than b fewer/less c think/find

Notice 1 Tu as raison (lit., You have reason); J'ai faim. 2 a le plus b mieux c moins 3 a Je le/la trouve... b Je trouve le Louvre ... c Ils le/la trouvent ... d Ils trouvent le Louvre ... e Je sais que ... f Tu sais que ... g On sait qu'il y a ... h Tu sais qu'il y a ... i C'est unique au monde. 4 a 3 b 4 c 2 d 1 e 7 f 5 g 6

Grammar explanation: comparisons a plus sympa b plus charmant c plus de livres d le/la plus célèbre e le meilleur restaurant f un plus jeune homme g moins difficile h moins de jours i le moins cher j le pire film

Practice 1 a (Est-ce qu') il y a seulement trois étudiants ici ? b Il y a des livres chez moi. c Je trouve qu'il y a moins de chiens dans le parc aujourd'hui. 2 a Paris est plus grande que Toulouse. b Je trouve ce restaurant trop petit. c Tu vois quelle adresse ? / Quelle adresse est-ce que tu vois ? d Il faut travailler pendant la semaine.

Put it together 1 Example: Il y a tellement d'endroits à Toulouse que je voudrais visiter… L'endroit le plus important de la ville est la place du Capitole. L'architecture est très unique ! Après ça, à mon avis il faut voir le jardin japonais !

CONVERSATION 3

Figure it out 1 a la musique de Jacques Brel b la musique moderne c le livre qu'elle lit maintenant 2 a in exchange b absolutely 3 a Le serveur est où ? b L'addition, s'il vous plait ! c à mon avis d J'aime ça plus que ... e Qu'est-ce que tu recommandes ?

Notice 1 a tu vas adorer b je voudrais c je te donne 2 a 2 b 3 c 1 d 5 e 4 3 a Dis-moi ... b Qu'est-ce que tu recommandes ? c Tu peux me recommander ... ?

Practice 1 a de l'eau, un taxi, plus/encore de temps, un autre verre b Example: Je voudrais en savoir plus sur l'architecture. Je voudrais en savoir plus sur la culture de ton pays. 2 a J'adore l'art classique. J'aime ça plus que l'art moderne. b À ton avis, quel livre est plus intéressant ? c Un instant, je dois te donner notre adresse !

Your turn: use the hack 2 Malheureusement, si je comprends bien, c'est à dire, à propos, j'ai l'impression que, franchement 3 Examples: a Bon, non. Malheureusement, mon diner est trop froid. b J'habite ici, c'est-à-dire, Paris est ma ville ! c Oui, j'ai l'impression qu'on a pas du lait d Franchement, je peux pas vivre sans café !

Put it together Example: Je pense qu'il faut lire 'Le tour du monde en 80 jours' de Jules Verne. Je le lis parce que je voudrais en savoir plus sur le monde à cette époque. Franchement, les livres de Jules Verne sont mieux que les livres modernes parce qu'il est plus descriptif dans ses histoires.

Check your understanding a faux b vrai c faux d vrai e vrai

MISSION SCRIPT – MODEL

Example: J'adore le resto Luigi's proche de chez moi ! Quand j'ai faim c'est mon premier choix pour les pizzas vraiment italiennes. Entre nous, on mange la meilleure pizza du monde dans ce resto ! Il faut gouter la napolitana si tu y vas !

UNIT 7

CONVERSATION 1

Figure it out 1 b It's not bad (C'est pas mal) 2 a le weekend dernier b Comment tu as trouvé ça ? c On a parlé de nos projets. 3 Why did you decide to go to ...? 4 a faux b vrai c faux d vrai

Notice 1 a Qu'est-ce que tu as fait ? b j'ai préféré c j'ai mangé d je suis allé(e) e on est allé f on a parlé g j'ai visité h on a visité i vous avez décidé de 2 a il y a b dernier c une fois d le café du coin

Grammar explanation: past verb forms
1 a j'ai b parlé c j'ai parlé 2 a J'ai regardé la télé hier. b Il a étudié le français ce matin. c Tu as choisi le restaurant ? d Elle a demandé quelque chose. 3 a Je suis sorti avec mes amis. b J'ai choisi ce musée. c Antoine a regardé le film le weekend dernier.

Practice 1 Example *J'ai rencontré ma femme il ya 20 ans* 2 a Tu dois aller au restaurant où j'ai mangé il y a deux jours. b On a aimé le film ! (Le film nous a plu !) c Elle est allée voir son frère à Dublin. 3 a Il y a trois mois, je suis allé au Canada. b J'ai trouvé le musée très intéressant ! c Ce matin, je suis arrivé en métro.

Put it together 1 Example: Hier, je suis allé chez mes parents. On a parlé de ma copine et de comment elle va. Le weekend dernier, j'ai mangé une pizza avec elle. 2 Example: J'ai visité Londres il y a un mois. J'ai décidé d'aller à cette ville pour visiter une ville typiquement anglaise avec ma famille. Ça m'a plu parce que j'ai vu tellement de choses très britanniques. J'ai trouvé ça très intéressant.

CONVERSATION 2

Figure it out 1 a vrai b faux c faux 2 a Elle a appris quelques nouveaux mots et ella a pratiqué quelques phrases avec Julie. b (Elle a commencé) il y a seulement quelques mois 3 I forgot! You told me that (said that to me) already! 4 tu as étudié; j'ai étudié; j'ai appris; j'ai pratiqué, tu as fait; tu as commencé; j'ai commencé; j'ai décidé; j'ai acheté; j'ai oublié; tu m'as dit

Notice 1 a 3 b 1 c 2 2 a j'ai étudié b j'ai appris c j'ai pratiqué d j'ai commencé e j'ai décidé de f j'ai acheté g j'ai oublié

Grammar explanation: three easy patterns for the top 'irregular' past verbs

1

French	Meaning
on a fait	we made – we did
j'ai lu	I read
il a vu	he saw
elle a compris	she understood

Practice 1 a J'ai trouvé ce restaurant il y a neuf mois. b J'ai commencé à apprendre le français il y a trois ans. c Il m'a rencontré il y a une semaine. 2 a Je vois le film. b Je vais voir le film demain. c J'ai vu le film la semaine dernière. 3 a Ça prend trop de temps donc j'ai décidé d'habiter ici jusqu'à l'automne. b Une fois, j'ai pris l'avion jusqu'au Canada tout seul. c L'été dernier, j'ai pris le train depuis l'Espagne jusqu'en Italie. d Est-ce que tu as besoin du dictionnaire ? Je l'ai ici. e Je dois dire que le livre est plus facile à lire cette fois que la dernière fois.

Put it together Example: Je suis allé au mariage de mon cousin à la montagne il y deux jours. On a bu des cocktails et on a dansé ! J'ai vu toute ma famille ! J'ai dit à mon cousin: "on a passé un moment extraordaire". C'était vraiment génial ! Je suis rentré hier.

CONVERSATION 3

Figure it out 1 a ma prononciation b accent c grammaire 2 a vrai b faux c faux

Notice a Tu savais que b Je pensais que c Je voulais

Practice 1 a Je pensais que tu étais occupé(e). b Tu pensais qu'elle était ici ? c Cécile avait le livre. d On savait pas. e Je voulais manger avec toi. 2 a Tu peux me dire quelle est la différence entre ces deux mots ? b Tu as dit ça si vite ! Qu'est-ce que ça veut dire ? c Est-ce que tu as compris ? d Ma prononciation est comment ? J'ai bien dit ce mot ? e Je voulais dire l'autre mot. f L'autre jour, j'ai demandé à mon prof, 'comment est mon accent ?/mon accent est comment ?' et elle a dit 'pas mal.' g J'ai pratiqué ma grammaire toute la semaine. h J'ai écrit quelques phrases. Tu peux les vérifier et me dire si elles sont correctes ? i Tu m'as beaucoup aidé. Merci !

Your turn: use the hack 1 a Demain, je fais du ski. b Lundi prochain, on mange une omelette. c La semaine dernière, ils 'cherchent' un chat. d Il y a trois jours, j'apprends un nouveau mot en français.

Put it together Example: L'an dernier, j'avais peur de parler français. Je pensais que mon accent était trop fort et je voulais arrêter et parler en anglais seulement. Mais je trouve que le français est une langue sympa alors j'ai décidé de parler de mon weekend sans penser à mon niveau de français. Maintenant, c'est plus simple !

COMPLETING UNIT 7

1 un chien 2 non 3 un peu de viande

MISSION SCRIPT – MODEL

Example: Il y a vingt ans, je suis arrivé à la Gare de l'Est pendant la nuit. Je pensais : 'comment est-ce que je vais trouver mon hôtel dans cette grande ville ?' J'avais pas de plan et je parlais très peu français. Mais j'ai trouvé un taxi et le chauffeur de taxi était très sympa. Il m'a amené jusqu'à l'hôtel. On a parlé et il m'a dit que mon français était très correct. Une très bonne première soirée !

UNIT 8

CONVERSATION 1

Figure it out 1 a improving (tu fais des progrès) b recently (récemment) c le coq au vin 2 Je suis content(e) de te revoir! 3 a Récemment, Lauren a commencé à faire la cuisine. (Elle prend des cours.) b Lauren va faire une mousse au chocolat. 4 a quoi de neuf b ça fait longtemps c en ce moment 5 It's important to practise.

Notice 1 a Continue comme ça !, 'continue like that!' b Quand j'essaie de..., 'when I try of it to-make' 2 a Ça fait b quoi jusqu'à maintenant ? c vite d à faire

Practice 1 a Ça fait longtemps !; Je suis content(e) de te revoir ! b Je vois que…; Dis-donc, quoi de neuf ? c Ben, en ce moment…; Recemment, j'ai commencé … d Et tu as appris quoi ? 2 a Je sais que... b Tu sais que … ? c Tu as vu … ? 3 Example: Récemment, j'ai commencé à prendre des cours de danse. En ce moment, je cherche un nouveau travail. 4 a Tu fais quoi ? b Tu vas boire quoi ?

Put it together Example: Récemment, j'ai commencé à lire un roman chaque weekend. C'est intéressant de me perdre dans l'histoire ! La dernière fois, c'était un livre d'espionnage. J'ai lu trois livres pour le moment et j'espère en lire vingt cet été !

CONVERSATION 2

Figure it out 1 a Faux. Lauren prend pas le métro. b Faux. Jacques va souvent au travail en voiture. c Faux. Lauren va au restaurant où on mange la meilleure soupe à l'ognon. d Faux. Jacques prend parfois son déjeuner dans un café. Il déjeune normalement à la maison (chez moi). 2 At first it was strange (bizarre), but now she has a routine (elle a une routine). 3 Il me semble que ... Conversation lead 4 a moi aussi/moi non plus; rarement/ normalement b je me promène; je fais du vélo/je prends pas le métro; je vais en voiture

Notice 1 le matin, 2 avant le travail, 3 l'après-midi, 4 avant, 5 en ville, 6 dans le quartier, 7 partout, 8 le même, 9 à la maison, 11 de temps en temps, 12 rarement, 13 souvent, 14 toujours, 15 parfois, 16 jamais, 17 en voiture, 18 pour le déjeuner

Vocab explanation: using faire to describe what you do 1 faire une promenade 2 faire la cuisine

Practice **1** a Je fais souvent du sport. b Hier, à 15h, j'ai fait du shopping. c Voilà mon amie, Julie. d Le concert commence à 18h et finit à 20h.

Put it together Example: Chaque jour, je me lève à 7h et je prends le bus à 8h pour aller au travail. Après le travail, j'adore faire du sport et lire des articles sur Internet. Je joue souvent au tennis le weekend et je lis un blog sur les voyages le lundi parce que je veux voyager en Europe un jour !

CONVERSATION 3

Figure it out **1** a faux b vrai c vrai d faux **2** a J'espère aller au parc b pour jouer au foot; avec des copains c J'ai déjà prévu de faire du shopping d avec quelqu'un **3** I'd love to

Notice **1** a Qu'est-ce que j'amène ? b À quelle heure ? c Tu peux m'écrire l'adresse ? d Je peux te montrer sur le plan.

Grammar explanation: conditionals
a J'adorerais b On serait c Elle voudrait

Practice **1** a Je dois mettre quoi ? b Ça finit à quelle heure ? / Ça va finir à quelle heure ? / À quelle heure ça va finir ? c Tu connais l'adresse ? d Le rendez-vous / la soirée est où ? e Je dois arriver quand / à quelle heure ? f Je peux amener du vin ? **2** Example: a Tu fais quoi plus tard ? b J'ai du temps libre plus tard pour le concert. Tu viens ? **3** Example: a Ça serait amusant / parfait /impossible. b J'aimerais bien mais je suis occupé(e) (e). **4** a Tu pourrais me demander la prochaine fois ? b Je sortirais mais il est trop tard. **5** a you would prepare b it would be c I would travel d he would say e you could

Put it together **1** Example: Ah, l'été. À ta place (if I were you), je prendrais le soleil et je passerais tout mon temps sur la plage ! Je mangerais du poisson et je boirais des cocktails. Je devrais pas travailler, comme ça j'aurais le temps de lire des romans. Comme la plage est proche d'ici, je voudrais aller en vélo. **2** Example: Je pourrais voyager le mois prochain mais on va partir d'où et à quelle heure notre le samedi ? Tu sais que je préfère dormir tard le weekend ! Comme on passe tout notre weekend en montagne, je dois amener une tente ? Je pense que ça serait amusant de dormir sous la tente, non ?

Your turn: use the hack **1** a Je pense qu'ils vont pas gagner. b On va au restaurant ensemble ! C'est génial ! c Alors, on danse ? d Supermarché plus tard ?

COMPLETING UNIT 8

1 faire du vélo **2** non **3** le dimanche

MISSION SCRIPT – MODEL

Example: J'habite tout près de la mer. Tous les jours, avant le petit déjeuner, je fais du jogging sur la plage. Après je mange des oeufs, du pain et des fruits. Je travaille toujours jusqu'à midi et puis je mange avec ma femme. On mange beaucoup de poisson et de légumes. L'après-midi, je travaille encore. Je suis traducteur et j'adore mon travail. J'aimerais apprendre encore beaucoup de langues et visiter beaucoup de pays. Mais je suis content de ma vie. Le soir, on lit un livre ou on regarde un film et le vendredi, on sort avec des amis. On prend jamais la voiture, on va partout toujours à pied.

UNIT 9

CONVERSATION 1

Figure it out 1 a It's Lauren's last week (semaine) in Paris. b Lauren and Jacques are planning to go shopping (faire du shopping). c There are a lot of things to see (à voir) on the avenue. 2 a I'm going back (returning) to the United States soon. b That's a pity ! c That depends, y'know. 3 a à la campagne b les montagnes c le lac et la forêt d proche de chez moi e sous le soleil

Notice 1 a Lauren va rentrer aux États-Unis bientôt. b Lauren va ramener beaucoup de cadeaux pour sa famille c Lauren va les acheter sur l'avenue des Champs-Élysées 2 a me rappeler b te rappeler c m'a rappelé 3 a 3 b 5 c 6 d 1 e 4 f 2 4 la campagne, les montagnes, le lac, la forêt, les arbres, le soleil 5 Example: a J'habite à la campagne/en ville. b Je préfère rester au soleil/sous les arbres. c Le climat est meilleur près du lac.

PRACTICE

2 J'habite dans une petite ville. Près de chez moi, il y a des champs avec des vaches. 3 Mon amie Florence habite à Paris dans un tout petit appartement. Près de chez elle, il y a une boulangerie et un magasin de chaussures.

Grammar explanation: using manquer for 'to miss' a Tu me manques. b Ils/Elles me manquent. c Elle nous manque. d Je manque à Antoine. e Mon frère va me manquer. f Ta copine te manque ?

Vocab explanation: describing the weather 1 a Il fait beau aujourd'hui. b Il fait mauvais. C'est dommage ! c Tu as pas froid ? Tu sais qu'il fait froid sur la côte. 2 Example: En Angleterre, il fait gris et il fait froid. Il pleut pas aujourd'hui, on a de la chance !

Grammar explanation: changing gender and number for adjectives a (m) prêt (f) prête b (m) grand (f) grande c (m) chaud (f) chaude d (m) fatigué (f) fatiguée

Put it together Example: J'adore aller voir ma famille en Irlande. Quand je prends le bus à ma ville, je vois beaucoup de collines vertes. On les appelle les 'drumlins'. Dans ma région, il y a beaucoup de lacs aussi ! En été, il fait pas chaud mais il pleut pas trop. Quand on peut, on nage dans les lacs. Ça me manque beaucoup !

CONVERSATION 2

Figure it out 1 a faux b vrai c faux 2 a un souvenir typique de Paris (un béret classique) b Elle est aventureuse. c Il est jeune. d Ils sont plus traditionnels et ils ont bon gout. e C'est moins cher. 3 a impressionnante b aventureuse c typique d classique e jeune f ennuyeux g nouveaux h traditionnels i pas facile 4 a rappelle b vraiment c trouverait d enfin e déjà

Notice 1 a Je dois acheter quoi ? b Mes parents sont plus traditionnels. c ça me rappelle d super ennuyeux 2 a simple/facile, dur /difficile b unique, typique c stupides/ nuls, intelligents d modernes, traditionnels e aventureuse, timide f vieux, jeune 3 a Mon grand frère. b Mes grands frères. c Ma grande sœur. d Mes grandes sœurs. e Le magasin était ouvert. f La boulangerie était ouverte. g Les magasins sont ouverts. h Les boulangeries sont ouvertes.

Practice 1 C'est le moins cher./C'est la moins chère. 2 Column 1: timide, laid/laide, désagréable, pessimiste, fier/fière, drôle. Column 2: old, odd. Column 3: jeune, typique. Column 4: adventurous, handsome/pretty, nice, optimistic, modest, serious 3 Examples: a Je suis aventureuse. b Mon travail est fascinant. c Mon père est drôle. d Sa maison est spacieuse. e Ma mère est courageuse.

Put it together Example: Alors, ma cousine est très intéressante ! Elle est super active car elle fait du ski et elle adore aller partout en vélo. Elle est aussi très intelligente ! Mon père est plus timide. Il vient chez nous le weekend et il regarde la télé. Il est sympa et patient.

CONVERSATION 3

Figure it out 1 a Lauren's brother needs a new headset to play video games. (pour jouer aux jeux en ligne) b The headset is a little bit expensive. (un peu cher) c Lauren is going to pay with her debit card (avec sa carte de crédit) 2 payer cash; avec sa carte de crédit; at that price (à ce prix-là) 3 a le rouge b le vert 4 b 5 serait

Notice 1 a ça a l'air b quel genre de ...? 2 a celui-ci/celle-là b le noir/la noire c le petit/la petite d le nouveau/la nouvelle 3 a un peu cher b payer en cash c la marque d la caisse 4 a des Adidas b un Kleenex c un Pepsi d un Mac

Practice 1 a a l'air d'être b dormir c a l'air 2 a Combien coute celle-ci ? b C'est de la bonne qualité ? c Je peux l'utiliser maintenant ? d Vous acceptez les cartes de crédit ? e Je peux payer seulement en cash. 3 a les rouges b la marque c à la caisse d la grande 4 large; long; short; light; heavy

Conversation strategy: use the set phrase celle-là, les noirs/noires, le grand/la grande, les vieux/vieilles, les plus chers/chères, Pas celui-ci, celui-là ! / Pas celle-ci, celle-là !

Put it together Example: Je cherche des nouvelles chaussures de sport. Je veux faire du footing très souvent alors je dois choisir une bonne marque. J'aime les jaunes. Oui, celles-ci ont l'air solides et de bonne qualité. Je peux payer avec ma carte de crédit ?

COMPLETING UNIT 9

1 près d'un lac, à la campagne 2 non 3 aventureuse et ouverte 4 pour regarder des vidéos en ligne

MISSION SCRIPT – MODEL

Example: Dans ma ville préférée, il fait toujours beau temps. C'est entre la mer et la montagne. À la mer, on peut nager. À la montagne, on peut faire du ski. La ville est grande mais il y a beaucoup de parcs avec des arbres. On prend le métro ou le vélo. On a pas besoin de voiture. Il y a des grandes avenues avec des bâtiments historiques et aussi des quartiers modernes avec des gratte-ciels immenses. Les gens dans cette ville sourient beaucoup et sont jamais stressés. Ma ville préférée me manque tellement !

UNIT 10

PUT YOUR CONVERSATION STRATEGIES INTO ACTION

Example: Enchanté. Je m'appelle David. On peut se tutoyer ? Merci de parler avec moi aujourd'hui. J'apprendre le français parce que j'adore. Oui, je parle espagnol aussi. Pardon, je n'ai pas compris. Tu peux répéter lentement, s'il te plait ?

COMPLETING UNIT 10

2 Léa, Versailles, huit mois/8 months, italien/Italian, lire

ACKNOWLEDGEMENTS

Though my name and face may be on the cover, there are so many people whose voices and ideas are in these pages.

I owe a debt of gratitude to my French teacher **Léa Tiralarc** who helped me maintain my French over the past several years, and who I consulted with for this course to ensure that the conversation flowed naturally, with modern, relevant French. My *québecoise* flatmate **Marie-Ève** also played a big role in pushing my French to the next level over a summer of telling jokes and organizing events in French.

There aren't enough praises I can sing about my editor **Sarah Cole**, who first reached out to me with the exciting prospect of collaborating with *Teach Yourself*. She worked with me over two years with unwavering support and passion for my vision of a modern language course. I cannot imagine that any other publisher could have brought so much life to these courses.

Melissa Baker worked behind the scenes to juggle timetables and perform more than a few miracles to ensure all the pieces of this publishing puzzle came together. **Eric Zuarino** and **Eleni Yiannoulidou** worked with me over many months to make large and small improvements to each chapter, and **Matthew Duffy** kept the project moving forward. I am grateful to the rest of the **Teach Yourself** team in both the UK and US, who showed incredible enthusiasm in creating a totally new kind of language course.

I owe a huge thank-you to the brilliant people at Team FI3M: **Bálint, David, Kittichai, Dávid, Joe, Ingo, Joseph, Adam, Holly and LC**, who kept my website, *Fluent in 3 Months*, running while I was busy writing these courses and made sure we continued to do innovative work. Thank you all.

Finally, my partner **Lauren**, without whom this course never could have come to light. She is the Pepper Potts to my Tony Stark - she makes sure my crazy ideas run smoothly and professionally, and she came up with many of the cleverest concepts that you see in these pages. Her perfectionism and academic background turned my ideas for a good course into a truly great one.

NEW SPELLING REFORM

A set of changes to French spelling rules came into effect in 2016, as recommended by the Académie Française. Officially, both traditional and new spellings are acceptable but all school materials will now reflect the new rules.

In this book, we have resolutely followed the new spelling convention. Here's a brief overview of the main changes:

Spelling rule	New way	Traditional way
1 The *accent circonflexe* is no longer required on the vowels **i** and **u**.	aout *August* maitresse *school teacher* le gouter afternoon snack connaitre *to know*	août maîtresse le goûter connaître
This change doesn't apply where it is necessary to distinguish between two words that sound the same but mean different things.	mur *wall* mûr(e) *ripe*	mur mûr(e)
2 The hyphen (trait d'union) inside words disappears.	piquenique *picnic* tirebouchon *corkscrew* weekend	pique-nique tire-bouchon week-end
A dash is now inserted between all the words that make up a number.	deux-cents *200* trente-et-unième *31st*	deux cents trente et unième
3 'Silent' letters get deleted.	ognon *onion*	oignon

There's a little more to this reform, but the main idea is to respond to 'the natural evolution of the French language, to make it more regular and easier to learn, and to simplify antiquated ways of spelling'.

This is music to a language hacker's ears because even French natives find it very difficult to spell things right!

Ouf ! Phew!